KT-453-790

Hemispheric Specialization and Psychological Function

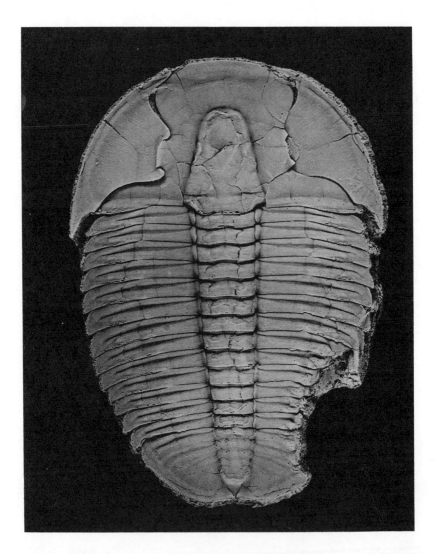

Frontispiece The earliest known behavioural asymmetry from around half a billion years ago. A Middle Cambrian fossil trilobite *Elrathia kingii* showing a healed arcuate scar which resulted from injury during predation. Such injuries seem to have occurred predominantly on the right side. From L. E. Babcock and R. A. Robinson (1989). Preferences of Paleozic predators, *Nature*, **337**, 695–696. Figure (KUMIP 204773) reproduced with permission including that of the University of Kansas Museum of Invertebrate Paleontology.

Hemispheric Specialization and Psychological Function

JOHN L. BRADSHAW
Monash University, Melbourne

CHESTER COLLEGE

ACC. No.	DEPT.
900221	

CLASS No.

612.825 BRA

LIBRARY

JOHN WILEY & SONS
Chichester·New York·Brisbane·Toronto·Singapore

Copyright © 1989 by John Wiley & Sons Ltd,
Baffins Lane, Chichester,
West Sussex PO19 1UD, England

All rights reserved.

No part of this book may be reproduced by any means,
or transmitted, or translated into a machine language
without the written permission of the publisher.

Other Wiley Editorial Offices

John Wiley & Sons, Inc., 605 Third Avenue,
New York, NY 10158-0012, USA

Jacaranda Wiley Ltd, G.P.O. Box 859, Brisbane,
Queensland 4001, Australia

John Wiley & Sons (Canada) Ltd, 22 Worcester Road,
Rexdale, Ontario M9W 1L1, Canada

John Wiley & Sons (SEA) Pte Ltd, 37 Jalan Pemimpin 05-04,
Block B, Union Industrial Building, Singapore 2057

Library of Congress Cataloging-in-Publication Data:

Bradshaw, John L.
    Hemispheric specialization and psychological function/John L.
Bradshaw.
        p.   cm.
    Includes bibliographical references.
    ISBN 0-471-92318-4
    1. Cerebral dominance.   2. Left and right (Psychology)   3. Brain–
–Localization of functions.   I. Title
    QP385.5.B7   1989
    612.8'25—dc20   89–16611
                                                          CIP

British Library Cataloguing in Publication Data:

Bradshaw, John L.
    Hemispheric specialization and psychological
    function.
    1. Man. Brain. Hemispheres. Physiology
    I. Title
    612'.825

    ISBN 0-471-92318-4

Typeset by Inforum Typesetting, Portsmouth
Printed and bound in Great Britain by Biddles Ltd, Guildford

Contents

Acknowledgements   vii

Preface   ix

Chapter 1.   Asymmetries in nonliving and living systems   1

Chapter 2.   Clinical studies of human cerebral asymmetry   23

Chapter 3.   Studies with commissurotomies   54

Chapter 4.   Studies with normals   74

Chapter 5.   Models of hemispheric interaction   110

Chapter 6.   Language and the right hemisphere   121

Chapter 7.   Evolutionary aspects of language and tool use   148

Chapter 8.   Handedness   159

Chapter 9.   Sex differences   179

Chapter 10.   Developmental aspects   192

Chapter 11.   Hemisphericity and cognitive style   203

Author index   212

Subject index   216

Acknowledgements

This book was conceived when Professor Carlo Umiltà of the Istituto di Fisiologia Umana dell'Università di Parma, who had visited and worked with me at Monash in 1983, invited me to give a course of lectures at Parma in 1988. I soon realized how out-of-date our earlier *Human Cerebral Asymmetry* (Prentice Hall, 1983) had become. Moreover I now needed something which was more integrative and pitched at a slightly lower level, and which was well illustrated. This book was developed from that series of Parma lectures, and much of it was written there; I am profoundly grateful to Carlo for inviting me, and giving me such excellent facilities and stimulating company.

My long-term colleague Norman Nettleton and graduate student and collaborator Jane Pierson have both helped me enormously with ideas and criticisms during the years we have worked together. I must also acknowledge our draughting artist Rosemary Williams and photographer Vlad Kohout who have put so much into the illustrations, and my daughter Catriona Bradshaw who typed much of the manuscript. Above all I am deeply grateful to my wife and latterly colleague and research assistant Judy Bradshaw, who typed the rest of the manuscript and improved it in innumerable ways.

Preface

Psychology has now been studied and taught at universities in Europe and the English speaking world for over a century. During that time it has ramified and split into numerous branches, many of whose practising members really have very little to say to each other. The subdiscipline of neuropsychology as such is relatively recent, thought it has its roots in two major traditions, experimental psychology (particularly with respect to perceptual and cognitive processes, and motor control and language), and clinical psychology. In the latter case the areas of interest relate to brain mechanisms of behavior, as adduced from studies of brain injury or local dysfunction. In both cases an early European tradition may be discerned—on the one side Wundt, Helmholtz and Mach as early experimentalists, and on the other Broca and Wernicke who as skilled clinical observers were able to take advantage of 'nature's experiments'.

In the last two decades experimental neuropsychology has flowered, as experimental psychologists, neurologists and clinical neuropsychologists have come to realize that new experimental techniques, when applied to both clinical patients and normal subjects, and allied with clinical observations of the traditional sort, can provide valuable converging information about the organization of brain and mental processes. Inevitably, interpretations are largely reductionist.

In many ways, modern experimental neuropsychology has developed into a microcosm of experimental psychology generally. While other areas continue to attract attention, for example movement control and its disorders (e.g. Parkinsonism), and memory and memory dysfunctions (e.g. the Korsakoff and Alzheimer syndromes), one particular area has attracted an inordinate amount of interest. This is the area of human laterality or cerebral asymmetry. Many researchers have been satisfied at documenting laterality effects (sensory, cognitive and motor) for their own sakes. Others have hoped thereby to further their understanding of pattern recognition, language and motor skills. Others are intrigued by individual differences and by, for example, sex, developmental and environmental effects upon such complex mental functions. Yet others hope to use the undoubted cerebral localization of many of the functions of focal interest as a window into the general question of brain–behavior relationships. It is intriguing to note that there is now a renewed interest in the strong probability of their being parallel (analogous, if not always directly homologous) asymmetries in nonhuman species.

While the study of human lateral asymmetries took off in the late 1960s, it was not until the early 1980s that any texts appeared which attempted, under single authorship (as opposed to edited compilations), to integrate and interpret the plethora of reported findings. Since then (and four important texts appeared between 1981 and 1983) there has again been a hiatus. This book is a renewed attempt to bring the reader up to date. Since, however, in my filing system I have now nearly 5000 relevant references, I have attempted to approach the task somewhat differently from for example our previous work (Bradshaw and Nettleton, *Human Cerebral Asymmetry*, Prentice Hall, 1983). Rather than meticulously referencing every statement, I have referred the reader to major integrative reviews given as 'Important Readings' at the end of each chapter. These reviews have been carefully chosen as providing a balanced and complete overview of the particular aspects which they address, and apart from a very few necessary exceptions, they all date from 1983 onwards. Occasionally, because a statement is controversial or a finding is very new or insecure, I have found it necessary also to reference experimental reports and include them in the list. Sometimes also I have listed items as 'Important Readings' without referencing them in the text. Such items are of major significance, and cover much of the subject matter of the entire chapter, rather than discrete sections.

The chapters are generally organized in an order that has become almost conventional, because that is the logical way to address the problem, though inevitably some newcomers appear. Thus after describing the burgeoning field of laterality in nonhuman species (findings in the last two or three years have revolutionized the area), the book discusses clinical, commissurotomy and normative studies of human cerebral asymmetry. Three chapters then follow, on theoretical models of hemispheric specialization and interaction, language in the 'minor' (right) hemisphere, and language, tool use, dextrality and bipedalism in human evolution. Another three chapters follow on handedness, sex, and developmental aspects, dealing with individual and developmental differences in cognitive abilities and their possible lateralization. Finally, after an overview, the vexed question of cognitive style is discussed (another possible individual difference), and certain recent popular overgeneralizations and extravagant claims concerning 'hemisphericity', education of the right hemisphere, and remediation are examined.

The book is likely to be of use to senior undergraduates (as it is not too technical or abstract, and is abundantly illustrated and contains useful reading lists), graduate students, teachers, researchers entering the field and requiring a 'state of the art' summary or overview, established workers who wish to check up on specific areas, and specialists in other fields, e.g. educational psychologists, workers in rehabilitation, clinical psychologists and neurologists.

While I have attempted to address most major areas of relevance, and hope to have sighted (and cited) most important integrative reviews up to mid 1988, the field is far too dynamic for me to be able to offer anything completely free of personal bias, or totally comprehensive or exhaustive. No doubt my selection of topics has at times been idiosyncratic and I apologize to anyone whose work I have omitted or misunderstood. I hope that at least for the next few years this text will provide some kind of overview, a retrospect and a prospect which will suggest fruitful lines of future research. The provision of a 'Summary and Conclusions' section at the close of each chapter is aimed to provide both a general overview and a balanced judgement of any controversial aspects previously discussed in detail. Each chapter commences by introducing the topics to be covered. This book does not offer a unified theory of lateral asymmetry, and I doubt if one is likely in the foreseeable future. If at times I appear uncritical, it is because much of our information is so new that we cannot yet assess it against the test of time.

1

Asymmetries in nonliving and living systems

Human cerebral asymmetry is just one aspect of a more general asymmetrical tendency which we exhibit, and indeed share with other living and extinct species. The evolution of dextrality and left-brain control of speech and praxis, while of interest in its own right, also opens a window into such questions as the localization of brain function, consciousness, and why for example a mirror apparently reverses an observer's left and right sides, but not top and bottom. (Left and right of course are egocentric, unlike the 'absolutes' up/down.) Inevitably this brings us to such issues as handedness and sex differences, clinical deficits, and the development of verbal and perceptual abilities. In this chapter, which largely summarizes material presented in greater detail elsewhere (Bradshaw, 1988), we shall see that we share with other species a number of often loosely related asymmetries, which may in turn stem from underlying biochemical or even nuclear effects.

Upon initial confrontation, we appear, like most vertebrates, to be laterally symmetrical about the midline. This appearance, however, is both superficial and misleading. Beneath the skin surface our unpaired organs (the gut, heart, liver, spleen) are asymmetrically disposed; nor are even our paired organs completely symmetrical. Thus females usually have one breast slightly larger than the other, and well over 2000 years ago Greek sculptors were aware that the left testicle in males hangs lower than its fellow (see Figure 1). It is, however, also the lighter of the two, not the heavier, as the ever rational Greeks believed. In cases of hermaphroditism, undifferentiated gonads on the right have a greater potential for developing into testes, and those on the left for becoming ovaries.

If we look into a double-reversing mirror, i.e. via two mirrors so placed at an angle to each other that we can now see ourselves as others see us, not left–right

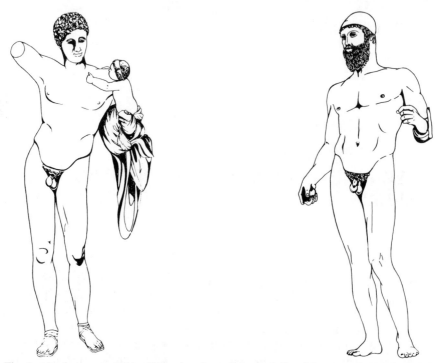

Fig. 1   As demonstrated by these sketches of classical Greek bronzes and sculpture, it has been known for over 2000 years that the left testicle in males typically depends lower than its fellow.

reversed as in a single normal mirror, we may be struck by asymmetries in our own face, asymmetries to which we have so habituated through years of experience of our own mirror image that we are no longer sensitive to them; they are now revealed by the double reversal which initially opposes our habituating mechanisms. We can circumvent the need for double mirrors and highly familiar faces such as our own if we resort to another trick, the photographic construction of left–left (L ⌐) and right–right (Я R) composite faces (Kolb, Milner and Taylor, 1983). Thus we can take a full-face portrait and prepare its mirror image by printing through a reversed negative. If we cut the original and its mirror image vertically down their exact midlines, and jux-tapose two left halves (L ⌐), i.e. creating a complete composite face made entirely from the original left side, and similarly create a right–right (Я R) composite, the two composites are immediately seen as somehow dissimilar. Moreover the L ⌐ composite (using the term L,R here to refer to what is perceived, from the observer's rather than the owner's viewpoint) always seems to resemble its original (LR) more closely than the Я R composite. The fact that this occurs both with normal and mirror-reversed originals indicates

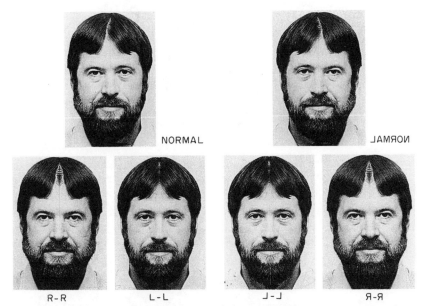

Fig. 2   From an original photograph of a typically asymmetrical face, we can construct a left–left and a right–right composite. (In this illustration L and R happen to refer to the *owner's* left and right, not, as in the text, to what is *perceived* from the observer's viewpoint.) When asked to choose which of two symmetrical composites more closely resembles the normal asymmetrical original, people usually choose the composite constructed from the side *seen* on the left of the currently inspected original, whether normal or mirror-reversed.

that the effect is perceptual; we take more notice of the half-face seen on the left (Figure 2). We can simplify the task even further. Instead of performing the above three comparisons, i.e. L⅃ versus original, Я R versus original, and the results of both comparisons with each other, to determine which of the two composites more closely resembles an original, we can create two composite happy–sad faces, one the mirror image of the other, and ask which of the two is happier (or sadder). Again, people typically choose the face which has the left side (as seen) of the mouth showing the target emotion, and only a single comparison is now needed (Figure 3). This situation arises because the left side of a display, whether or not we steadily fixate its center (here e.g. the nose), is preferentially processed by the contralateral right side of the brain, the right hemisphere (RH) which, as we shall shortly see, is generally superior at judgements involving patterns, faces and emotion (Chapters 2 and 4). Indeed these asymmetries tend to be stronger without fixation, and they may occur with inverted faces (a procedure which tends to destroy the images' face-like qualities), and perhaps even with composites of laterally symmetrical nonfacial stimuli, e.g. trees (Figure 4).

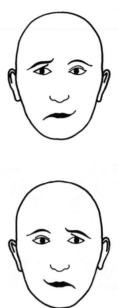

Fig. 3   The bottom face is identical to the top face, merely left–right reversed. In each case one half portrays a sad and the other a happy expression. If asked which of the two faces is the happier, people tend to choose the face whose left half (as observed) contains the happy expression (see J. R. Jaynes *The Origins of Consciousness and the Breakdown of the Bicameral Mind.* Boston: Houghton Mifflin, 1976, for other versions of such a demonstration).

Not only is the perceived left side of a face more salient, because of its direct access to the viewer's right cerebral hemisphere, but the *owner's* left side (perceived by the viewer on the right side) tends to produce stronger emotional responses, being more directly under control of emotional centers in the RH. These effects, which can be objectively measured and plotted, will be discussed in more detail in Chapter 2. Because we face each other, we see the 'weaker' right side of our opponent's face to our left and so largely via our 'stronger' RH. Conversely, mouth asymmetries during *speech* are stronger on the owner's *right* side, in terms both of measured amplitude and velocity of movement (see Figure 5). Thus the right side of the mouth opens faster and wider than the left, as it is connected (again contralaterally) to the left hemisphere (LH) which controls speech in almost everyone. Interestingly, such speech asymmetries tend to be greater for more complex movements, and for females, as so often is the case with motor asymmetries (see below, and Chapter 9), while as we shall see *males* tend to be more laterally asymmetrical ('lateralized') with *cognitive* tasks.

Fig. 4   The bottom tree is identical to the top tree, merely left–right reversed. The two trees in the middle are symmetrical left–left and right–right composites. When asked which of these two middle trees (i.e. the symmetrical composites) more closely resembles an asymmetrical original (top and bottom), there is a slight tendency for people to choose the composite constructed from the left side of the currently observed original.

If the world were left/right reversed (i.e. if we passed, like Alice, into a 'looking-glass' world, or merely viewed it through a mirror or via reversed slides), we would only notice changes in the case of artificial human creations (see Figure 6)—such artifacts as roads, taps, screws, writing; the natural world would appear much the same as before, as Corballis has shown (see e.g. Corballis and Beale, 1983). Thus the fact that most of us may experience difficulties in remembering which is left, or how to turn off a tap, or as children to write N, S, Z rather than И, Ƨ, Ƨ, indirectly indicates how nearly *symmetrical* we are. Indeed, if we were perfectly symmetrical, we would not notice if we had entered an Alice world, even one filled with directional (reversed) human artifacts, as logically it would be the same whether *we*, or the *world*, underwent such reversal, and reversal of a perfectly symmetrical object (ourselves!) could

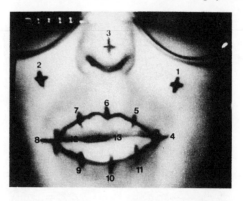
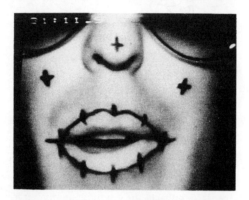
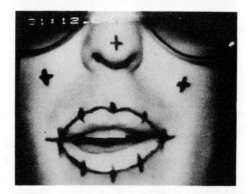

Fig. 5 While speaking, the right side of a person's mouth (i.e. the left as *observed* on the photograph) is typically more mobile than the left. (From M. E. Wolf and M. A. Goodale, Oral asymmetries during verbal and nonverbal movements of the mouth. *Neuropsychologia*, 1987, **25**, 375–396. Reproduced with permission of authors and publishers, Pergamon Press.)

Fig. 6   Natural scenes look much the same whether viewed as normal photographs, or left–right reversed. The same is certainly not true of human creations which include, for example, writing, road traffic, etc.

not alter it. Many animal species have difficulty in learning to make consistent left (or right) turns to commands which do not intrinsically convey the requisite directional information (which an arrow, for example, does), or to make one kind of nondirectional response (e.g. salivation) to a stimulus on one side of the body (e.g. a tickle) but not on the other. If asked to discriminate between mirror-image obliques, e.g. / and \ , animals, children and even adults, especially perhaps left handers who usually tend to be less asymmetrical than right handers (see Chapter 8), may have difficulty. To overcome this problem they may develop such strategies (as sometimes shown by pigeons) of consistently tilting the head always to one and the same side, to convert / and \ into | and — (or | and —); of course the animal must remember always to tilt its head the *same* way, and *that itself* requires some pre-existing asymmetry!

It is of course advantageous for most animals to be able to make left/right

Fig. 7   A sphere is the optimal and simplest packaging shape for a free-floating organism (e.g. many of the Radiolarians). A sessile creature (e.g. a Coelenterate) may adopt a flattened pie-shaped radial symmetry, while an animal which moves along the ground (e.g. a flatworm) is left with lateral symmetry. (Figures 6 and 7 reproduced with permission from J. L. Bradshaw, *Basic Experiments in Neuropsychology*. Amsterdam: Elsevier, 1986.)

generalizations, and not to regard something occurring on their left as quite different from when it happens to occur on their right. Only humans seek to impose such distinctions, maybe because we need the added coding flexibility which such extra distinctions permit, or perhaps because we tend to be more consistently asymmetrical than other vertebrate species. As we shall see, while in many species *individuals* may be markedly asymmetric, at the *population* level consistencies *between* individuals tend to be far less pronounced than in our own species, though current research seems rapidly to be closing the gap.

For a free-floating organism supported on all sides by a medium (e.g. water), and exposed to no unidirectional forces (light, gravity), a sphere is the optimal packaging unit. If under gravity it sinks to the bottom, or floats to the surface, it is likely to differentiate top–bottom into a flattened radial pie-shaped symmetry. If it then commences unidirectional locomotion, it needs sensors at the front and a propulsion system behind, thus leading to a laterally symmetrical wormlike configuration, which may itself be further modified or obscured as in coiled snails, flatfish, etc. (see Figure 7). However, despite such gross physical forces which may shape organisms in the direction of lateral symmetrization, weaker subatomic forces may have an asymmetrical effect. Thus the weak nuclear force is responsible for the β decay of radioactive isotopes; emitted neutrons give rise to protons and electrons, which are circularly polarized (in opposite directions to each other) along their axes of emission. Thus an electron always has a (notional) left-hand spin. Additionally the biochemistry of living organisms is based upon chiral (handed) molecules, with one of the two possible series of enantiomers (mirror-image isomers) predominating. Thus the L-α-amino acids which rotate linearly polarized light anticlockwise, and the D-sugars which rotate it clockwise, occur to the virtually complete

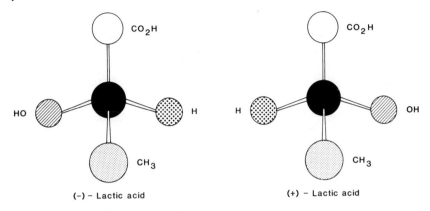

Fig. 8 The three-dimensional molecular arrangement of the four bonds of the carbon atom can lead to two possible configurations (enantiomers), one the mirror image of the other, as shown here in the two possible forms of lactic acid. Living protein is normally constructed exclusively from one alone.

exclusion (in living things) of the opposite optical isomers. This may be a consequence of the arrangement of the four bonds of the carbon atom, one configuration being the mirror image of the other (Figure 8); it is therefore possible to build regular structures only from entirely one or other chirality. Moreover when racemic mixtures of certain amino acids are bombarded by β particles, the D-isomers may be destroyed more quickly than the L-isomers. Alternatively, interactions due to the weak force may make one molecule more energetically favorable than its mirror image, via an atom's outer shell of electrons which are largely responsible for chemical interactions, thus affecting the formation of bioactive molecules. Such effects, perhaps amplified by certain clay substrates which may have catalyzed the formation of early biotic molecules, may have selectively favored one mirror-image form of a molecule. The helices and superhelices formed by L-amino acids are thereby also asymmetrical, and probably determine the structure of certain fibrous compounds in developing neurites, the cytoskeleton of cells, flagellae of sperm, bronchial cilia, etc.; all the twists in such structures must be in the same direction for the system to function. Indeed in Kartagener's syndrome this may not happen, and *situs inversus* (transposition of heart and certain other asymmetrically located organs from the normal position to the opposite side of the body), immotile sperm, respiratory problems, etc., may result. Finally, the asymmetric cytoskeletal architecture present in the maternally derived cytoplasm of the zygote will be preserved in all its descendants, being determined by the arrangement of fibrils formed by the structural proteins; this situation may perhaps account for a slightly greater maternal (extrachromosomal?) than paternal inheritance of handedness (see Chapter 8).

In many species of arthropod, insect and vertebrate there are consistent asymmetries at the species level, e.g. mouth parts, mandibles, lungs, antlers, eyes (in flatfish), tusk (of the narwhal) and even genitalia, though the direction *between* species may not always be consistent. There are numerous biochemical and hormonal asymmetries in the hypothalamus of the rat, to do with reproductive function. In the domestic chick, males (and females injected upon hatching with testosterone) have a larger habenular nucleus on the right, an observation which is compatible with Geschwind's claims (see Chapters 6 and 8) that testosterone retards brain growth on the left. The most primitive fossil chordates (the cornute calcichordates from the Cambrian to the Devonian epochs) were very asymmetric around the head; the more advanced mitrate calcichordates (which some but not all believe may foreshadow vertebrates) became externally almost symmetrical, while retaining an asymmetry of the central nervous system. Scars on fossils of the extinct Paleozoic arthropods, trilobites, indicate an asymmetrical distribution of healed injuries, suggesting that contemporary predators attacked preferentially from the right (Frontispiece). In true vertebrates (amphibia, reptiles, fish, birds) the epithalamic habenular nuclei (which connect to the photoperiodic pineal and limbic regions, and which again respond to testosterone) are highly asymmetric, especially in males. In the salamander, and in mice, rats, rabbits and cats, the RH is the larger (Kolb *et al.*, 1982).

Behavioral asymmetries were thought to be restricted to our own species, and to be disadvantageous, leading to turning biases, and interfering with abilities to generalize between similar events occurring on opposite sides of the body; conversely, *cognitive* asymmetries might assist in the development of spatial or directional maps, where ability to make consistent left or right turns, if required, could be important under certain circumstances. We shall see that there is some evidence of superior perceptual learning in strongly asymmetrical animals. Manipulative dexterity, for which our species is pre-eminent, is also prominent in rodents, racoons, cats, bears, monkeys and apes. Individual animals were long known to be lateralized, though populations were thought to be composed of equal numbers of left and right 'dominant' individuals, and not to be influenced by selective breeding for one or other chirality (Collins, 1985). We now know that the traditional picture with rodents (turning biases), birds (a host of behavioral asymmetries), and primates (handedness and brain asymmetries) has greatly changed (Bradshaw, 1988).

BIRDS

When pigeons learn pattern discriminations, the right eye (which connects directly to the LH) is a superior acquisition system, suggesting a LH dominance for the acquisition of visually guided behavior. However, asymmetrical intertectal interactions may also contribute, as, with commissural section (section of the fibres interconnecting the two sides of the brain), the asymmetries may reverse. With passerines, the LH largely mediates song control, an asymmetry strikingly analogous to our own LH control of speech, and one of the earliest nonhuman asymmetries reported. Damage to the LH in young chaffinches, or early in the season before the commencement of song learning in canaries which annually develop a new repertoire under the influence of rising testosterone levels, permits the RH to take over function. (We shall see in Chapters 6 and 10 that in human infants the RH can take over speech functions if LH injury is sufficiently early and massive, though such inter-species similarities with respect to functional plasticity may be instances of analogy rather than homology.)

In parrots, calls (which are often complex and may be imitative) currently appear to be bilaterally represented; consequently if the degree of lateralization does not always correlate with the capacity for vocal learning, we should be wary of claiming that in our own species unilateral articulatory control is required to avoid hemispheric competition for output, which could result in e.g. stuttering (see Chapters 6 and 7). Many species of parrot, however, are left footed for food manipulation, and this is again a characteristic which is likely to be analogous rather than homologous to our own handedness. However, while these findings might seem to suggest that the left foot of the parrot is comparable to the human right hand, one can alternatively argue that if the beak is used primarily for manipulation, then *it* is analogous to our own right hand. The parrot's left foot then performs the role of our own left hand (if we are dextral), positioning the object for the beak to act upon it.

In the bird visual system, there is complete decussation, so that occlusion of one eye permits direct stimulation of the ipsilateral hemisphere via the opposite eye. Moreover injection of neurotoxins into one or other side of the brain can unilaterally suppress memory formation. Learning which is lateralized to the left forebrain of domestic chicks includes imprinting, visual discrimination learning, auditory habituation and attention switching. The left forebrain is more likely to activate a pecking response, and also to inhibit it when no longer rewarded, while emotional responses to attack, novelty and copulation tend to be activated by the RH and inhibited by the LH (Andrew, 1983; Rogers, 1986). However, the sexes differ in how brain lateralization is manifested, which itself is subject to further developmental changes. Thus only males, for the first few weeks after hatching, exhibit structural asymmetries in certain visual pathways whereby each eye projects to the opposite side of the thalamus. In females, both eyes project to both sides. Thus while both sexes exhibit similar asymmetries with respect to learning, attack, novelty and copulation (see above), they can only be demonstrated, in young males, by direct testing via one or other eye; in females, however, as in males, they can be demonstrated by chemical inactivation of one or other hemisphere. These asymmetries may be important for the early imprinting process, though the function of such sex differences is then unclear. Indeed testosterone can even reverse asymmetries in male chicks, and light seems to play a crucial role. Thus, *in ovo*, just before hatching, the chick's head is turned up on its left shoulder, shielding the left eye and ear, and only the right eye and ear can receive sensory inputs to activate the LH. Indeed consistent lateralization at a population level may fail to appear if the eggs are protected from light and sound before hatching, though at the level of the individual chick the brain remains (inconsistently) asymmetric. (A somewhat similar argument, position *in utero*, has been developed to explain head turning reflexes in human neonates, which could possibly underlie subsequent hand preferences, see Chapter 10.) Thus light determines the *direction*, not the *presence* of asymmetries, and indeed if light is shone, prior to hatching, into the normally occluded left eye, with occlusion now of the normally exposed right eye, the direction of asymmetries reverses for both sexes. Genes, hormones and environmental influences all therefore contribute to the manifestation of lateral asymmetries. The same is probably true with humans. One interpretation of the chick findings is that the LH may habituate faster to novelty, and so may be better able to withhold responses to irrelevant stimuli and so categorize higher-level information; conversely the RH may subserve spatial relations and low-level passive emotional responding. These conclusions come close to the analytic–holistic distinction which has been proposed vis-à-vis human brain asymmetry (see Chapter 7). However, asymmetries in chick and rodent (see below) may be subject to complex sex and developmental effects and interactions.

RODENTS

Mice have strong individual asymmetries for paw preferences for food reaching, but at a population level no consistent biases so far have emerged. Selective breeding may alter the strength of pawedness, but not its direction; females show stronger asymmetries for pawedness than do males (see Figure 9), exactly as is the case with our own handedness and other motor asymmetries (Collins, 1985). Moreover mice showing (or bred for) stronger paw preferences have greater brain asymmetries in the orbitofrontal cortex and striatum (both involved in movement) and the hippocampus (where extracorporeal space may be represented); they may also have overall bigger brains and greater reproductive success, with higher testosterone levels, leading to masculinization and aggression (see Bradshaw, 1988, for details). Rats, similarly bred for stronger lateralization, may learn more quickly to escape from shock in a T maze (i.e. they have better directional and spatial skills, and are better able to discriminate between left and right, being more lateralized); they are also better at learning new positions of escape to a platform hidden beneath the surface of murky water.

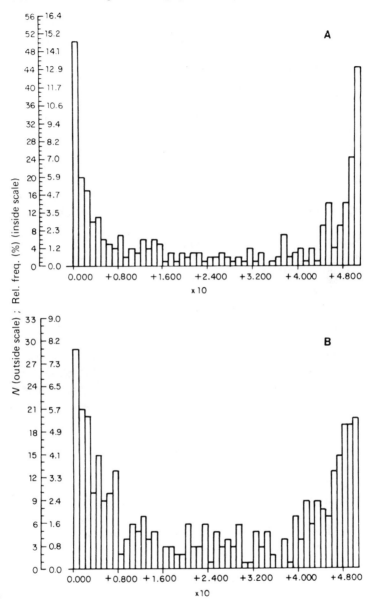

Fig. 9 Distribution of right paw entries in a food reaching task for 341 female mice (A) and 368 male mice (B). Note the greater lateralization of female mice. (Figure from R. L. Collins, On the inheritance of direction and degree of asymmetry. In S. D. Glick (Ed.), *Cerebral Lateralization in Nonhuman Species*. New York: Academic Press, 1985. Reproduced with permission.)

Rat brain asymmetries have been studied by four major groups, namely those of Diamond, Robinson, Denenberg and Glick (see 'Important Readings'). Diamond's group has shown that, in males, the olfactory bulb of the RH is larger (olfaction is particularly important, spatially, for this species); the cortex of the RH is thicker in posterior (sensory) regions, unless the males are castrated at birth. The asymmetry is reversed for females unless they, in turn, are similarly ovariectomized. Similar effects were noted, in terms of sex and development, for the hippocampus, though generally differences in strains and in exposures to enriched or impoverished environments may be important for these asymmetries. The fact that these cortical asymmetries tend to be stronger for males is again reminiscent of the cortical cognitive (but not the motor) situation in our own species; moreover it is compatible with Geschwind's hypothesis (see Chapters 6 and 8) that testosterone somehow retards LH growth.

Robinson's group showed that RH (but not LH) damage may lead to transient shifts in catecholamine levels on both sides of the cortex, substantia nigra and locus coeruleus, with transient changes in emotional behavior. There is debate as to whether these emotional changes involve only the RH, or are mediated via the commissures, as the effects of commissurotomy seem to vary between studies.

Denenberg's group demonstrated complex effects of early (preweaning handling) and later (postweaning) environmental enrichment upon subsequent behavioral asymmetries in unilaterally lesioned rats. They showed that early handling leads to sexual precocity, weight increase, a better resistance to stress, reduced emotionality, more exploration and better avoidance learning, together with increased brain asymmetries. The subsequent presence or absence of environmental enrichment may determine whether or not a RH lesion increases or decreases activity, though generally RH damage leads to increases in spontaneous activity. As with the studies of Diamond's group, complex interactions involving sex and strain may be present, and it is unclear how the two forms of early intervention, handling and environmental enrichment, interact, perhaps via different critical milestones of development. Nevertheless the general picture is that the RH mediates emotional reactivity, with inhibitory transcommissural influences from the LH

Glick's group has been concerned largely with asymmetric turning tendencies in rats. Thus normal rats may rotate spontaneously at night, or after drug treatment in the daytime. For any one individual, the dominant or preferred direction tends to remain constant. These turning preferences may be predicted by neonatal asymmetries in tail posture (cf. the prediction of subsequent hand preferences by head posture asymmetries in human neonates, see Chapter 10). Unilateral damage to the subcortical nigrostriatal motor system, which contains the neurotransmitter dopamine (DA), and which is modulated by the frontal motor cortex, leads to ipsiversive turning (i.e. in the same direction as

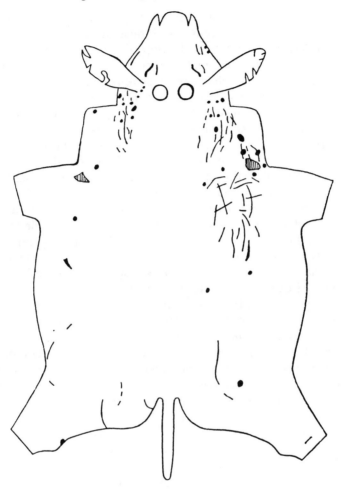

Fig. 10 A composite diagram showing the distribution of scars recorded on the skins of 48 adult male impala. (From P. J. Jarman, The development of a dermal shield in impala. *Journal of Zoology (London),* 1972, **166**, 349–356. Reproduced with permission of author and publisher, The Zoological Society of London.)

the side of lesion). Normal rats have left–right asymmetries in DA concentration in the two striata, and high doses of *d*-amphetamine (*d*-AMPH) increase this asymmetry, leading to daytime rotation in the direction contralateral to the side with the higher DA levels. DA concentrations are normally higher in the striatum contralateral to the rat's turning preference, which we now know tends to be to the right. Moreover the left frontal cortex tends to be more active. Rats lacking clear spatial biases may be hyperactive, and show learning difficulties in spatial tasks, with problems in discriminating left from right, just like some human dyslexic children; moreover such rats, and dyslexic children, may be helped by *d*-AMPH which helps to develop a directional sense, and, apparently paradoxically, in the light of amphetamine's normal action as a stimulant, to reduce hyperactivity. (Amphetamine probably improves the ability to direct attention.) Cocaine inhibits DA reuptake into the striatum, and thereby also enhances rotation, though all of these effects may show strong sex differences.

There is some evidence that humans may show similar drug-induced or natural turning biases. Thus when people's directional turning tendencies are unobtrusively measured during the working day, females show a greater average rate of rotation, though it is consistently right-sided males (in terms of hand, foot and eye dominance) who show rightwards (clockwise) turning preferences; females and mixed dominance males show the opposite tendency. We have ourselves found that when *required* to rotate blindfolded through two complete revolutions, in either direction, dextrals, especially females, showed a rightwards bias and sinistrals a leftwards tendency. When attempting to walk in a straight line, blindfolded, subjects, especially females and dextrals, deviated to the right. Several studies with schizophrenics, who are thought to suffer from overactive LHs, and are known to have greater concentrations of DA in the LH, have shown strong rightwards turning tendencies.

Before discussing primate asymmetries, it is interesting to note that the ultrasonic calls of mouse pups, made to evoke maternal attention, are perceived categorically in the frequency domain, just like human speech; moreover they are similarly perceived by the mother preferentially via the right ear/ LH system, though only if she has been exposed to them beforehand, with the result that the calls have come to have biological significance for them. The distribution of scars on the skins of male impala, the result of inter-male contests, is also highly asymmetric. There are many more on the right side (see Figure 10), indicating that the contestants may turn to the left when facing an adversary, which is again compatible with RH mediation of such emotional, agonistic, precopulatory activity. Dogs prefer to wipe adhesive tape from their faces with their right paw; the RH may be longer and higher, though not wider, and the Sylvian fissure on the right may be lower, though these brain asymmetries seem not to correlate with paw preferences. Conversely, when reaching for food in a tube, cats tend to prefer the left paw, and again females are the more lateralized. These sundry findings are reviewed in greater detail in Bradshaw (1988).

PRIMATE ASYMMETRIES: BRAIN MORPHOLOGY

Asymmetries in the peri-Sylvian (speech-related) cortex are prominent in humans, and have been observed for a century (Galaburda, 1984; LeMay,

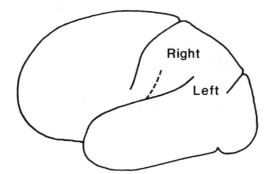

Fig. 11 Left (solid line) and right (broken line) Sylvian fissures, the right shown superimposed (and mirror-reflected) upon the appropriate part of the left hemisphere. The Sylvian fissure is generally longer on the left, but terminates at a lower level than the right. (Figure redrawn from samples published by A. B. Rubens, Anatomical asymmetries of human cerebral cortex. In S. Harnad, R. W. Doty, L. Goldstein, J. Jaynes and G. Krauthamer (Eds.), *Lateralization in the Nervous System*. New York: Academic Press, 1977 and reproduced with permission from J. L. Bradshaw and N. C. Nettleton, *Human Cerebral Asymmetry*. Englewood Cliffs, N.J.: Prentice Hall, 1983.)

1985). Thus the Sylvian fissure, that major landmark separating the temporal from the frontal regions, is longer in the LH, and continues further in a horizontal direction on that side before tending upwards. Its posterior end, the Sylvian point, is higher on the right side (see Figure 11), an asymmetry which is apparent as early as the sixteenth week of gestation, and is evident even in our fossil ancestor, *Homo erectus*. The temporal planum, especially the superior portion of the superior temporal gyrus (an important language area through which the Sylvian fissure passes) is larger on the left (see Figure 12), even in the fetus. The same holds true for another speech area, the parietal operculum, where recent pictures by nuclear magnetic resonance imaging have suggested a good correlation between asymmetries and handedness. In grosser terms, the left occipital pole is wider and protrudes more posteriorly, and anteroparietal and postero-occipital regions are larger on the left; conversely, the right frontal pole extends beyond the left, thus giving the brain what has been described as an overall counterclockwise torque (see Figure 13). There are also suggestions that the LH may have a higher ratio of grey to white matter, though it is disputable as to whether it is more 'important' to have more cell bodies, more synapses or longer axons; presumably it depends upon the nature of the requisite cognitive functions. Many of these asymmetries appear also in Old World monkeys (see Chapter 7), suggesting that an expansion of prefrontal and parietal integration cortices in the LH occurred in an early primate ancestor common to monkeys and ourselves; thus during primate evolution, the Sylvian fissure has migrated from a nearly vertical to a horizontal posture.

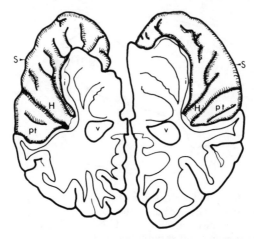

Fig. 12   Standard asymmetry of the planum temporale (pt), the roughly triangular region lying posterior (inferior in the diagram) to the transverse auditory gyrus of Heschl (H) and bound laterally by the Sylvian fissure (S). This pattern of asymmetry is seen in approximately two-thirds of normal human brains. (Figure from N. Geschwind and A. M. Galaburda, *Cerebral Lateralization: Biological Mechanisms, Associations and Pathology*. Cambridge, Mass.: Bradford-MIT Press, 1987. Reproduced with permission.)

This is probably due to increasing development of the inferior parietal lobule, especially in the LH, which in our own species has come to subserve speech after a lengthy process of preadaptation.

PERCEPTUAL AND MOTOR ASYMMETRIES IN THE MONKEY

Rhesus monkeys spontaneously using the left hand may learn a tactile discrimination task quicker than those using the right, and those without consistent preferences may be fastest of all (see Bradshaw, 1988, for details); while in our own species sinistral and ambilateral athletes and tennis players occur with otherwise unexpected frequency, this situation contrasts with the rat studies (above) which showed that the absence of asymmetries may hinder the acquisition of a spatial task. The resolution of this conflict probably depends upon the relative contributions of cognitive, sensory and motor components in the task, and the element of surprise occasioned by left-handed action in contact sports. However, some animal studies offer results contrary to the human model; commissurotomized (split-brain, see Chapter 3) monkeys may learn to discriminate lines, differing slightly in slope, faster when viewing

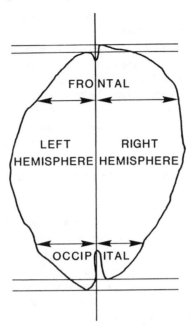

Fig. 13   Asymmetries of frontal and occipital regions. The wider right frontal and left occipital regions, and the more extensive left occipital and right frontal poles give the brain an overall counterclockwise torque. (Redrawn from CT scans of A. M. Galaburda, M. LeMay, T. L. Kemper and N. Geschwind, Right–left asymmetries in the brain. *Science*, 1978, **199**, 852–856, and of C. H. Chui and A. R. Damasio, Human cerebral asymmetries evaluated by computed tomography. *Journal of Neurology, Neurosurgery and Psychiatry,* 1980, **43**, 873–878 and reproduced with permission from J. L. Bradshaw and N. C. Nettleton, *Human Cerebral Asymmetry*. Englewood Cliffs, N.J.: Prentice Hall, 1983.)

through the right visual field (RVF) which projects to the LH. Monkeys lesioned in the RH are better able (than LH-lesioned animals) to perform spatial discriminations which involve detecting the position of a dot within a square. However, as with humans, monkeys show a RH superiority for face processing, and in the auditory modality the parallels to our own species are even closer: there is a right ear advantage (REA, i.e. a LH superiority as the right ear projects mainly to the LH) in the discrimination of species-specific calls (Petersen *et al.*, 1984); conversely LH lesions (in regions corresponding to our own receptive speech area, see Chapter 2) affect monkeys' abilities to discriminate between two forms of their vocalization, and to perform complex delayed conditional discriminations between auditory and visual stimuli. Furthermore, again exactly as in our own species, there is in baboons a left ear advantage (LEA, i.e. a RH superiority) for discriminating between members of various acoustic classes and for discriminations which involve voice onset time (VOT, e.g. as between the speech sounds /b/ and /p/), even though, of course, in our own species, this task would be thought of as speech related.

Turning to hand preferences, monkeys may favor the right hand for fine manipulations, and the right forelimb is generally larger, perhaps reflecting greater use; gorillas may grasp with the right hand, and, like ourselves, hold an infant with the left arm while (tripedally) locomoting. Generally, there appears to be a left-hand preference for visually guided reaching and grasping in prosimians (MacNeilage, Studdert-Kennedy and Lindblom, 1987), especially under conditions of an obligatory bipedal stance, with a right-hand preference for manipulation and practised performance in stereotyped situations. These primate patterns of handedness may be structural, a functional adaptation to feeding and a precursor to our own manual preferences. They may stem from the need to use the right hand for postural support, thus freeing the left for reaching. Later in primate evolution, when the forelimbs were freed from involvement in such postural support, the right was able to undertake manipulative functions. However, such an account must also somehow encompass the evidence for other behavioral asymmetries in phylogenetically lower species (see above) if it is to play a role in the evolution of human handedness, and we shall see later that handedness is an imperfect predictor of language lateralization, especially in sinistrals. However, while this ancestral and hypothetical left-hand preference for visually-guided reaching may be submerged in our own species, there is some evidence that dextrals may under certain circumstances be better with the left hand for fast, visually guided, ballistic reaching. However, it does seem maladaptive for Man to have now lost a left-hand bias in reaching (the LH/right hand system presumably having taken over *both* functions) as an object would have to be transferred from right to left hand if it is to be bimanually manipulated or worked on by the right hand. Moreover during infancy a right hand bias for reaching *precedes* the appearance of bimanual manipulation. When the latter appears, infants often switch reaching preference to the formerly nonpreferred hand, to facilitate using the preferred hand for more active manipulation, and only later revert to using the right hand for both reaching and manipulation, necessitating a fumbling intermanual transfer.

SUMMARY AND CONCLUSIONS

Despite a superficial appearance of bilateral (left–right) symmetry, we are asymmetrical with respect to internal (and some external) organs, the two sides of the face, and of course hand preferences. Human handedness patterns probably account for left–right asymmetries in human artifacts, asymmetries which are grossly absent in the natural world. While many animal species cannot easily learn to perform left–right discriminations at a sensory or motor level, a situation which reflects their evolution in a largely symmetrical environment, recent evidence suggests the frequent presence of subtle asymmetries in both living and nonliving systems. Thus the biochemistry of living organisms exhibits a chirality which may itself stem from asymmetric action of subatomic forces, and which in turn may modify cytoplasmic and maybe even neural and corporeal structures. Thus in the animal world asymmetries are being found at both the individual and the population level.

The bird brain exhibits many parallel asymmetries to that of the human. The LH may be dominant for the acquisition of visually guided behaviors (in pigeons), for song control (in passerines), for imprinting, visual discrimination learning, auditory habituation and attention switching (in chicks), while (again with chicks) the RH may subserve spatial relationships and emotional responsivity. Morphological and functional asymmetries are also apparent in the rodent brain, though as with birds there may be strong sex differences; again the RH seems to subserve emotional reactivity, while the LH may, as in our own case, be better equipped to process species-specific vocalizations categorically. Rats also tend, like humans, to make rightwards turns.

In many species of primate, asymmetries are present in the peri-Sylvian and parieto-temporal regions. The brain typically exhibits a 'counterclockwise torque'. Again there is a LH superiority in the discrimination of species-specific calls, with, additionally, it has been suggested, a left-hand preference for guided reaching and grasping, accompanied by a right-hand preference for manipulation and practised performance in stereotyped situations. These primate asymmetries may be viewed as preadaptations leading to our own cognitive and manual asymmetries.

IMPORTANT READINGS

Andrew, R. J. Lateralization of emotional and cognitive function in higher vertebrates, with special reference to the domestic chick. In J. R. Ewert and D. Ingle (eds.), *Advances in Vertebrate Neuroethology*. New York: Plenum Press, 1983, pp. 477–510.

Bradshaw, J. L. The evolution of human lateral asymmetries: New evidence and second thoughts. *Journal of Human Evolution*, 1988, **17**, 615–37.

Collins, R. L. On the inheritance of direction and degree of asymmetry. In S. D. Glick (ed.), *Cerebral Lateralization in Nonhuman Species*. New York: Academic Press, 1985, pp. 41–72.

Corballis, M. C. and Beale, I. L. *The Ambivalent Mind*. Chicago: Nelson Hall, 1983.

Denenberg, V. H. and Yutzey, D. A. Hemispheric laterality, behavioral asymmetry, and the effects of early experience in rats. In S. D. Glick (ed.), *Cerebral Lateralization in Nonhuman species*. New York: Academic Press, 1985, pp. 110–35.

Diamond, M. C. Rat brain morphology: Right–left, male–female, young–old, enriched–impoverished. In S. D. Glick (ed.), *Cerebral Lateralization in Nonhuman Species*. New York: Academic Press, 1985, pp. 73–88.

Galaburda, A. M. Anatomical asymmetries. In N. Geschwind and A. M. Galaburda (eds.), *Cerebral Dominance: The Biological Foundations*. Cambridge, Mass.: Harvard University Press, 1984, pp. 11–25.

Glick, S. D. and Shapiro, R. M. Functional and neurochemical mechanisms of cerebral lateralization in rats. In S. D. Glick (ed.), *Cerebral Lateralization in Nonhuman Species*. New York: Academic Press, 1985, pp. 158–84.

Kolb, B., Milner, B. and Taylor, L. Perception of faces by patients with localized cortical lesions. *Canadian Journal of Psychology*, 1983, **37**, 8–18.

Kolb, B., Sutherland, R. J., Nonneman, A. J. and Whishaw, I. Q. Asymmetry in the cerebral hemispheres of rat, mouse, rabbit and cat: The right hemisphere is larger. *Experimental Neurology*, 1982, **78**, 348–59.

LeMay, M. Asymmetries of the brains and skulls of nonhuman primates. In S. D. Glick (ed.), *Cerebral Lateralization in Nonhuman Species*. New York: Academic Press, 1985, pp. 234–46.

MacNeilage, P. F., Studdert-Kennedy, M. G. and Lindblom, B. Primate handedness reconsidered. *Behavioural and Brain Sciences*, 1987, **10**, 247–303.

Petersen, M. R., Beecher, M. D., Zoloth, S. R., Moody, D. B. and Stebbins, W. C. Neural lateralization of vocalization by Japanese macaques: Communicative significance is more important than acoustic structure. *Behavioral Neuroscience*, 1984, **98**, 779–90.

Robinson, T. E., Becker, J. B. and Camp, D. M. Sex differences in behavioral and brain asymmetries. In M. S. Myslobodsky (ed.), *Hemisyndromes: Psychobiology, Neurology, Psychiatry*. New York: Academic Press, 1983, pp. 91–128.

Rogers, L. J. Lateralization of learning in chicks. *Advances in the Study of Behavior*, 1986, **16**, 147–89.

2

Clinical studies of human cerebral asymmetry

Hemispheric specialization in humans may be studied with normal subjects (Chapter 4), with subjects whose hemispheres have been surgically separated (next chapter), or with clinical patients (this chapter) who have suffered localized, and lateralized, insult to one or other side of the brain, with a resultant characteristic dysfunction. (Note that lesions can be localized, e.g. to the posterior regions on *both* sides, without lateralization; deficits, e.g. prosopagnosia, may then be none the less unique, but cannot of course tell us anything about asymmetric function.) Relevant information is typically gained from identifying discrete patterns of deficit (syndromes) associated with one or more localized trauma. However, new methods of visualizing the abnormal (and normal) brain, both in static structural terms and dynamically as it functions, provide a necessary complement. One of the oldest methods of visualizing function is to record electrical activity, while its logical obverse, electrostimulation (with observation of behavioral change) is providing us with valuable new insights of a quite different kind. Behavioral change, whether produced experimentally or by such accidents of nature as localized head injury, are conveniently divided into verbal and nonverbal; in this and other chapters we shall see that this distinction does not neatly overlap with left and right hemisphere function. While language breakdown may take many forms, and its taxonomic classification is of great theoretical and clinical significance, and to a somewhat lesser extent similar observations may be made with respect to nonverbal deficits, we must be wary of trying to tie too closely together function and region; it is all too easy to lose sight of the fact that the brain functions as an integrated and unified whole, with disturbance to one system often affecting other remote systems. Moreover we should also be wary when attempting to cross such explanatory boundaries as lie between brain and behavior, machinery and mind. This chapter examines the clinical evidence for human cerebral asymmetry.

Before reviewing the effects of localized injury upon such apparently lateralized functions as speech, pattern recognition, attention and emotion, we should consider techniques, commonly employed in a clinical context, which reveal structural or functional asymmetries, e.g. CAT and PET scans, NMRI, rCBF, EEG and ERPs, electrostimulation, unilateral ECT and injection of sodium amytal (amobarbital, amylobarbitone).

Computerized (trans)axial tomography (CAT scans) involve three-dimensional x-ray image reconstruction by computer (Henderson *et al.*, 1984; Koff *et al.*, 1986; Yeo *et al.*, 1987). This static and mildly invasive (x-ray) technique shows the presence *in vivo* of morphological brain asymmetries. On the other hand, positron emission tomography (PET) scans provide a dynamic picture of current function, with relatively good spatial if poor temporal resolution of e.g. LH involvement during language tasks. Radioactively tagged 'glucose' (a metabolically useless analog of true glucose) is taken up by currently active brain areas as if it really were a source of energy, and (being chemically slightly different) becomes trapped. Its abundance can then be visualized via externally located detectors. The technique of nuclear magnetic resonance imaging (NMRI, see Kertesz *et al.*, 1986) provides a static image like a CAT scan, though of far higher quality, and is much less invasive. The brain (or body) lies within a powerful electromagnetic field, which aligns the direction of spin of protons (hydrogen atom nuclei); when struck by a pulsed radio signal, they return a characteristic echo, whose intensity depends upon the concentration of hydrogen and therefore of water, which itself has a markedly differential abundance in various brain structures. There is some evidence of a correlation between morphological asymmetries in the human brain, as indexed by CAT and NMRI scans, and language lateralization, handedness and intellectual abilities, though such claims are also disputed.

Regional cerebral blood flow (rCBF) may change markedly as a function of mental activity (e.g. language in certain LH regions), via feedback mechanisms (Risberg, 1986). These involve dilation of blood vessels due to metabolic demand, signalled by highly local carbon dioxide increases. Early techniques involved unilateral injection of ^{133}Xe (which attaches to red blood cells) to one of the internal carotid arteries; this painful and potentially risky technique permitted multiple external scintillation detectors to follow the nearly instantaneous arrival and subsequent clearance of the radioactively tapped tracers, though only one hemisphere could be tested at a time. With computer processing, brain activity areas can be topographically displayed on a color monitor, with different hues being assigned to different levels of blood flow. Subsequently a less invasive approach involving inhalation of ^{133}Xe was developed, which also permitted bilateral assessment. However, the procedure still suffers from poor spatial ($\sim$ 1 cm) and temporal resolution, and only permits surface measures. The new procedure of single proton emission computed tomography (SPECT) should permit deep-structure analysis, though problems of resolution will remain. Generally, rCBF indices demonstrate that much wider brain areas are active during e.g. speech than was previously thought, especially prefrontal regions, leading to the possible need to reassess the classical limits of Wernicke's and Broca's areas (see below). Of course, activity does not necessarily imply participation in processing. Indeed the surprising observation of apparently increased blood flow during language tasks in RH regions, which if damaged do not normally result in aphasia, suggests the possibility that *inhibition* of an area may require energy, as well as excitation.

Very recently, Posner *et al.* (1988) described the amalgamation of an advanced brain mapping technique for measuring blood flow (using PET measurements within defined cortical regions) to an information processing model of the steps involved in certain basic language functions. Thus PET can image rCBF after a bolus intravenous injection of ^{15}O-labelled water, the low-level radionuclide having such a short half-life (123 seconds) that repeated measurements can be taken from the same subject performing different tasks. Typically the tasks form a multilevel subtractive hierarchy, with each higher level adding a smaller number of processing operations to those of its subordinate control. The rCBF measurements resulting from the simpler task are then subtracted from those resulting from the next hierarchical level to obtain a precise image of the brain areas active in performing the additional processing operations. Thus in tracking the stages of reading aloud, the level of sensory processing can be visualized by contrasting (i.e. differencing) simple visual fixation, with fixation together with visual presentation of words which require no overt behavioral response. To localize the level of motor programming and articulatory output, fixation together with visual word presentation can be contrasted with the additional requirement of pronouncing the presented word. Finally this latter repetition task can be contrasted with a semantic association condition where the subject gives a single word-use for each stimulus word, e.g. 'eat' on the presentation of 'cake'. A color-coded topographical map by brain areas of the differences in activation levels for each pair of cognitive tasks then reveals functional localization for each processing stage, e.g. sensory input and involuntary word-form processing at the first contrast, output coding and motor control in the second, and semantic processing in the third (see Figure 1).

Electrical measures (EEG, ERPs, see e.g. Davidson, 1988) are the oldest of the indices of brain activity during mental processing; they are noninvasive, and of excellent temporal if of poor spatial resolution. Again the relationship between cognitive and electrical activity is unclear—high activity *could* simply indicate that a deficient area is 'trying hard'. Moreover any electrophysiological asymmetries could merely reflect underlying morphological (i.e. structural,

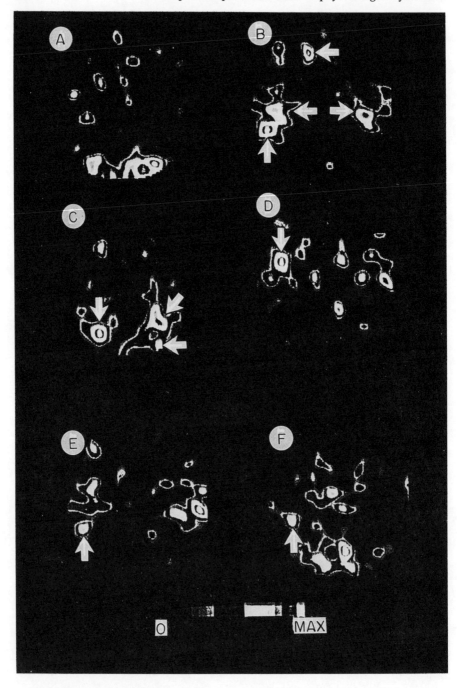

rather than functional) asymmetry. Electroencephalographic (EEG) measures during language and visuospatial processing generally indicate an inverse relationship between mental effort and the amplitude of α; i.e. engagement of a hemisphere results in α suppression. Many studies find α decreases in the LH during verbal tasks. Computer displays can map such patterns of area activity (e.g. brain electrical activity mapping, BEAM), as in PET and rCBF. Event-related potentials (ERPs) or evoked responses represent the averaging of the EEG over 1 sec epochs following multiple presentation of a stimulus, to enhance the very small (5–25 μV) signal embedded in the higher-amplitude EEG. Thus the ERP sums each repetition of a stimulus, while the EEG within which the ERP is embedded cancels, as it is not timelocked to the stimulus like the ERP. Such ERPs are quantified in terms of latency and amplitude, e.g. P_1, N_2 or P^{100}, N^{350} where P and N reflect positive and negative components, 1 and 2 their locus in a sequence, and 100 and 350 their latency in msec. The problem is that more than 50 repetitions may be needed for satisfactory averaging, and such practice effectively changes the task characteristics for the subject. ERPs have been used to plot phonetic, semantic, lexical and syntactic involvement in language, the use of words in ambiguous contexts, polysemous words, homophony etc., and typically indicate left/right, anterior/posterior differences, and also sex and handedness differences, and possibly differential effects in schizophrenics and stutterers. Instead of measuring ERPs to words etc., as above, one can present clicks or flashes while the subject performs lengthy verbal or spatial processing tasks now of a much more naturalistic kind. Thus smaller ERPs to clicks may result over the LH during verbal tasks, i.e. the ERPs to the irrelevant (to the LH) clicks decrease. Corresponding effects may occur over the RH for spatial tasks. In addition to EEG and ERP indices, the electrophysiologist may measure slow-potential changes, e.g. the contingent negative variation (CNV), preceding or following expected verbal or nonverbal processing.

The following three approaches do not strictly employ the assessment of

---

◀ Fig. 1 Subtraction rCBF images for various information processing stages in language tasks. (Figure from S. E. Petersen, P. T. Fox, M. I. Posner, M. Mintun and M. E. Raichle, Positron emission tomographic studies of the processing of single words. *Journal of Cognitive Neuroscience*, **1**, 155–170 (1988). Reproduced with permission.) Horizontal slices A and C represent passive visual and B and D auditory input tasks; A and B are taken 1.6 cm above the AC–PC line (a landmark) and C and D 0.2 cm below it. Slices A, B, C and D represent rCBF changes (differences) at these two levels between fixation alone and (visual or auditory) presentation of words. Active areas (arrowed) differ between the two presentation modes. Slice E represents activity for passive auditory word presentation at 1 cm above the AC–PC line (cf. slice D at a slightly different level). Slice F shows a similar focus of activity, during a rhyme detection task on visually presented words; thus the temporoparietal region is implicated in some type of phonological coding common to visual and auditory words. (Original figure in color.)

lateralized output, as above, but nevertheless possess certain other conceptual similarities:

(i) Electrostimulation of peri-Sylvian speech cortex in conscious patients during surgical exploration for epileptic foci, as pioneered by Ojemann (1983). Such stimulation acts like a temporary lesion, blocking functional activity; thus it rarely elicits but may sometimes block expressive speech, or may lead to errors in a perceptual task like phoneme discrimination. Errors may often be highly specific, e.g. to certain word classes, though there is substantial individual variability in the exact loci for a given function, with variability relating to sex (the frontal regions may be more important for males), language ability, prior experience and prior brain injury. Of course the patient populations are far from normal, often with long-standing epilepsy and consequent plastic reorganization of brain functions. However, for a given individual, there is often extremely discrete representation of unique language functions at a given site. The general picture is of a peri-Sylvian system which simultaneously subserves both motor sequencing and phoneme decoding, and which is surrounded by a verbal short-term-memory system extending frontally, parietally and temporally. The anterior extent of this short-term-memory system may be more important for retrieval, and the posterior extent for storage functions, as evidenced by the effects of electrostimulation during separate retrieval and storage phases of tasks undertaken by the patients. Specialized language loci may lie at interfaces between these systems, e.g. naming functions in posterior temporal sites, with syntax specializations in midtemporal zones. The more central peri-Sylvian region (though still extending frontally, temporally and parietally) seems, from the perceptual and motor errors occurring during electrostimulation, to be important both for the identification of phonemes and for orofacial movement sequencing. Thus it may even be the substrate of the long-hypothesized motor theory of speech perception, whereby to comprehend incoming speech sounds adequately, we have to be able to simultaneously match them, in an anticipatory fashion, with subvocal or prevocal precursors of the actual articulatory gestures which would be required to produce them. This region is separate from the adjacent face motor cortex, and outputs to the posterior portion of the third frontal gyrus, immediately in front of the face motor cortex. Thus much of the LH seems to be fundamentally motor, be it for motor sequencing, temporal ordering or precise perceptual timing, with anterior temporal, and parietal, lobe involvement also in manual sequencing. There is little evidence of a comparable RH involvement. Ojemann's electrostimulation studies reveal that the cortex has a generally columnar–mosaic organization, each column (0.5 to 1.0 cm diameter) having different functions from its neighbors. The thalamus may also be important in speech initiation, alerting and attention, as evidenced by electrostimulation therein, perhaps triggering the appropriate cortical mosaic columns.

(ii) Unilateral electroconvulsive therapy (ECT). This 'kick it and fix it' approach which for poorly understood reasons may alleviate severe depression, perhaps 'resetting' brain activity, or flooding the brain with neurotransmitters, has been found to be as efficacious as bilateral ECT, without that older procedure's disturbing side effects and language disruption. Indeed a double dissociation may appear, depending upon the side stimulated, e.g. language decrement following LH stimulation, and visuospatial deficits after RH involvement. Moreover the effects may be modified in predictable directions (see Chapters 8 and 9) by the effect of sex and handedness.

(iii) The Wada amytal (amobarbital, amylobarbitone) test. The same observation may be made here. Barbiturate anesthetic is injected into the left or right internal carotid artery, which supplies the ipsilateral hemisphere. The effects are typically a transient loss of function; the contralateral hand drops flaccidly, and if the LH is injected the patient stops counting—effectively a reversible hemispherectomy. The technique is risky, and is only used presurgically to identify the language hemisphere, which may be necessary in the case of sinistrals, or those who suffered perinatal injury, whose cerebral organization tends to be nonstandard. Effects are brief—around five minutes— and only permit direct assessment of motor functions. Moreover narcotization of a hemisphere may be subtotal, because of individual differences in branching of cerebral arteries from the carotids; carotid branches to the brainstem can further bias results. However, the procedure typically reveals LH language lateralization in 90–95% of dextrals, and 65–70% of sinistrals.

VERBAL SYNDROMES

Aphasia has been known for at least four to five thousand years, as revealed by readings from Egyptian papyri. It is an acquired loss of language due to cerebral damage, and is characterized by paraphasic errors (i.e. errors in word production), impaired comprehension as well as production, anomia (word finding difficulties), and disturbances of grammar and of phonology. Thus it does not just involve *spoken* language, and should be distinguished from dysarthria (due simply to disturbed neuromuscular control). It is usually also accompanied by apraxia, acalculia and other cognitive disabilities. Its taxonomy stems from Lichtheim over 100 years ago, and modern 'diagram-makers' still largely follow his model (see Figure 2), on the basis of the overlap of the topographical distribution of language functions and the topography of arterial occlusions, injuries etc. Thus a modern taxonomy would look like Table 1 (Kertesz, 1985, and see also Benson and Geschwind, 1985).

The relevant brain areas may be schematically represented as shown in Figure 3. The two most important and interesting aphasias from the viewpoints

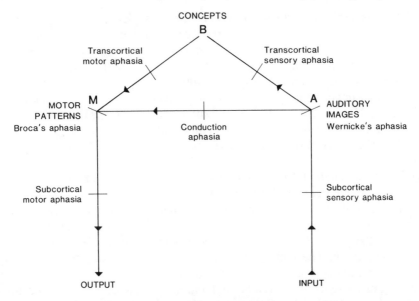

Fig. 2 'Lichtheim's house'. Over 100 years ago the pioneering neurologist L. Lichtheim (On aphasia. *Brain*, 1885, **7**, 433–484) conceptualized the relationship between the various types of observed aphasia (lower case) in terms of breaks (slashes) in the flow of information between or within processing regions (upper case). Variations of this connectionist approach have persisted until now.

of history and cerebral lateralization are *Broca's* and *Wernicke's*, though note that modern thinking is tending to move away from a rigid distinction between motor and sensory/semantic aphasia, as implied in the above traditional categorization. Broca in the 1860s claimed 'nous parlons avec l'hémisphère gauche', and described a frontal syndrome adjacent to the motor face area of the LH, known to be important in programming language. Broca's aphasia is effortful, nonfluent, slow, awkward, telegraphic, agrammatic and of limited vocabulary; thus there may be numerous meaningful substantives, but few syntactically significant function words—functors, e.g. 'the', 'to', 'if', 'and' etc. This type of aphasia results not just from a need for economy of effort, but is known now to involve a true syntactic disorder, as complex syntax and functors may not be comprehended or repeated. Thus it is no longer correct to claim that comprehension is relatively unimpaired. Wernicke's aphasia was identified in Germany ten or fifteen years later, as an apparent complement to Broca's syndrome. The receptive speech area of the LH is affected in the posterior temporal lobe and adjacent to the primary auditory cortex. Damage traditionally was held to affect comprehension rather than production, which stays fluent, of normal or above normal rate, effortless, of normal prosody,

Table 1 Modern taxonomy of aphasia

	Spontaneous speech	Fluency	Comprehension	Repetition	Naming
Broca's	Hesitant, agrammatic	Poor	Good	Poor	Poor
Pure motor	Phonetic errors	Impaired	Good	Impaired	Impaired
Global	Stereotypic utterances	Poor	Poor	Poor	Poor
Wernicke's	Paraphasic, jargon	Good	Poor	Poor	Poor
Word deaf	Normal	Good	Poor	Poor	Good
Conduction	Phonemic errors	Good	Good	Poor	Good
Transcortical sensory	Normal to semantic jargon	Good	Poor	Good	Poor
Transcortical motor	Scant, mute	Poor	Good	Good	Impaired
Isolation	Mute	Poor	Poor	Good	Poor
Anomic	Circumlocutory	Good	Good	Good	Impaired

syntax, grammar, phrase length, melody and inflection. However, the speech is devoid of content and is replete with neologisms, paraphasic substitutions, circumlocutions, and meaningless jargon. Other traditional categories of aphasia include global (where the lesion encompasses both Broca's and Wernicke's areas), conduction (where the arcuate fasciculus interconnecting Broca's and Wernicke's areas is damaged), transcortical and anomic aphasia.

Problems with such a taxonomy emerged as early as Jackson in the nineteenth century, who observed that locating damage that destroys speech, and localizing speech, are two quite different things. Head in the first quarter of this century showed a similar contempt for the diagram-makers, and Marie at the turn of the century claimed that there is only one aphasia, a general language disturbance due to damage to Wernicke's area, with all other categories merely variations thereof, due to extension of lesions into sensory and motor areas. This holistic tendency contrasts with that of the early localizationists, though there has been a recent emphasis on the effects of complex disconnections between cortical and subcortical areas, rather than simply between cortical centers of behavior. There are certainly many transitional forms of aphasia, disagreements, and problems of 'elastic' and ill-defined and disputed area boundaries, and change and evolution of aphasic types during recovery. Thus

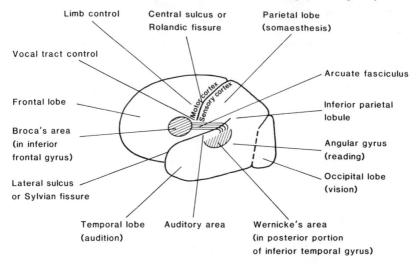

Fig. 3   The major surface features and language related areas of the left hemisphere.

the limits of vascular supply extend beyond the limits of certain functional areas; the gyri and sulci landmarks do not necessarily map on to discrete cytoarchitectonic regions, which are themselves perhaps the true loci of processing. Moreover a small lesion within a functionally defined area will probably produce a (heuristically) different pattern of deficits than one at the confluence of a number of such modules. Thus a whole network of differentially specialized modules may be functionally disturbed by a critical focal lesion; conversely, the same complex function may be impaired as a result of damage in any of several areas, each of which is a component of an integrated network subserving that function.

Furthermore performance deficit after localized injury need not indicate that that area mediated performance or function; rather, the damaged area may now release from inhibition another inhibitory area, so that mediation in some third locus is now inhibited. Yet again, reorganization after injury may itself be responsible for residual anomalies; thus defective performance may stem from a damaged area performing suboptimally, or another unspecialized area taking over function unsuccessfully, or noise or inhibition from a damaged and previously functional area interfering with another otherwise competent area which could have performed satisfactorily in isolation. We should therefore be wary of blindly 'glueing' flow-chart diagrams upon brain anatomy (and see Marshall, 1984, 1986); patients vary, in age at injury and at testing, in premorbid intelligence, education and personality, rate of illness progression, likelihood of seeking help, and strategies adopted in circumventing disability. Thus the paralexic naming response of 'stone' for the visually presented word 'rock' may simply be an adaptive strategy, in a word-finding struggle, rather than evidence of e.g. RH involvement (see Chapter 6). Indeed Caramazza and McCloskey (1988) argue vehemently against group classifications of e.g. the aphasias or the alexias of the sort attempted here on the basis of multipatient studies. They are not, strangely enough, unhappy about the possibility (see above) that performance decrement stems more from a change in function of a whole integrated system; indeed they believe that the study of highly specific or discrete dysfunctions *can* be used to derive information about the componential operation of the normal cognitive system. However, their concern is that averaging across patients assumes homogeneity at several levels—lesion site and extent, experimental technique, and the *prior*, presumably normal, cognitive system; such homogeneity cannot be easily verified without appealing in a dangerously circular fashion to observed performance, which is itself being used to ultimately derive general statements about the nature of the normal system. In consequence they reject attempts at taxonomic classification of e.g. the aphasias and the alexias (or movement disorders also, presumably), and argue for studies at the single case rather than the group level when we attempt to draw inferences about normal cognitive functioning from an analysis of patient performance. However, such a pessimistic viewpoint must inevitably limit the generality of any possible conclusions.

Until now, we have been considering a largely cortical mediation of language, while recent evidence indicates that subcortical structures such as the thalamus and basal ganglia (respectively a relay station, and a motor initiation center) are important for speech initiation and fluency (Crosson, 1985). Thus Broca's anterior cortex may formulate speech programming, word finding, phonology and syntax; Wernicke's posterior cortex may monitor the accuracy of these resultant formulations, prior to the actual motor programming, with respect to semantic content, and if necessary initiate corrections via *subcortical* thalamic connections between the anterior and posterior cortex. The equivalent *transcortical* route, the arcuate fasciculus, meanwhile monitors phonology and corrects errors before actual speech output, operating as an editor. Finally, the extent of inhibition from the basal ganglia upon the thalamus, which itself regulates reticular activation of the anterior Broca cortex, may determine the actual speech release. This would account for the dysarthria, difficulties in word finding, hesitancy and dysfluencies which result from damage to the left thalamus. The basal ganglia, of course, coordinate all classes of skilled movement, including speech; they receive input from the cortex, and they output via the thalamus back to the cortex, to integrate intention into sequential movements.

Despite the above caveats concerning the creation of a rigid taxonomy of the aphasias, acquired dysfunction in the reading of written language (alexia, the term preferred by neurologists, or dyslexia, as preferred by cognitive neuropsychologists) is still best understood in terms of five (often disputed) major categories (and see e.g. Benson and Geschwind, 1985, and Marshall, 1984). Reading of course is consciously and deliberately learnt, unlike speech which is naturally acquired, often against great odds, e.g. infantile isolation or deafness. *Pure alexia* (*alexia without agraphia, or posterior alexia*), the first category, leaves writing and spelling unimpaired, unlike the other four syndromes. It requires damage to the occipital visual areas of the LH (with resultant field defects), together with callosal (especially splenial) disconnection, usually via occlusion of the left posterior cerebral artery. Thus words in the left visual field (transmitting initially to the RH) cannot reach the LH, via the damaged corpus callosum, while LH occipital damage prevents direct access of the 'reading center' in the angular gyrus. Consequently the patient can see (the RH occipital cortex is intact, though field defects result from LH occipital damage), and can write (with an intact angular gyrus), while being unable to read his/her own writing. Any residual reading capacity is often via a painful sequential sounding out, letter by letter. This account is of course classically connectionist, and runs into trouble with patients who do not experience right homonymous hemianopia (loss of vision in the right half of the visual field), though according to Coltheart (1983) this condition is almost always present. Such letter-by-letter reading means that patients fare worse with longer words. It could represent either the survival of one (the phonological, see below) route, or alternatively it could merely be a compensatory form of reading, with no relevance for nomal reading, after the loss of the other route of direct lexical access. The second and third of the five major categories (see above) into which the alexias have traditionally been divided, *agraphia* and *central alexia*, are not central to our major considerations, and will not be discussed further. The fourth syndrome, *surface dyslexia*, is of interest mostly by contradistinction to deep or phonological dyslexia (below); regularly spelled words (e.g. 'hat', 'dog') and nonwords ('gife', 'boze') may be read better than irregular ones (e.g. 'yacht', 'sword') which may be wrongly regularized. Thus 'pint' may be read with a short vowel as in 'hint', and 'bear' may appear as 'beer'. With *phonological dyslexia* the patient cannot read nonwords; it is often considered to represent a subset of the symptoms of *deep dyslexia*, where in addition to the above deficit in reading nonwords, reading ability may depend upon semantic properties (concrete words being read better than abstract) and syntactic aspects (content words being read better than grammatical functors). Deep dyslexia will be discussed in detail later (Chapter 6) but is of interest being characterized by semantic paralexic substitutions (synonyms) during reading. Thus 'crocus' may be read as 'tulip', 'rock' as 'stone', 'hedgehog' as 'porcupine', though many other kinds of error also occur. As mentioned, nonwords (e.g. 'gife', 'boze') typically cannot be read, together with grammatical functors ('and', 'if', 'be'—while 'bee' presents no problem); abstract or nonimageable words ('length', 'holiness') may present more difficulties than concrete/

imageable ones ('dog', 'brick'), though again this is sometimes disputed. Some claim that deep dyslexia represents residual language functions in the RH (though see Chapter 6); it certainly requires major LH injury, and may appear during partial recovery from global aphasia. If the (disputed) RH hypothesis is correct, direct semantic access routes ('reading by sight') may remain intact in the RH, with loss of the phonological or mediated access ('reading by sounding out') mechanisms of the LH. Alternatively, the RH may directly generate elicited images, which are read off and partially transmitted to the LH for report.

Alternative psychological accounts (by contradistinction to the largely neurological approach undertaken above) of acquired reading disorders have been proposed (see e.g. Coltheart, 1983, 1985) and some aspects will be considered later in Chapter 6, though they are largely beyond the scope of this volume. However, such models generally assume that there are at least two major routes in reading—the nonlexical (phonological) process, and direct lexical access. The former, where such a question *is* addressed (and it often is not), is probably seen as a true LH mechanism, and involves the transformation of the orthographic representation (graphemes) into phonological (phoneme) form without the involvement of semantic processing. It is the only system which could cope with nonwords or novel words. Such spelling-to-sound transformations need not necessarily occur at the level of single letters; they could operate at the level of letter clusters, syllables or even morphemes (the smallest meaningful units). Transformations could even operate via a parallel simultaneous segmentation of the letter string in all possible ways, with each segment then automaticaly accessing all words which contain those segments in the equivalent positions; this procedure would then activate the corresponding pronunciations, from which would be derived the likely pronunciation of the target word or letter string. In surface dyslexia, neurological damage has perhaps resulted in a reduction in the pool of words upon which the above process of analogy can operate. All three mechanisms (single letter reading, letter groups, or derivation by analogy) could of course simultaneously operate. The second major route of direct lexical access, where there is no intermediate phonological stage, is possibly less firmly established in the LH, though there is little real speculation to date upon this issue. It is necessary for the correct reading aloud of exception or irregular words. *Regular* words can of course be correctly read by either the nonlexical (phonological) route or the route of direct lexical access. The two routes may be separately lost in acquired dyslexia, and if their neurological substrates are sufficiently apart, there may be a clear dissociation. If close together, there may always be some damage to both processes.

NONVERBAL SYNDROMES

We can consider these under the headings of the agnosias (including prosopagnosia), deficits of orientation and construction, hemineglect and hemi-inattention, emotionality, and music and singing.

The agnosias

Agnosia (see e.g. Damasio, 1985; Warrington, 1985) occurs when a normal percept is stripped of its meaning, in a patient, otherwise normal, who cannot recognize an object or its significance, or correctly manipulate it. Apart from *prosopagnosia* (see below), it has classically been divided into *apperceptive* and *associative* agnosia. Apperceptive agnosia is seen as a disability in constructing a stable representation of visual form, with a consequent impairment of higher-order recognition processes. It has been described as a post-Rolandic syndrome, often associated with RH damage, where there are problems in identifying anomalies in sketchily drawn scenes, or in identifying and isolating familiar overlapping figures, or in recognizing incomplete outlines (Gollins figures, Mooney faces, fragmented letters), or in recognizing unusual views, unevenly lit figures or where there are deviations from prototypical representations. On the other hand associative agnosia is traditionally seen as a deficit in accessing semantic (i.e. associative and functional) knowledge about an object, following the derivation of an intact perceptual representation of visual form. Intriguing recent observations include selective loss or preservation of certain categories (e.g. foods), or problems in making e.g. food/nonfood or animate/inanimate distinctions (see e.g. Humphreys and Riddoch, 1987a; Warrington and McCarthy, 1987; Warrington and Shallice, 1984). However, Humphreys and Riddoch (1987b) query the usefulness of this classical distinction between apperceptive and associative agnosia. They argue that it is too simple to provide a full description of the many kinds of deficit in visual object recognition. Moreover recent theories of information processing and object recognition in the normal brain dispute the old idea of a purely linear, serial, hierarchical relationship between the operations of elementary perception, object recognition, and classification and categorization; current ideas concerning e.g. cascade processing emphasize considerable overlapping and paralleling of the traditional stages. Moreover while associative agnosia has often been thought of as a LH syndrome, a meta-analysis of case studies by Humphreys and Riddoch fails to support such a view; indeed as we shall see at least some RH contribution may be likely in the semantic (as compared to the phonological–articulatory) aspects of language. Humphreys and Riddoch conclude that there is in fact little correlation between side of lesion and diagnoses of apperceptive and associative agnosia, and propose a new classification of the agnosias without appealing to locus of lesion.

Though not hitherto closely associated with the above controversy, *prosopagnosia* has likewise oscillated in terms of what has been thought of as the likely side of lesion. One of the theoretically most interesting syndromes, this acquired inability to recognize faces was originally associated with posterior RH damage. After a period during which the need for bilateral injury was stressed, with each hemisphere perhaps differentially specialized for different aspects of face processing, the pendulum of opinion seems now to be swinging back to a major RH involvement in prosopagnosia proper (though see Damasio and Damasio, 1986). We have of course an amazing capacity to recognize maybe thousands of faces, often after only a single exposure, despite the 'paraphernalia' of hats, spectacles and beards, the changes wrought by aging, and the aging of our own memories. Face recognition depends upon both whole-face 'gestalt' recognition, where the RH may play a major role (see Chapter 4), and piecemeal feature-by-feature analysis, which probably appeals to LH mechanisms. A prosopagnosic cannot recognize a familiar face, even his/her own, though it is seen *as* a face. Any subsequently successful recognition may depend upon other sensory modalities (e.g. sound of voice), or distinctive features (presence of a mole in a characteristic location). The syndrome is quite separate from any inability to discriminate between *unfamiliar* faces, and may not in fact even be restricted to faces. It may include other potentially ambiguous generic stimuli which require context-related individuation; there are therefore problems in recognizing individual members which closely resemble each other (like faces) in a particular category, and where successful recognition depends upon association and context of an 'episodic' (i.e. arbitrary) nature. Thus farmers, car enthusiasts, tailors and birdwatchers have recently been reported as displaying prosopagnosia-like disabilities in recognizing individual cows, cars, clothes or birds (Damasio, Damasio and Tranel, 1986). Other such generic stimuli of a potentially ambiguous nature with which prosopagnosics may experience difficulty include food, animals, abstract symbols, coins, handwriting, furniture (e.g. chair types), playing cards and personal possessions. While this seems to indicate a problem of evoking the specific historical context of a potentially ambiguous stimulus, it is not just a matter of episodic memory failure *per se*; there is not a confusion between one's own and others' possessions, and cars are misrecognized by make rather than by owner. Nor do pure prosopagnosics usually have any accompanying deficit in other visuospatial capacities, e.g. discrimination of unfamiliar faces, figure–ground segregation, stereopsis, recognition of objects from noncanonical (i.e. nonstandard) directions or when unevenly illuminated or incompletely presented. Nor do they usually experience problems of spatial localization or unilateral neglect, though they do typically also suffer from a color deficit.

Interestingly, it has been reported that in some cases galvanic skin responses (GSRs, an index of unconscious activation) associated with actual recognition may be preserved, despite functional (cortical?) agnosia; this phenomenon is curiously reminiscent of 'blindsight' where, after damage to the visual cortex the patient may deny seeing anything, yet may still be able to point to where 'unseen' flashes occur, presumably via preserved midbrain visual mechanisms to which consciousness does not have direct access (Weiskrantz, 1986). There is also another experimental paradigm, now involving category-specific interference, which demonstrates that a prosopagnosic may show signs of covert recognition while unable overtly to recognize faces (De Haan, Young and Newcombe, 1987). Thus the patient showed a normal pattern of interference from simultaneously presented distractor faces in a politician versus nonpolitician name-classification task, and he was faster in matching the identities of familiar than of unfamiliar faces, even though he performed at chance level when overtly classifying the faces.

Debate continues about the lateralization of prosopagnosia. The early studies finding a RH association tended to employ discrimination of unfamiliar faces, in an attempt to equate for task difficulty between patients, and so were not strictly testing for prosopagnosia (the failure to recognize *familiar* faces). While the need for a bilateral lesion is frequently emphasized (Damasio and Damasio, 1986), nevertheless the RH component seems to be consistently occipitotemporal, while the LH component is usually quite variable. One possibility is that bilateral lesions are required because, with unilateral RH lesions, LH feature-analytic strategies may suffice. Indeed prosopagnosics *do* tend to rely upon certain distinctive features in a manner reminiscent of LH processing. Thus there may be an asymmetric spatial distribution and/or temporal occurrence of bilateral involvement. Indeed prosopagnosia may be commoner when RH lesions follow rather than precede LH injury, and a nonpaired RH injury (i.e. one without any accompanying damage to the LH) may more commonly lead to prosopagnosia, even if transient, than a nonpaired LH lesion. We may therefore rely more upon RH mechanisms, especially perhaps for the important configurational aspects of faces, so that a previous LH lesion would be relatively silent until the occurrence of a second RH lesion.

Is there therefore a unique processor, perhaps largely located in the RH, which is dedicated to the processing of faces? This would be over and above a general RH superiority for pattern processing and emotions, which of course are also largely cued by face movements. There are four major arguments in support of such a thesis (Levine, 1989). Our face-recognition ability is more prodigious than that of any other similar class of stimuli, though it could simply be that we are more familiar with such important stimuli. Secondly, face recognition appears to have a unique developmental history, though recent work suggests that neonates may learn to recognize voices just as readily, and the reported developmental dip in face-recognition ability at puberty may also be found with voice recognition (see Chapter 4). Thirdly (and again see Chapter 4) faces are more susceptible to inversion (which destroys the configurational or relational aspects of a stimulus) than is the recognition of other mono-orientational stimuli. However, expertise with other such material (e.g.

dog breeds by breeders) which develops an awareness of configurational (RH?) properties also leads to an inversion effect. Finally, specific lesions to the inferior visual association areas (inferior occipital and temporal) are involved. (In the macaque, neurons in the superior temporal sulcus of the visual cortex have been identified which respond primarily to faces—human or monkey, real or photographed, full or sideways view; however, in view of the fact that a different area is involved from that of humans, not too much should perhaps be made of such findings.) However, why then are prosopagnosics so comparatively rare, given that these areas are not infrequently vulnerable? One possibility (and cf. the discussion of deep dyslexia in Chapter 6) is that only certain individuals, given that lesion, are likely to manifest prosopagnosia, due perhaps to idiosyncracies of neural organization. This would explain why hemispherectomies or split-brain patients tested via a single hemisphere fail to evince prosopagnosia, while they nevertheless demonstrate face-processing strategies in accordance with the hemisphere interrogated. (Shortly we shall discuss hemineglect whereby patients with unilateral injury may fail to attend to events occurring on one or other side of the midline. It has long been asked why the isolated hemispheres of split-brain patients do not behave similarly, and it is interesting to note that this has in fact now been demonstrated with appropriate testing procedures.) Finally, the fact that prosopagnosia-like symptoms can occur with other kinds of generic stimuli also argues against there being a unique faces-specific processor, unless lesions typically fail to be restricted to a sufficiently circumscribed region within which such a processor could be located.

Orientation, construction and drawing

Lesions to the LH may affect dynamic route-finding abilities, e.g. around a hospital ward or city (though the RH has also been implicated), and the ability to disembed hidden figures, while RH injury may affect the capacity to manipulate static images and maps without reference to one's own progression through that space (e.g. as in mental rotation), and to perform figure completion tests (see e.g. Damasio, 1985). In the context of construction and drawing LH damage can lead to oversimplification, loss of detail, poor discrimination of elements but with an intact overall configuration and pattern of spatial interrelationships; conversely RH injury results in haphazard, inappropriate combinations of correctly discriminated features, with faulty overall configurations, proportions and spatial interrelationships, (see Figures 4a and 4b). Thus while the RH has long been considered silent, unimportant, unconscious and automatic, its nonverbal visuospatial roles (often vaguely defined, by exclusion) have only comparatively recently become apparent. These may include size discrimination, directional perception, stereopsis and depth, part–whole interrelationships, recognition of anomalies, incomplete pictures,

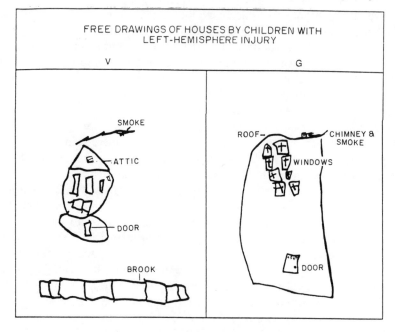

Fig. 4a   Free drawings of a house produced by children with LH and RH damage. Labels indicate elements named spontaneously by each child.

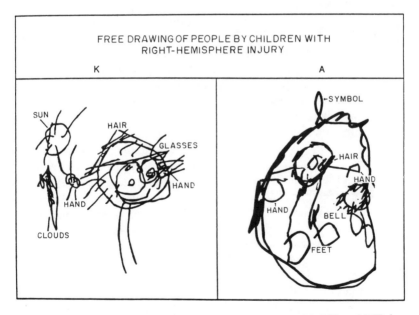

Fig. 4b Free drawings of a person produced by children with LH and RH damage. Labels indicate elements named spontaneously by each child. (Figures 4a and 4b reproduced with permission from J. Stiles-Davies, J. Janowski, M. Engel and R. Nass. Drawing abilities in four young children with congenital unilateral brain lesions, *Neuropsychologia*, 1988, **26**, 359–371.

objects viewed from unusual angles, humorous juxtapositions, and contextual relationships (Warrington, 1985).

Hemineglect, hemi-inattention

At some point it is clear that there must be limits upon the amount of information which an organism can simultaneously process. Such *filtering* may be more evident at the level of response preparation than with perceptual processing; it is far more difficult to perform and monitor the success of two motor operations simultaneously, than it is to attend simultaneously to two or more channels of incoming information, though even then if both channels occupy the same sensory modality (e.g. two different spoken messages, one to each ear), the solution may be rapid alternation between them. Division of attention is always at some cost, and evidence is available that neuronal responses to attended items may be enhanced, with corresponding suppression of neural activity for unattended material. The correlates of overt attentional foci will of course be head, eye and possibly hand movements towards the current focus (orientational and fixational responses); recently it has been shown that, in the visual modality at least, attention may be *covertly* directed to loci *other* than the current observable *overt* focus (see *Neuropsychologia*, 1987, **25** , whole no. 1A). After detection that a peripheral event may be of possible importance, orientational head movements and eye foveation may be directed by the midbrain superior colliculus and the frontal eyefields of the anterior cortex, regions which work largely in parallel (see below for a detailed discussion of the relevant anatomy and physiology). Pattern processing may then proceed in the occipital (striate) cortex, with object recognition developing in the extrastriate regions and particularly in the inferior temporal lobe. In the posterior parietal cortex, sensory and motor attentional fields may be mapped. It is this region which is uniquely involved in the syndrome of unilateral neglect.

This syndrome is characterized by inattention towards or neglect of events on the (usually) left side of body space, in the absence of primary sensory or motor defects (Heilman, Watson and Valenstein, 1985; Mesulam, 1985). The patient may brush up against a doorpost on the left, ignore food on the left side of the plate or tray (until perhaps it is rotated!), shave, groom or dress only the right side, read only from the right side of a page, leave a large margin on the left, copy only the right side of drawings, ignoring either the left side of an entire picture (see Figure 5) or the left sides of all objects within a picture, cancel only lines on the right side of a page (see Figure 6), or bisect a line to the right of its true midpoint. Lesions causing left neglect are usually large and of sudden onset or rapidly progressive. Five separable components have been identified. With *hemi-inattention*, there is failure to respond to unilateral events unless attention is drawn to them. Thus the patient can be bribed or forced to attend left, but normally is reluctant to respond in the side of

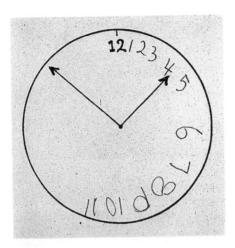

Fig. 5 This left-neglecting patient, when asked to draw (from memory) the numbers on a prepared clock face, which already showed the hands and 12 o'clock, placed all the remaining numbers 1 to 11 on the right side of the face, completely ignoring the left side.

extracorporeal space to the left of the midline, and may be slower to initiate a response towards the neglected left hemispace even when the response is initiated and terminated entirely within the intact right half space (Posner *et al.*, 1987). *Hemispatial neglect* involves the classical defects of drawing, line bisection, eating off one side of the plate etc. With *hemi-akinesia*, in the absence of gross motor defects there is failure to raise an arm contralateral to the lesion, or, unless encouraged, to orient head or eyes to stimuli contralateral to the lesion. With *allesthesia*, a patient touched on the left side will report the event as occurring on the right. *Extinction* is often the most intractable, with failure to respond to one side during simultaneous bilateral stimulation, even when unilateral performance on the 'bad' side is relatively intact. Clinically, right side extinction is less rare than right neglect, which may not depend upon the former. Extinction as a phenomenon is reminiscent of the larger tactual, visual-field, and ear asymmetries found with normal subjects during competitive bilateral stimulation (e.g. with dichhaptic and dichotic inputs, see Chapter 4).

Unilateral neglect may be considered with reference to more than one coordinate system (Bradshaw, Pierson-Savage and Nettleton, 1988): the body midline (currently preferred), head coordinates (dissociable from body coordinates by head turn), retinal coordinates (dissociable by eye turn), and gravitational coordinates (dissociable by the subject or patient tilting or adopting a horizontal posture). Several recent studies have shown that neglect may be modified by turning or tilting head, eyes or body (Ladavas, 1987). We must

Fig. 6   This left-neglecting patient, when asked to cancel (draw a line through) all the lines scattered at various orientations across the page, completely ignored lines to the left, despite repeated prompting.

therefore conclude that the brain does not merely register events impinging upon the proximal receptor surfaces, but for good reasons maps events occurring out in space beyond the body before they are directly encountered. Thus the auditory system maps the contralateral sound field, and is affected by gaze direction. The superior colliculus controls eye, pinna and head orientation, and may combine spatial representations of sight and hearing. In the visual cortex, eye and head position, including tilt, may alter the firing of retinotopic cells, and the EEG is modified by lateral movements of hands as well as eyes.

Such considerations do not presuppose that attention is necessarily overt, involving the direction of fovea and hands; thus we can manipulate the direction of *covertly* focussed attention in normal subjects, as if it were an attentional spotlight focussed to a point in the visual field other than where the fovea is directed, and measure reaction times to visual targets occurring at fixation, or at an attended locus away from fixation, or at an unattended locus. With such procedures, valid or invalid location cueing can be employed, or differential frequencies of target occurrence in different locations, and performance transitions may occur at the vertical (and horizontal) meridian. We may therefore covertly orient attention, and program overt eye movements or manual responses, all within a single frame of reference.

Neglect is not a unitary phenomenon; different sensory modalities and different processes are disturbed by lesions in various loci. Important factors, as in all such clinical disorders, include locus of lesion, rapidity and nature of the pathology, the interval between damage and testing, and premorbid processing strategies. Important areas involved in attention to meaningful events include cortical polysensory convergence areas (especially the inferior parietal lobule), frontal regions (the eyefields and motor areas), the basal ganglia, thalamus and mesencephalic reticular activating system. Visual information goes to the cortex either directly via thalamocortical (retinogeniculostriate) routes, or indirectly via midbrain (retinotectal) pathways; the former may be responsible for pattern vision, identifying 'what?', while the latter 'where?' system is more concerned with spatial location. After receipt in the primary visual projection area, signals are sent to the inferior parietal lobule (where a spatial map is probably maintained) and the cingulate gyrus (a limbic center involving inwardly motivational aspects). Both regions then project to the prefrontal cortex, where spatially appropriate motor responses (a 'motor map') can be prepared, including orienting and visual and haptic exploration within extrapersonal space. The main difference between the roles of these frontal regions and the superior colliculus may be that the former are more concerned with significant events, while the latter mediates a general 'awareness' (probably unconscious) of and responsivity towards all peripheral occurrences; the inferior parietal lobule, on the other hand, may register a spatial template ('sensory map') of important events whether or not orienting head or eye movements occur.

Rizzolatti and Gallese (1988) describe from experiments with primates the roles of the two important cortical structures, the parietal and frontal lobe; the latter they divide into the frontal eyefields and inferior area 6. The frotal eyefields are a visuomotor center for saccadic eye movements. Lesions result in decrements in spontaneous and evoked saccades in a contralateral direction, and neglect of contralateral events, especially those in *far* extrapersonal space. Deficits seem to be attentional and not just oculomotor. Inferior area 6 seems to be important in transforming somatosensory and visual information into motor acts. It contains a somatosensory representation of movements independent of the main motor cortex, and responds strongly to objects moving within the subject's *close* peripersonal space, especially when *approaching* the subject. It contains visual receptive fields located around tactile fields, the two forming a single responsive region for the skin and closely adjacent space. Representations are anchored to body coordinates and do not change position with eye movements, indicating that visual information is coded in terms of *body* rather than retinal coordinates. Activity occurs with face and arm movements, especially for reaching and for movements *towards* the mouth.

Unilateral lesions lead to attentional deficits for near contralateral peripersonal space, in contrast to the far extrapersonal decrements resulting from
frontal eyefield damage. There are indications that the inferior perietal lobule,
which seems to largely parallel the role of inferior area 6, may be more
important in Man. Again, lesions lead to deficits in organizing limb movements
in near peripersonal space, and hemi-inattention. It seems to compute the
spatial position of objects in craniocentric coordinates, integrating retinal locus
and fixational direction.

Left neglect after RH injury is commoner, more severe and longer lasting
than right neglect after LH injury (Heilman, Watson and Valenstein, 1985;
Mesulam, 1985), though the latter syndrome may of course be masked by
incapacitating trauma from LH injury. It is also possible that there are
anterior–posterior differences confounding the left–right asymmetry. An appealing hypothesis is that while the LH may unilaterally mediate language and
speech for the entire organism, the RH in a complementary fashion subserves
the representation of extracorporeal space, not only contralaterally (i.e. with
respect to objects falling to the left of the midline), but also ipsilaterally (right
side), while the LH can only subserve contralateral (right) hemispace. Thus if
the RH is damaged, only right hemispace can be subserved by the surviving
LH. This idea that hemineglect stems from a disordered representational
schema of extracorporeal space is compatible with evidence that patients'
inabilities to recall buildings on the left side of a street depend upon their
imaginary standpoint at one or other end. However, such an account cannot
explain patients' difficulties (see above) in shifting attention *leftwards* even
when the target towards which attention is shifted still occurs within the 'intact'
right hemispace. Nor is it compatible with evidence that RH damage is
associated with lowered affect, defective alerting, poorer arousal, slower
performance by either hand, all suggesting that the RH mediates bilateral as
well as contralateral arousal (see below). Such observations are supported by
studies with normal subjects, indicating that temporoparietal RH activity is
activated by important events on either side, while the LH is only aroused
contralaterally. Nor again can the idea of a representational schema, on its
own, account for the apparent importance of the commissures in hemineglect.
Thus while significant neglect is generally absent after commissurotomy and
hemispherectomy, the commissures nevertheless seem to play a role in integrating hemisphere–hand and hemisphere–hemispace mapping, when a hand
crosses the midline. Consequently if a commissurotomy patient tactually
bisects a line with the right hand in left hemispace, the disconnection prevents
the right hand from being influenced by the RH, which normally subserves the
left hemispace for intentional movements; instead, the right hand remains only
under the motor control of the contralateral LH, which will now direct it back
to its own hemispace, thus generating abductive errors to the right. Similar
arguments apply for an abductive leftwards tendency for the left hand,

abductive tendencies which in normal subjects will be counteract
opposite hemisphere via intact commissures. Hemispheric differen
capacity to direct attention, overt and covert, sensory and mo
therefore to be even more important than asymmetries in the schematic
representation of extracorporeal space.

In our discussion of prosopagnosia (above) we noted that recognition of
some kind may apparently occur without conscious awareness, a phenomenon
which we noted was reminiscent of blindsight and indeed also of certain
memory disorders (e.g. the Korsakoff syndrome), where the patient may
continue to acquire new skills without ever being able consciously to remember
the circumstances and events surrounding their acquisition. It has recently
been shown (Marshall and Halligan, 1988) that there may be a similar
dissociation between overt and covert perception in a case of (left) visuospatial
neglect; two drawings were simultaneously presented of a house, in one of
which the left side was on fire. The drawings were judged to be identical, yet
when asked to select which house she would prefer to live in, the patient
reliably continued to choose the house which was not burning. To this list we
may add recent reports of pure alexics (see above) who, while explicitly unable
to identify words, nevertheless perform above chance on word/nonword
decisions and forced-choice semantic categorization tasks (Coslett and Saffran,
1989).

Emotionality

Damage to the LH typically results in the negative 'catastrophic' reaction of
crying, swearing, depression, refusals and dysphoria, while with RH injury
either indifference, anosognosia and minimizing responses may occur, or even
positive affect, euphoria and jocularity (Gainotti, 1983; Grafman *et al.*, 1986;
Otto, Yeo and Dougher 1987; Silberman and Weingartner, 1986). It could of
course be argued that dysphoria after LH injury and accompanying aphasia is
not inappropriate, and even that euphoric indifference after RH damage is just
another form of neglect. Unilateral amobarbital injections reveal similar if
transient effects to trauma, as does unilateral ECT, which slows down the
affected hemisphere. Thus RH ECT may be as psychiatrically efficacious as
bilateral ECT if it retards the activity of the depressive, negative RH. Such a
formulation suggests that the LH (mediating positive affect) and the RH
(negative affect) are in a state of mutual inhibition; however (see Chapters 4
and 5), the idea of a mutual inhibitory balance is far from being universally
accepted on other grounds, and we can also ask whether the syndromes reflect
pathological *under*arousal of one hemisphere, or pathological *over*arousal of
its fellow. Nevertheless there are claims that manics may prefer global holistic
strategies, and depressive may show an obsessive attention to detail, though
again ideas of cognitive style (see Chapter 11) reflecting differences in hemispheric processing strategies (see Chapter 4) are somewhat controversial. Even

so, there is good evidence that schizophrenics and maybe depressives show abnormal visual field and ear asymmetries.

Otherwise silent RH lesions have been implicated in pathological laughing, and similar silent dysfunctions of the LH have been cited as causing pathological crying, i.e. due again to a presumed disinhibition of the intact contralateral hemisphere. Similarly gelastic (laughing) epilepsy has been related to LH foci, and dacrystic (crying) epilepsy to RH seizures and increased ipsilateral activation. Hysterical symptoms (loss of sensation and loss of movement without obvious organic causes) are said to be commoner on the left side of the body (i.e. in regions mediated by the RH). Damage to the RH certainly leads to aprosodia (loss of natural pitch, tonality and inflections in speech), both expressive and receptive (Ross, 1985). Finally, lower GSR values have been reported for the right hand during depressive episodes, though there is uncertainty about whether GSR effects are excitatory or inhibitory, ipsilateral or contralateral. The role of the frontal cortex may be to inhibit the subcortical limbic structures primarily involved in emotion; indeed the proximity of a LH lesion to the frontal pole correlates positively with degree of depression. However, do the two hemispheres mediate *opposing* emotions, or are all emotions mediated by the RH? It is of course true that there are probably more negative than positive emotions anyway, and the various negative emotions (disgust, fear, anger) may be differently lateralized, with different behavioral consequences. Moreover a hemisphere may be 'disadvantaged' for several possible reasons—because it operates less efficiently, or because it is relatively inactive—and in any case 'more active' does not necessarily mean 'better functioning': hyperarousal (e.g. of the LH in schizophrenia) can be equally maladaptive.

Although this chapter deals with clinical evidence for laterality differences in e.g. emotion, emotional studies with normals (Bryden and Ley, 1983) are best dealt with here. Such normative studies can be considered under two headings: visual field and ear asymmetries, and facial asymmetries. Dichotic and even monaural advantages (see Chapter 4) for the left ear (LEAs) have been repeatedly shown for the recognition of emotional sounds (cries, shrieks, laughter), and for emotionally intoned sentences (angrily, happily, sadly); a double dissociation is even reported, i.e. a right ear advantage (REA) for reporting the verbal content, and a LEA for the emotional aspects. An advantage for stimuli presented to the left visual field (LVF, i.e. contacting the RH) occurs in discriminating emotional faces and emotions *irrespective* of the faces themselves. The usual LVF advantage for face processing is increased with emotional faces, suggesting that emotionality confers a RH advantage over and above the requirements for processing patterns and faces. There are also claims of leftwards conjugate lateral eye movements (cLEMs) in response to emotional questions, though the whole issue of cLEMs is controversial (see Chapters 4 and 11).

Turning now to facial asymmetries, as discussed in Chapter 1, when we present composite faces, one side happy, one sad, for decisions about which of two such mirror-image composites looks happier, the left side of such composites is usually seen (by the RH) as more strongly portraying one of the two possible interpretations; thus if the left side is happy, the whole face seems happier than if the left side is sad and the right happy. Moreover the owner's left side of the face typically produces stronger emotional expressions, such that in face-to-face confrontation, the weaker right half of the communicator's face falls within the perceiver's stronger LVF/RH. The face is of course the primary organ of recognition, communication and emotional expression, as Darwin himself observed in a pioneering study over 100 years ago. The musculature of the human face is perhaps more highly developed than in any other species, perhaps reflecting our social needs. We can divide facial emotions into posed, voluntary or deliberate, and spontaneous, involuntary or automatic (Borod and Koff, 1984; Weber and Sackeim, 1984). In the former category, movements originate in the motor cortex, and travel monosynaptically via the cortico-bulbar tracts to the internal capsule, the pons, the medullary pyramids (where decussation, or crossing over to the opposite side, occurs), down to the facial nucleus and the seventh cranial nerve. Its ventral portion may subserve largely bilateral innervation, perhaps more for the upper musculature and for surprise, horror, frowning. The dorsal portion seems to be largely contralateral, and to innervate the lower muscles which portray sadness, contempt, disdain, smiling, doubt and (again) horror and surprise. Overall, from still photo and video analyses, deliberately posed negative emotions (especially disgust, anger, sadness and grief) seem to show stronger left-side intensities, and perhaps likewise happiness, though other positive emotions may be more bilateral, perhaps because they are normally relatively more spontaneous and involuntary. Interestingly, people who can voluntarily wiggle their ears or wink one eye or unilaterally smile are usually more successful with the left side, suggesting that motility and voluntary expression is easier on that side.

Turning now to spontaneous, involuntary and automatic displays of emotion, we find that the innervation is more complicated. It may originate in the thalamus and/or the globus pallidus and continue on to the facial nucleus via multisynaptic extrapyramidal pathways. Other areas are probably also involved, including orbitofrontal regions, the medial tip of the temporal lobes, the hypothalamus, brainstem, pons and midbrain. Such spontaneously elicited expressions, e.g. in response to films and jokes, tend to show bilateral representation for positive emotions, just as with posed or voluntary expressions above, while negative emotions may possibly be more left sided. There are claims that electromyelogram (EMG) asymmetries, while subjects spontaneously respond to emotional questions, show greater right-sided zygomatic activity after positive questions, and greater left-sided activity after negative questions, while for deliberately posed expressions zygomatic activity may be greater on the left side for either kind of question.

In conclusion the nature of asymmetries in the facial expression of emotion is still controversial; the locus of the musculature (upper or lower) and the nature of the emotion (positive or negative) may be very important. Overall, the RH is closely concerned with general arousal processes, including emotion, and may be specialized for vigilance towards and activation by negative aspects of the environment. Hence to avoid danger, it is ready to respond to the total, global situation, it is specialized for sustained vigilance and attention, and it is particularly sensitive to possibly aversive stimulation, resulting in lower left-side pain and touch thresholds.

Music and singing after unilateral intervention or injury

Singing may be preserved after LH damage; RH amobarbital suppression may affect singing but not speech, though the resultant speech may be monotonous, with incorrect pitch though maybe intact rhythm. Dissociation of amusia (loss of musical capacities) and aphasia is not uncommon, and was reported long before LH mediation of speech was known, though not all aspects of music are necessarily mediated by the RH (Henson, 1985). Thus just as with prosopagnosia, amusia is not necessarily a consequence of injury to a single brain centre, though as a generalization the RH largely subserves melodic tonality, and the LH rhythmic sequentiality (see Chapter 4). Amusia may be *receptive*, with impairments in pitch perception, instrument recognition, chord analysis, melody recognition or reading musical notation; alternatively it may be *expressive*, with impaired production of known or new melodies, vocally or instrumentally produced, with or without inabilities to transcribe music. Amusia, however, is as yet poorly understood, and is bedevilled by patient bias, as recent amusics, unless they are professional musicians, are far less likely to present for treatment than aphasics. Moreover studies with normals often show big differences in the nature (strength or direction) of asymmetries, between skilled and unskilled musicians.

SUMMARY AND CONCLUSIONS

New methods of visualizing the brain (CAT and PET scans, NMRI, rCBF and EEG techniques) have all demonstrated morphological and functional asymmetries, though their interpretation is not always completely straightforward. Electrostimulation, unilateral ECT and unilateral amobarbital suppression provide further behavioral evidence of asymmetrical function. However, analysis of the effects of unilateral injury, especially of the cortex, has provided most of our information. Thus after LH trauma there may occur apraxia, alexia or aphasia, with various manifestations (pure, surface or deep; Broca's, Wernicke's, transcortical, etc.) as an apparent function of locus and extent of cortical injury; however, such taxonomy and 'diagram making' should be undertaken with some caution, as alternative interpretations may be possible. Nevertheless connectionist principles in a recent guise seem to re-emerge when the role of subcortical structures (thalamus and basal ganglia) is considered.

Syndromes associated with RH damage tend to be less sharply defined than their LH counterparts. Nevertheless they include prosopagnosia (though bilateral damage may be required; and patients may fail to recognize other forms of potentially ambiguous generic stimuli which require context-related individuation, and not just faces), difficulties with orientation, construction and drawing, hemi-inattention and hemineglect (probably commoner and more severe after RH than LH damage), and emotional disturbances. While the RH may be overactive during intense emotion, or may be released from inhibition by LH damage, with a resultant 'catastrophic' reaction, opinion is divided concerning whether the RH mediates all forms of emotional activity, or whether it subserves the negative rather than the positive aspects. The RH certainly seems to be involved with general arousal processes, and may be specialized for vigilance towards important and possibly threatening aspects of the environment. Studies with normals (tachistoscopic, dichotic, or measured asymmetries of posed or involuntary facial expressions) all support the idea of a RH role in emotionality. While music has traditionally been thought of as a province of the RH, this may be strictly true only of the melodic aspects; indeed clinical (and normal) studies all indicate that face recognition, emotionality and music are probably all subserved by both hemispheres, though in different ways under different circumstances.

IMPORTANT READINGS

Benson, D. F. and Geschwind, N. Aphasia and related disorders: A clinical approach. In M.-M. Mesulam (ed.), *Principles of Behavioral Neurology*. Philadelphia: F. A. Davis, 1985, pp. 194–238.

Borod, J. C. and Koff, E. Asymmetries in affective facial expression: Behavior and anatomy. In N. A. Fox and R. J. Davidson (eds.), *The Psychobiology of Affective Development*. Hillsdale, N.J.: Erlbaum, 1984, pp. 293–323.

Bradshaw, J. L. and Nettleton, N. C. *Human Cerebral Asymmetry*. Englewood Cliffs, N.J.: Prentice Hall, 1983.

Bradshaw, J. L., Pierson-Savage, J. M. and Nettleton, N. C. Hemispace asymmetries. In H. A. Whitaker (ed.), *Contemporary Reviews in Neuropsychology*. New York: Springer-Verlag, 1988, pp. 1–35.

Bryden, M. P. and Ley, R. G. Right hemispheric involvement in the perception and expression of emotion in normal humans. In K. M. Heilman and P. Satz (eds.), *Neuropsychology of Human Emotion*. New York: Guilford Press, 1983, pp. 6–44.

Caramazza, A. and McCloskey, M. The case for single patient studies. *Cognitive Neuropsychology*, 1988, **5**, 517–28.

Coltheart, M. The right hemisphere and disorders of reading. In A. W. Young (ed.), *Functions of the Right Cerebral Hemisphere*. New York: Academic Press, 1983, pp. 171–201.

Coltheart, M. Cognitive neuropsychology and the study of reading. In M. I. Posner and O. S. M. Marin (eds.), *Attention and Performance XI*. Hillsdale, N.J.: Erlbaum, 1985, pp. 3–37.

Coslett, H. B. and Saffran, E. Evidence for preserved reading in pure alexia. *Brain*, 1989, **112**, 327–60.

Crosson, B. Subcortical functions in language: A working model. *Brain and Language*, 1985, **25**, 257–92.

Damasio, A. R. Disorders of complex visual processing: Agnosias, achromatopsia, Balint's syndrome, and related difficulties of orientation and construction. In M.-M. Mesulam (ed.), *Principles of Behavioral Neurology*. Philadelphia: F. A. Davis, 1985, pp. 259–88.

Damasio, A. R. and Damasio, H. The anatomical substrate of prosopagnosia. In R. Bruyer (ed.), *The Neuropsychology of Face Perception and Facial Expression*. Hillsdale, N.J.: Erlbaum, 1986, pp. 31–8.

Damasio, A. R., Damasio, H. and Tranel, D. Prosopagnosia: Anatomic and physiologic aspects. In H. D. Ellis, M. A. Jeeves, F. Newcombe and A. Young (eds.), *Aspects of Face Processing*. The Hague: Martinus Nijhoff, 1986, pp. 268–77.

Davidson, R. J. Electroencephalographic measures of cerebral asymmetry: Conceptual and methodological issues. *International Journal of Neuroscience*, 1988, **39**, 71–89.

De Haan, E. H. F., Young, A. and Newcombe, F. Faces interfere with name classification in a prosopagnosic patient. *Cortex*, 1987, **23**, 309–16.

Gainotti, G. Laterality of affect: The emotional behavior of right and left-brain-damaged patients. In M. S. Myslobodsky (ed.). *Hemisyndromes: Psychobiology, Neurology, Psychiatry*. New York: Academic Press, 1983, pp. 175–92.

Grafman, J., Vance, S. C., Weingartner, H., Solazar, A. M. and Armin, D. The effects of lateralized frontal lesions on mood regulation. *Brain*, 1986, **109**, 1127–48.

Heilman, K. M., Watson, R. T. and Valenstein, E. Neglect and related disorders. In K. M. Heilman and E. Valenstein (eds.), *Clinical Neuropsychology* (2nd edition). New York: Oxford University Press, 1985, pp. 377–401.

Henderson, V. W., Naeser, M. A., Weiner, J. M., Pieniadz, J. M. and Chui, H. C. CT criteria of hemispheric asymmetry fail to predict language lateralization. *Neurology*, 1984, **34**, 1086–9.

Henson, R. A. Amusia. In J. A. M. Frederiks (ed.), *Handbook of Clinical Neurology*, Vol. 1 (45): *Clinical Neuropsychology* (gen. eds. P. Vinken, G. Bruyn and G. Klawans). Amsterdam: Elsevier, 1985, pp. 483–90.

Humphreys, G. W. and Riddoch, M. J. On telling your fruit from your vegetables: A consideration of category-specific deficits after brain damage. *Trends in the Neurosciences*, 1987a, **10**, 145–8.

Humphreys, G. W. and Riddoch, M. J. The fractionation of visual agnosia. In G. W. Humphreys and M. J. Riddoch (eds.), *Visual Object Processing: A Cognitive Neuropsychological Approach*. Hillsdale, N.J.: Erlbaum, 1987b, pp. 281–306.

Kertesz, A. Aphasia. In J. A. M. Frederiks (ed.), *Handbook of Clinical Neurology*, Vol. 1 (45): *Clinical Neuropsychology* (gen. eds. P. Vinken, G. Bruyn and G. Klawans). Amsterdam: Elsevier, 1985, pp. 287–331.

Kertesz, A., Black, S., Polk, M. and Howell, J. Cerebral asymmetries on magnetic resonance imaging. *Cortex*, 1986, **22**, 117–27.

Koff, E. I., Naeser, M. A., Pieniadz, J. M., Foundas, A. L. and Levine, H. L. Computed tomographic scan hemispheric asymmetries in right and left handed male and female subjects. *Archives of Neurology*, 1986, **43**, 487.

Ladavas, E. Is the hemispatial deficit produced by right parietal lobe damage associated with retinal or gravitational coordinates? *Brain,* 1987, **110**, 167–80.

Levine, S. C. The question of faces: Special in the brain of the beholder. In A. W. Young and H. D. Ellis (eds.), *Handbook of Research in Face Processing.* Hillsdale, N.J.: Erlbaum, 1989, pp. 37–40.

Marshall, J. C. Toward a rational taxonomy of the acquired dyslexias. In R. N. Malatesha and H. A. Whitaker (eds.), *Dyslexia: A Global Issue.* The Hague: Martinus Nijhoff, 1984, pp. 211–32.

Marshall, J. C. The description and interpretation of aphasic language disorder. *Neuropsychologia,* 1986, **24**, 5–24.

Marshall, J. C. and Halligan, P. W. Blindsight and insight in visuospatial neglect. *Nature,* 1988, **336**, 766–7.

Mesulam, M.-M. Attention, confusional states and neglect. In M.-M. Mesulam (ed.), *Principles of Behavioral Neurology.* Philadelphia: F. A. Davis, 1985, pp. 125–68.

Naeser, M. A. and Borod, J. C. Aphasia in left handers: Lesion site, left side and hemispheric asymmetries on CT. *Neurology,* 1986, **36**, 471–88.

Ojemann, G. A. Brain organization for language from the perspective of electrical stimulation mapping. *Behavioral and Brain Sciences,* 1983, **6**, 189–230.

Otto, M. W., Yeo, R. A. and Dougher, M. J. Right hemisphere involvement in depression: Toward a neuropsychological theory of negative affective experiences. *Biological Psychiatry,* 1987, **22**, 1201–15.

Posner, M. I., Petersen, S. E., Fox, P. T. and Raichle, M. E. Localization of cognitive operations in the human brain. *Science,* 1988, **240**, 1627–31.

Posner, M. I., Walker, J. A., Friedrich, F. A. and Rafal, R. D. How do the parietal lobes direct covert attention? *Neuropsychologia,* 1987, **25**, 135–46.

Risberg, J. Regional cerebral blood flow in neuropsychology. *Neuropsychologia,* 1986, **24**, 135–40.

Rizzolatti, G. and Gallese, V. Mechanisms and theories of spatial neglect. In F. Boller and J. Grafman (eds.), *Handbook of Neuropsychology.* Amsterdam: Elsevier Science Publishers, 1988, pp. 223–246.

Ross, E. D. Modulation of affect and nonverbal communication by the right hemisphere. In M.-M. Mesulam (ed.) *Principles of Behavioral Neurology.* Philadelphia: F. A. Davis, 1985, pp. 239–58.

Silberman, E. K. and Weingartner, H. Hemispheric lateralization of functions related to mood. *Brain and Cognition,* 1986, **5**, 322–53.

Warrington, E. K. Agnosia: The impairment of object recognition. In J. A. M. Frederiks (ed.), *Handbook of Clinical Neurology,* Vol. 1 (45): *Clinical Neuropsychology* (gen. eds. P. Vinken, G. Bruyn and G. Klawans). Amsterdam: Elsevier, 1985, pp. 333–49.

Warrington, E. K. and McCarthy, R. A. Categories of knowledge. *Brain,* 1987, **110**. 1273–96.

Warrington, E. K. and Shallice, T. Category specific semantic impairments. *Brain,* 1984, **107**, 829–54.

Weber, S. L. and Sackeim, H. A. The development of functional brain asymmetry in the regulation of emotion. In N. A. Fox and R. J. Davidson (eds.), *The Psychobiology of Affective Development.* Hillsdale, N.J.: Erlbaum, 1984, pp. 325–51.

Weiskrantz, L. *Blindsight: A Case Study and Implications.* Oxford: Clarendon Press, 1986.

Yeo, R. A., Turkheimer, E., Raz, N. and Bigler, E. Volumetric asymmetries of the human brain: Intellectual correlates. *Brain and Cognition,* 1987, **6**, 15–23.

3

Studies with commissurotomies

Commissurotomy operations provide us with the second major source of evidence of hemispheric specialization in humans. Indeed in terms of impact they may be regarded as the primary source, even though as we saw clinical evidence far antedates that of commissurotomy, going back more than a century, and recent work with normals (next chapter) is pre-eminent if only in terms of sheer bulk. Not only are the findings often apparently so dramatic (if inevitably somewhat contrived) that they reach the popular press, but such fundamental questions as the unity (or otherwise) of conscious experience seem, at least in principle, to be capable of direct experimental investigation. Indeed, as we shall see, this has been recognized for well over a century, and only a satisfactory surgical procedure has been lacking until relatively recently. While both clinical and commissurotomy patients inevitably share some brain and behavioral abnormalities, commissurotomy and normative studies are more similar at an experimental and procedural level than either is to the clinical approach. Of course it is not just the nature and extent of conscious awareness, and the unihemispheric mediation of language and nonverbal functions, which may be addressed by studying commissurotomy patients; there are other such issues as whether during learning a memory trace is stored on one or both sides, and how it may be transferred between hemispheres. Animal studies have in particular addressed this last problem. Newer techniques with human patients permit us to discuss the representation of language in the minor (right) hemisphere, and that hemisphere's system of beliefs, hopes, knowledge and aspirations, independent of that of the verbal left hemisphere. We can also study deliberate and unconscious methods of extra-callosally transferring information ('cross-cueing'), and the independent processing capacities of the two hemispheres when divided or joined. This chapter examines the evidence, from the effects of surgical disconnection of the hemispheres, for human cerebral asymmetry.

'The "corpus callosum" is the greatest leap anywhere made by Nature in her brain work' (T. H. Huxley, 1863, cited by E. G. Jones: Anatomy, development and physiology of the corpus callosum. In A. G. Reeves (ed.), *Epilepsy and the Corpus Callosum*. New York: Plenum, 1985, p. 3). We shall deal here with two related though independent issues which interdigitate via the corpus callosum: hemispheric specialization, and cerebral duality.

For 150 years there has been speculation on the possible duplex nature of consciousness, though only recently, largely through the studies of the Nobel laureate Sperry, has the problem been amenable to empirical investigation. Thus in the 1840s the otherwise obscure English physician Wigan noted that each cerebrum is a distinct and perfect whole as an organ of thought, and that a separate and distinct process of thinking may be carried out in each hemisphere separately. By 1860 Fechner argued that if it were possible (which he thought unlikely) to divide the brain down the midline, something like personal duplication would result, and that the two hemispheres, while beginning with the same moods, predispositions, knowledge and memories, would thereafter develop differently, according to the external relationships into which each entered. However, at the turn of the century, McDougall disagreed that the stream of consciousness could be so divided, and even bargained with the renowned physiologist Sherrington that if ever he (McDougall) should become incurably ill, Sherrington should sever McDougall's commissures to resolve the issue. The compact was never taken up. Indeed, the problem is still theoretically unresolved, and in practice we require sophisticated and artificial procedures to demonstrate anything like a division of consciousness; in fact a 'split-brain' patient seems surprisingly normal to the casual observer, so much so that Tomasch observed that the corpus callosum has hardly any psychological function, and seems to serve only to keep the hemispheres from sagging. Lashley, with equal irony and pessimism, remarked that it serves only to facilitate the spread of seizures.

Of the three major forebrain commissures, the corpus callosum, anterior and hippocampal commissures, the first is the largest (see Figure 1). Its anterior third (genu) interconnects the frontal lobes for largely motor functions, while its middle portion (trunk) interconnects parietal and temporal regions with largely somatosensory representation, and its posterior third (splenium) interconnects the occipital (visual) areas (see Figure 2). The anterior commissure has largely temporal connections, but seems able to partially stand in for the callosum's visual functions. The role of the hippocampal commissure is still largely uncertain. (For further details of callosal anatomy, see e.g. Jones, 1985). Recently there have been controversial claims of a relatively larger callosum in females, sinistrals and schizophrenics, all of whom on other behavioral criteria seem more likely to demonstrate nonstandard lateralization, though which might come first, the morphology or the behavior, is hard to tell; however, a recent MRI study has failed to find sex or

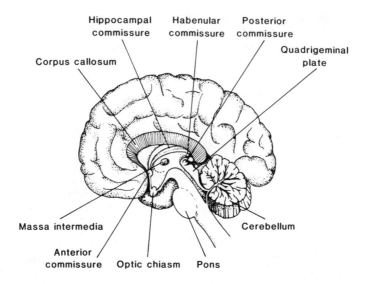

Fig. 1   The major commissural systems and associated structures. (Figure redrawn from an original in R. W. Sperry, The Great Cerebral commissure. *Scientific American*, 1964, **210**, January, 42–52. Copyright © 1964 by Scientific American, Inc. All rights reserved.)

handedness differences in callosal size (Kertesz *et al.*, 1987), despite continued claims that the critical region is the posterior trunk, interconnecting parieto-temporal regions important for language, praxis and spatial processing.

To comprehend the significance of experimental studies with com-missurotomized (and normal) subjects, it is important to remember that apart

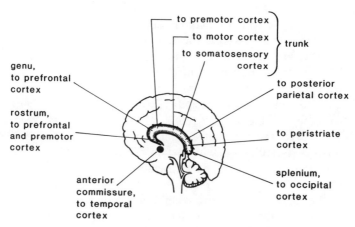

Fig. 2   Topography of commissural fibres in the corpus callosum.

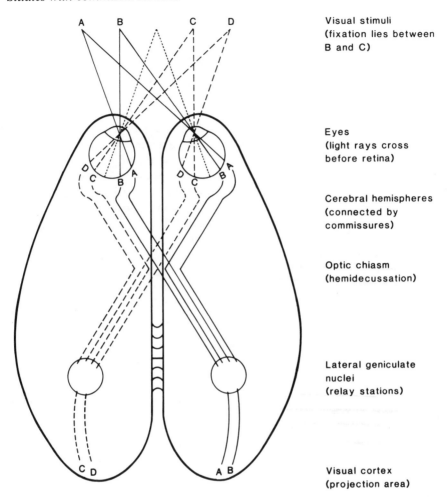

Visual stimuli
(fixation lies between
B and C)

Eyes
(light rays cross
before retina)

Cerebral hemispheres
(connected by
commissures)

Optic chiasm
(hemidecussation)

Lateral geniculate
nuclei
(relay stations)

Visual cortex
(projection area)

Fig. 3   The human visual system. As a consequence of hemidecussation, points A and B to the left of the fixation point (unlabelled) project to the right hemisphere, and points C and D to the right of fixation project to the left hemisphere, whichever eye is stimulated.

from olfaction (which is ipsilateral) most aspects of sensory representation are largely contralateral—entirely so for vision in lateral-eyed animals, and largely so for hearing and touch. Frontal-eyed animals, however, like ourselves, with overlapping visual fields, exhibit hemidecussation at the optic chiasm (see Figure 3). Consequently in each eye the nasal hemiretinae (which lie closest to the nose, and which, because of the cross-over of light rays in the lens, receive stimulation from the periphery ipsilateral to their respective eye) transmit their information to the contralateral (opposite) hemisphere. The temporal hemi-retinae, on the other hand, which lie adjacent to the side of the head, transmit their signals to the ipsilateral (same-side) hemisphere. Thus for whichever eye we address, stimuli falling in the left visual field (LVF) go initially to the RH, while those in the right visual field (RVF) travel initially to the LH. While with lateral-eyed animals each *eye* transmits information to its opposite hemisphere, in our case each *visual field* operates in this way. This situation strictly applies only to pattern vision, via the retinogeniculostriate pathways ascending to the visual cortex; the retinotectal system which mediates 'where?' rather than 'what?', and which may be preserved in case of 'blindsight', is rather more complicated and is undivided by the commissurotomy operation. Moreover albino animals of all species, including our own and including Siamese cats, exhibit curious departures from the normal groundplan discussed above, often with disturbing perceptual consequences (Carroll *et al.*, 1980). Motor control, at least that originating via the pyramidal system from the motor cortex for fine regulation of the distal extremities, is also largely contralateral, with decussation occurring at the medullary pyramids; the phylogenetically older extra-pyramidal motor system which handles the grosser and more automatic aspects of movement control is, however, largely bilateral, as is control of axial and proximal musculature.

ANIMAL STUDIES

Even with the commissures intact, nonhuman species may not always show perfect 'intermanual' transfer (Doty, Ringo, and Lewine, 1986); thus for difficult spatial patterns a discrimination acquired via one paw may not be available when tested with the 'naive' paw. Likewise, interocular transfer (train a visual discrimination through one eye with the other eye covered, switch the eyepatch around and test via the 'naive' eye, in a lateral-eyed animal) may also be incomplete, especially with complex discriminations in phylogenetically lower animals. Such observations, and similar tactual ones with very young children where anatomical evidence also suggests the possibility of callosal immaturity, indicate that commissural transmission may be of limited fidelity. With frontal-eyed animals, we must either substitute 'visual fields' for 'eyes', or we must first sever the optic chiasm, which will restrict the input from each eye to the *ipsilateral* hemisphere (see Figure 4 for the effects of division of commissures and/or chiasm with uniocular viewing). If the commissures are also completely severed *before* training, all intermanual, interocular or interhemispheric transfer is typically lost, except perhaps for very simple, subcortical, gross discriminations, e.g. of brightness or location, reminiscent of the 'blindsight' phenomenon. It is possible to simultaneously train opposite competing visual discriminations, one in each hemisphere, and the response

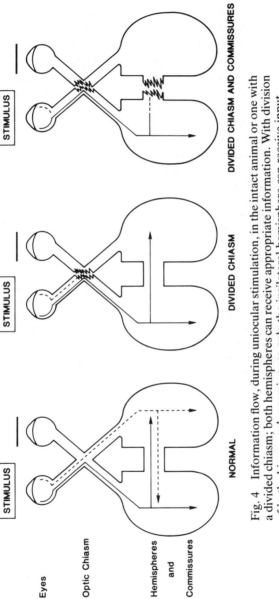

Fig. 4 Information flow, during uniocular stimulation, in the intact animal or one with a divided chiasm; both hemispheres can receive appropriate information. With division of both chiasm and commissures only the ipsilateral hemisphere can receive input.

elicited when testing occurs with both eyes open may depend upon which hand is available to respond. It is even possible to bring about 'reversible' commissurotomies (see Chapter 2) by suppressing one hemisphere by means of the unilateral amobarbital technique, or via application of potassium chloride to one cortex, so as to bring about unilateral spreading depression. If one thereby suppresses one hemisphere, trains the other, lets the first recover, suppresses the trained hemisphere and tests the naive one, it is found that engrams (the physiological correlates of memory representations) do not *automatically* transfer, not even if *both* hemispheres are active and operational. Thus if direct sensory input is initially restricted to a single hemisphere, information is not automatically copied into the other hemisphere over the intact commissures; rather, the naive hemisphere, if tested (e.g. via the other eye with the chiasm sectioned) has to call up the trained hemisphere. Indeed it might in fact be redundant to store identical 'carbon copies' in each hemisphere; rather, different *complementary* information seems to be so stored (see Chapter 5).

HUMAN STUDIES: THE CLASSICAL PICTURE

The commissurotomy operation was first undertaken in the 1940s to relieve otherwise intractable epilepsy by limiting its spread. Findings from these subjects revealed no observable psychological effects, due, as we now know, to the use of insufficiently subtle testing procedures, and perhaps also because of sparing of the anterior commissure. Indeed even since then comparatively few patients have been studied, and all may to some extent be atypical due to prior morbidity; there are also great inter-subject variations in age at operation and at testing, in education, severity of illness, ongoing medication etc., and invariably preoperative abilities are unknown. The operation itself is also traumatic. The classical period of study by Sperry and his colleagues extended from the early 1960s and demonstrated the often dramatic effects of splitting the hemispheres into two apparently independent cognitive systems (Bogen, 1985; Gazzaniga, 1985; Sidtis and Gazzaniga, 1983; Zaidel, 1983). Initially there is typically a left-side apraxia to verbal commands (e.g. 'wiggle your left toe') which will often quickly resolve due either to increased RH language competence, or to increased ipsilateral motor control. Words or pictures tachistoscopically flashed to the RVF–LH system, too rapidly for fixational eye movements to occur, will easily be reported; this is not the case for LVF–RH presentations, for which there is typically a complete expressive aphasia. Nevertheless the left hand is able correctly to select objects corresponding to the LVF–RH presentations, and sometimes even to point to the correct written name if the word is short and simple and the writing clear. Thus it soon became clear that the RH (at least of such patients, though cf. Chapter 6) can comprehend simple spoken (and, occasionally, even written) instructions. The right hand was found to stay superior for writing, while the left hand often became better for drawing (especially the general outline) the pattern of interrelationships between components, or overall gestalt, while the right hand remained better for portraying fine detail or feature elements. Moreover the hands differed in tactile strategies for matching visually presented, unfolded, two-dimensional plans to felt three-dimensional objects: the left hand–RH system appeared to operate via holistic, gestalt spatial interrelationships, while the right hand–LH system 'preferred' an analytic, detailed, feature-dependent approach. If two pictures were simultaneously flashed one to each visual field, only the ipsilateral hands could correctly select targets from a range of unseen, tactually explored alternatives; nor could the subject say whether or not they were the same objects. Likewise one hand could not mimic an unseen gesture molded on to the other hand, something which very young children also are unable to do, possibly due to callosal immaturity. While the patient could name an unseen object palpated by the right hand, this was not possible when the left hand was used, though that hand would then be able correctly to select an appropriate target from a range of unseen alternatives, or even to choose something *functionally* similar (e.g. cigarette–ashtray; knife–fork), and correctly manipulate it. However, matching *between* hands was generally impossible, unless the objects were *easily* and *grossly* distinguishable by ipsilaterally conveyed (or noncortically coded) information, e.g. a hard heavy brick versus a soft light ball.

Subsequently it was shown that the undivided midbrain (retinotectal, collicular) visual system could cross-match the relative heights of contours which were broken at the midline, but which extended into the LVF and RVF; similar cross-matching proved possible for relative angles, offset, separation and movement, despite the division of the cortical geniculostriate system for true patterned vision. Indeed, when two dots were flashed one in each visual field (i.e. one on either side of fixation and therefore effectively in opposite hemispheres) at an asynchrony which would normally lead to an illusion of apparent directional movement, this too was experienced by the split-brain patients, again suggesting midbrain integrative processes. We shall shortly return to this issue.

We have already discussed how symmetrical composite faces can be constructed by abutting two left (or right) halves at the midline (see Chapter 1). By an extension of this technique one can construct 'chimeras', which involve the abutting of halves of two *different* objects at the midline, e.g. the left half of a pie and the right half of a rose. When these stimuli were flashed with the midline junction coinciding with the fixation point, commissurotomy patients typically reported seeing a single *whole* picture (e.g. a whole rose), with completion across the midline into the other visual field, and suppression of the latter's contents. Migraine patients may experience somewhat similar effects when the temporarily developing defects in their visual fields (scotomas) happen to overlie an intrusive object (e.g. a fly) upon a patterned background (e.g. regular wallpaper); the wallpaper is seen unbroken, but without the fly. Indeed the same thing happens with everybody's blind spot: you can make a spot on patterned paper 'disappear' if the (single) eye is correctly positioned. Moreover the chimera effect may even occur with *normal* subjects, if the two discrepant halves of the tachistoscopically flashed chimera are separated by a broad band. Thus each hemisphere of the split-brain patient may under these (artificial) circumstances perceive a different complete object, a phenomenon which is perhaps the logical converse of hemineglect (see Chapter 2). Under these circumstances the patient usually claims to see the right-half object as a whole, but with the left hand will select a left-half object, or draw it, again as a *whole*. The right half typically predominates if, on testing, phonological aspects are emphasized (e.g. 'choose an object rhyming with this test item'), while the left half predominates if the physical aspects receive emphasis (e.g. 'choose something which looks like the test item'). Indeed such patients also show similar dissociations when laterally tested with nonchimeric stimuli: the LH tends to match by function (e.g. cigarette and lighter, knife and fork) while the RH may match by appearance (e.g. rose and pie, spectacles and scissors).

Zaidel attempted to survey the limits of hemispheric competence, from perception to intelligence, language and personality structure in general, free from the constraints of brief eccentrically presented visual stimuli. Using a scleral contact lens fitted with a collimating system and a hemi-occluder to obscure one visual field, he devised a method to permit free scanning within a single visual field–hemisphere system. Others have since devised electronic eye-trackers linked to displays or to electronic 'windows' in such displays, so as to achieve similar ends. Zaidel found, in confirmation of the earlier 'conventional' studies, that the LH was better at the feature-analytic task of disembedding embedded figures, and that the RH could read, and even 'write' (e.g. by moving cut-out letters) as long as the material was very simple, but was extremely deficient in phonological processing capacities. One patient, however, late in recovery, proved capable of phonologically matching pictures by rhyme, e.g. bat : cat, or bat (animal) : bat (baseball). Of course arguments from the single case are always dangerous, especially so when so much long-standing cerebral reorganization is possible with conditions of the sort which require such radical surgery. Zaidel concluded that normally the RH reads by 'direct access'. We shall discuss later (Chapter 6) suggestions that the RH is also thereby better at processing high frequency, concrete, imageable words, and knows objects' qualities while normally being unable to say their names. Zaidel found that the LH, while the RH is being interrogated via the 'Z' lens, may try to confabulate about the meaning of RH input, presumably in an unconscious, unintentional 'best-guessing' fashion familiar to students of top-down processing systems in cognition. Indeed the LH may attempt a takeover, presumably via ipsilateral pathways, to complete the end of a word commenced by the RH–left hand system in a task involving writing or the assembly of cut-out letters. Zaidel believes that the RH shows characteristically human levels and modes of consciousness, and has the same desires, ambitions, morality, beliefs and family knowledge as the verbal LH, when interrogated nonverbally by e.g. pointing to alternatives or moving cut-out letters.

HIGHER-ORDER INFORMATION TRANSFER IN COMMISSUROTOMIZED PATIENTS

When using such systems as the 'Z' lens, and interrogating the verbal LH about what 'it' thought had been shown to the RH, researchers have at times reported unexpectedly high levels of general accuracy, in terms e.g. of broad, conceptual categories. This proved to be particularly striking with partial commissurotomies, as if the LVF words generated complex RH images among which the patient hunts, as if playing '20 questions', until the target is hit upon and the LH can verbalize the RH's input (Sidtis, 1985, and see Figure 5). These images were abolished with total section, when evidence of interhemispheric transfer became less clear. In a typical demonstration of such phenomena, pictures, photographs or drawings of mostly unfamiliar individuals are shown to the (nonverbal) LVF–RH system (perhaps via the 'Z' lens), together with the occasional family member or pet; the patient is to select with the left hand items liked, disliked, recognized etc.—an easy task—and to *verbalize* what they are, why they are liked or disliked. In such an example, the patient selects, says 'nice', and makes guesses indicative of positive affect, and if the experimenter then mentions e.g. 'son', the patient may recognize this as correct. Thus there is evidence of interhemispheric transfer of information sufficient for broad categorical recognition of RH input as relating to e.g. 'a family member', 'an entertainment personality' etc., even though the exact identity is not usually immediately available.

There is a technique for lateralizing visual input which relies on the fact that we can only turn our eyes so far, laterally, in either direction; if a stimulus is shown just beyond that point it will continue to lie in one or other peripheral visual field, as further eye turn is impossible. This technique has been used in tasks requiring commissurotomy patients to name e.g. letters presented to the LVF–RH system (Myers and Sperry, 1985): indeed such responses have occasionally proved possible, especially with the long presentations attainable by this method, and if the patient is previously informed about the target category (e.g. letters or digits), or is given beforehand a subset of possibilities. Sometimes the patient may even say a word to rhyme with the name of an object's picture flashed to the LVF (e.g. shoe → 'two'), especially if a list of possibilities had previously been provided; he/she may even be able to say whether or not two digits, one in each visual field, are identical. However, such

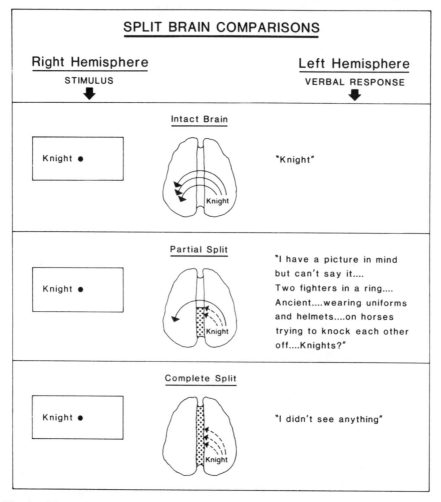

Fig. 5 Schematic representation of commissurotomy patient J. W.'s left-visual-field naming ability, with the corpus callosum intact (middle), and with the entire callosum sectioned (bottom). (Figure redrawn from J. J. Sidtis, Bilateral language and commissurotomy: Interactions between the hemispheres with and without the corpus callosum. In A. Reeves (Ed.), *Epilepsy and the Corpus Callosum*. New York: Plenum Press, 1985.)

an ability to name or categorize stimuli in the LVF seems to depend upon a strategy of mentally reciting alternatives, e.g. count up until you reach a number that somehow 'sticks out', so identifying the LVF digit.

To what extent may such demonstrations of apparent interhemispheric transfer of information in acallosal patients (and see e.g. Cronin-Golomb, 1986; Johnson, 1984a, 1984b; Lindeboom and Swinkels, 1986; Ramachandran,

Cronin-Golomb and Myers, 1986; Sergent and Myers, 1985) depend upon the use of sophisticated cross-cueing strategies, not necessarily deliberate but perhaps unconscious and automatic? Thus when a patient knows that a light flash can occur in one of four quadrants (upper or lower left or right) he/she can easily say 'upper left' (even though such information can only contact the mute LVF–RH system) by reading off fixational eye movements which occur *after* the disappearance of the brief tachistoscopic exposure. Similarly a patient can tactually discriminate between a sphere, cube, or pyramid, and verbally respond correctly while feeling with the left hand, by monitoring where his/her eyes go—e.g. to the wall clock (if a sphere), or to the rectangular door (if a cube); the third response alternative, 'pyramid', can even be given by default of the other two, with perhaps the verbal response 'then it *must* be the pyramid'. Loss of these abilities with blindfolding seems to confirm such conclusions. Moreover it has frequently been reported that during verbal responding the LH may apparently detect frowns initiated by the RH at an incorrect answer—and utter a correction.

While, as mentioned above, some commissurotomy patients have recently proved able to identify letters, digits or drawings presented to the LVF–RH system, if previously informed of the category or range of possibilities etc. (Johnson, 1984a, 1984b), one patient could even immediately name 'surprise' stimuli flashed to the LVF, e.g. a letter during a digit naming task, or vice versa, suggesting genuine interhemispheric transfer. In an experiment with the lateral limits technique (see above), a sample stimulus (a line drawing of a common object) was shown to one visual field, and the patient had to select a corresponding drawing in a choice array of alternatives presented to the same or opposite visual field as the original sample (Cronin-Golomb, 1986). Patients were able to do this, even with use of opposite visual fields, under two circumstances: when there was a concrete association between sample and choice (e.g. fish : duck—aquatic animals, a coordinate association; or shoe : sock—a contingent association where both relate to feet); they were also able to do it when the association was conceptual (e.g. telephone : envelope—where both items relate to communications). In another experiment, patients had to point to a line drawing in a choice array that was *exactly* identical to a sample drawing previously shown in the opposite visual field, the other choice alternatives being conceptually similar though not identical to the sample (e.g. yacht : rowboat, steamer . . .) or totally different. Patients chose the identical card correctly most often, followed by conceptually similar alternatives, and hardly ever chose unrelated alternatives. It is difficult to see how cross-cueing strategies could apply here, or in an experiment (Sergent, 1986) where two colour patches (red, green) were flashed for 100 msec one to each visual field; subjects pressed one key if *at least one* green was present, and the other if *no* green occurred. The interesting condition is where green occurs contralaterally to the responding hand, and red is in the ipsilateral field: a correct response is only possible if the hemisphere controlling the response can refrain from responding to the ipsilateral red, while at the same time 'knowing' that green is *also* present in the field contralateral to the responding hand, i.e. in the opposite disconnected hemisphere. Split-brain patients could do this task, and the difference in reaction time between this condition, and where green was ipsilateral, was too short for cross-cueing strategies to have been employed. Indeed such patients could distinguish (same/different) between red and green, versus two reds, or two greens, simultaneously presented to opposite visual fields, but only as long as the differences were relatively gross (as between red and green) rather than merely being different *shades* (e.g. two shades of red). Finally, the technique of semantic priming provides further evidence of interhemispheric transfer in the absence of callosal connectivity (Sidtis, 1985). Thus one word may be flashed to one visual field, followed by a second in the other; the subject has to respond (by a discriminatory button press) 'animal' or 'plant' to the second word (e.g. dog). If the first word (in the opposite visual field) also is an animal (e.g. cat), the second response may be facilitated, even if the patient cannot say what was the first word, e.g. if it had occurred in the LVF–RH system.

Thus commissural section seems not to preclude information transfer, though not every one accepts either the experimental controls or the conclusions (Gazzaniga, 1987), and we can ask whether the whole of the callosum was sectioned in every case; moreover what is the role of the other undivided forebrain—and midbrain—commissures? Indeed is there still the possibility of some sophisticated cross-cueing occurring, even though time constraints seem to militate against such an argument? It should be remembered that often what is transferred is apparently emotional tone, or general context or category information, though it may occasionally be actual identity. One is reminded of what happens with semantic paralexias in deep dyslexics (see Chapters 2 and 6): in such situations does the RH access meaning in broad *general* terms, and communicate the semantic result to the LH for *approximate* naming?

Sergent concludes, from reviews of her own and others' studies (see e.g. Sergent, 1986, 1987) that commissurotomy does not prevent all interhemispheric communication. Split-brain patients can report large, slow-moving stimuli in the LVF, and verbally give gross connotative or contextual information about such RH inputs. Moreover when the two hemispheres are provided with *separate* visual inputs, whose *combination* is essential for correct responding, the latter may prove possible in tasks involving spatial orientation, calculation and lexical decision, at speeds which preclude cross-cueing strategies, and without conscious awareness of the nature of the actual RH input. Thus subcortical connections may unify input, perhaps at a less detailed, more general and unconscious level, while the forebrain commissures may be essential for the transfer of complex, detailed, conscious information. The apparent lack of a disconnection syndrome in the coherent everyday behavior of such patients outside the laboratory, and the (subcortical) transfer of gross, contextual information, contrasts with traditional laboratory demonstrations of mental disunity at the perceptual level; such a paradox may stem, argues Sergent, from differences in operational criteria and kind of task.

AN INDEPENDENT PROCESSING CAPACITY IN THE TWO HEMISPHERES?

The traditional position is that commissurotomy patients do not possess an increase (or doubling) of processing capacity, except possibly in highly artificial circumstances, where automatic responding may be possible. So while such patients may show no increase in reaction time (RT) in one task while simultaneously performing a second task via the other hemisphere (normals usually do), they are nevertheless usually much slower, overall, than normals, and were so preoperatively due to their pre-existing epileptic condition; they may also perhaps be unable to regularly alternate (like normals) between hemispheres/tasks, or to maintain prolonged activation of a single hemisphere. Gazzaniga (1987) disputes this, and argues for some independent processing capacity in commissurotomy patients, on the basis of better performance (than normals) in a memory task requiring visual retention, when the information is distributed between the two hemispheres; thus with a complex visual array in both fields, normal subjects tend to combine it into a super-complex pattern, to the detriment of their performance, while patients can continue to separately handle each half, to their advantage. Thus under admittedly rare and artificial experimental circumstances, the commissurotomy patient may be able to break down a complex otherwise-unified visual array into two smaller subsets, each manageable by one hemisphere. Again of course we do not see an increase in total capacity, merely in this instance a somewhat artificial breakdown into two more efficiently manageable subsystems.

TWO SEPARATE WILLS OR CONSCIOUSNESSES?

There is still little agreement on the definition of consciousness. It is not amenable to easy empirical investigation, and so was long rejected by experimentalists as suspect, and remained the almost exclusive province of psychoanalysis. Its comparatively recent rehabilitation stems from interest in its obverse, unconscious processing in the context of selective attention. This latter area developed during World War II, when it became clear that we are limited capacity processors, who often cannot accept the quantity of information provided by the devices we have constructed to extend our sensory and motor ranges. (We have thus returned once more to the subject area addressed in the previous section, the allocation of processing resources.) Attention theorists originally believed that a processing bottleneck, with protective filtering-out of unwanted and selection of wanted information, occurred during perceptual input. However, partial report experiments soon rejected such early-selection ideas, showing that we are in principle capable of processing far more inputs than actually reach consciousness. There is currently debate about the extent to which such unattended and preconscious material can actually influence the way that we think, behave and respond in ambiguous situations. Nevertheless it is generally agreed that information-processing pressures and attentional selectivity are more significant at the point of choosing or initiating a response (i.e. late-selection theory), than at identifying a stimulus. However, even this is perhaps only true at the level of voluntary, deliberate (i.e. conscious) responding; we normally only choose to initiate one action at a time when its success requires careful ongoing monitoring. However, when such actions are highly skilled, they become automatic and unconscious, and several can be simultaneously carried out in parallel. Consciousness therefore seems to involve the monitoring and internal modelling of sensory and motor events where the outcome is uncertain; indeed we cannot normally monitor, or be conscious of, more than one such stream simultaneously. When a chimpanzee learns a complex new skill, e.g. involving careful manipulation, its concentrated dedication calls to mind a level of conscious preoccupation similar to our own under such circumstances. In fact comparative psychologists are nowadays finding it increasingly difficult to deny some level of conscious awareness to nonhuman species; the problem is how and where to draw the line. One potentially useful distinction is that between consciousness and *self* consciousness or self awareness ('meta' consciousness, perhaps). In the latter situation, a person, animal or system (as, hypothetically as yet, in artificial intelligence) observes *itself* behaving and problem solving, as an entity isolable from the rest of the environment. The ability to recognize images of oneself, as indexed by a differential response on seeing oneself, rather than another individual, in a mirror, may be limited to ourselves (above a certain age) and maybe the great apes. Thus the latter are said to manipulate mirrors to examine otherwise inaccessible regions of their own anatomies, or to evince distress when so observing dye upon their foreheads, and to attempt to wipe it off. However, other explanations for such behaviors have been proposed, and the issue is far from settled. Nor is it clear what would be the criteria for adducing self-conscious behavior (or even merely consciousness) to e.g. a sophisticated automaton. In animals, the ability to construct tools for some future purpose and then to use them was once suggested as just such a criterion. However, even here the boundaries between our own and other species are rapidly crumbling, and in terms of what are generally regarded as satisfactory definitions of tool using behavior, many nonprimate species would qualify. Indeed as we shall see in Chapter 7, the major hallmarks of humanity—tool use, language, bipedal locomotion and consciousness—are hardly unique.

Nor perhaps should we restrict (self) consciousness to the monitoring of skilled, purposive, nonautomatic behaviors. When we observe, remember or ponder, seated motionless in a chair, we surely continue conscious. Memory and learning may operate at three hierarchically distinct levels: habituation and sensitization (behaviors of which even single-celled creatures are capable), learning *how* to do something (procedural memory), and knowing *that* certain (often arbitrary) things have happened (declarative memory). While the rule-governed aspects of the second level might seem more important for perpetuating a successful existence, the third (declarative or episodic knowledge) may possibly be more characteristically human, in that we also preserve arbitrary contexts or instances independently of the derived rules or meanings. (A fourth hierarchical level might be *self* knowledge, *self* consciousness, *self* awareness, seeing *oneself* within such a declarative or episodic context of otherwise apparently arbitrary situations.) We may only be able to sustain such declarative or episodic knowledge if we already possess a pre-existing framework of automatized skills, knowing *how* to do things. In its absence, e.g. when very young and without a repertoire yet of skilled behaviors, we cannot know the arbitrary contextual aspects within which things are learned or performed. Perhaps for this reason we typically cannot remember events much before the age of two or three years, even though we may retain skills acquired then.

Jaynes (see Chapter 7) instead invokes *language* as a prerequisite for such consciousness, rather than episodic or declarative knowledge. He argues that until language and material culture reached a certain level of complexity (which, he says, was only within the last few thousand years, and took place in the vicinity of the Mediterranean Sea), humans behaved more like schizophrenics, and interpreted the need to behave in certain ways as commands received (via the RH, he says) from on high as it were. His theory is only mentioned here because of the (possibly undeserved) attention which it has received; it certainly ignores the fully human range of behaviors, including language and self-consciousness, evinced by Australian aborigines and American Indians, who were isolated from Mediterranean Man long before the date of his proposed 'origin' of consciousness and breakdown of the bicameral mind'.

So far we have discussed mind (the matrix of thought, modelling and consciousness) and brain (the presumed physiological substrate of mind). This is not the place to discuss the merits of such dualism, which of course is not universally accepted. Sperry (1984) holds that in normals, consciousness spans the two hemispheres via the integrative and inhibitory mechanisms of the commissures, with consciousness a new dynamic property emerging from the neural mechanism. (The concept of a new emergent property is best captured by analogy with the properties of molecular water, which cannot be readily predicted from a knowledge of the properties of its constituent atoms, hydrogen and oxygen). Thus Sperry believes that consciousness arises from these neural mechanisms but can also feed back and modify them, in much the same way that a quadruped, moving its limbs, is itself moved by these moving limbs.

If the LH is the seat of language, and we need language for consciousness, what is the status of the RH? Some have argued, including the Nobel laureate Sir John Eccles, that the RH behaves more like a preconscious automaton. Such a conclusion, however, ignores both the evidence for RH language mechanisms (see Chapter 6) and the question whether we *do* need language for consciousness. Certainly mutes, aphasics, adult left hemispherectomies, and the RHs of commissurotomy patients interrogated by that other Nobel laureate Sperry and his colleagues, indicate a full range of human hopes, beliefs and knowledge, even though access to actual speech may be lacking. Whether or not the RH is the seat of nonverbal imagery, can the commissurotomy operation result in the generation of two parallel independent streams of consciousness? Of course the two hemispheres of such patients must experience many factors which tend toward unification, e.g. shared sensory input, scanning eye movements, shared blood flows, cross-cueing strategies, midbrain integration, identical genotypes and past experiences. Such patients may perhaps only *behave* as if they have two minds, two wills, two independent streams of consciousness under extreme laboratory conditions, or perhaps early in the postoperative recovery phase; there are of course anecdotes of the right hand trying to restrain the left from a violent act, or one hand trying to hinder the other while dressing. Sperry's (1984) conclusion seems to be that each hemisphere does indeed have its own stream of consciousness, processing mode or speciality, while subcortical or attentional suppression of a hemisphere only occurs during prolonged abnormal laboratory conditions of extreme lateralization. However, Puccetti (1985), the philosopher of mind, argues that even normal people must have two ongoing streams of consciousness; his argument can be paraphrased as follows: if commissurotomy patients have two minds, and hemispherectomies still have one, then there must have been two to start with, the commissurotomy operation merely aiding the demonstration of a pre-existing duality. Thus he sees it as all an illusion that we are 'all alone' in our heads—and suggests that maybe the mute RH knows of the existence of its twin partner because it knows it is not doing the talking. Of course in normals callosal inhibition may usually conceal each hemisphere from 'introspective' access to the conscious contents of the other hemisphere, resulting in two mutually inaccessible sets of feelings. Indeed I cannot feel *your* sensations even if our two brains are interconnected, and even if due to such an interconnection I were to feel your foot being stepped upon, the resultant feeling for me would be mine, though of your foot. The converse of course is the *hemineglect* patient feeling something in his or her neglected leg *as if* it belonged to someone else. However, while the conclusion may or may not be correct (that we all possess more than one 'mind'), the logic probably is not so (that because a split-brain patient ends up with two 'minds' there must have been two to begin with). Thus if we continue tearing a hologram into successively smaller parts, it still preserves (ever more degraded) replicas of the original whole—yet those replicas can hardly be said to have been present in the original hologram, waiting to be released. However it *does* make sense to argue that the human mind is a 'sociological composite' (cf. Gazzaniga, 1985) of many frequently competing modules (we often say 'part of me wants to do x, another part seems to opt for y . . .'), while unifying attentional mechanisms normally select a single response output. Indeed, as we saw above, it is at the level of response selection, rather than e.g. stimulus identification, that probability and uncertainty seem to have their traditional effects upon performance efficiency, for example reaction times. Finally, other dimensions (than left–right) need neural integration, e.g. cortical–subcortical, anterior–posterior, and the role of the commissures is probably not (as traditionally conceived) limited solely to integration; there is good evidence (see Chapter 5) that the commissures are involved in inhibition, suppression, information duplication, and maybe even the provision of *complementary* patterns of interhemispheric information.

SUMMARY AND CONCLUSIONS

There has long been speculation upon the perceptual and cognitive consequences of severing the forebrain commissures. However, even their presence is no guarantee of complete interhemispheric transfer of information. Nor, if sensory input is initially restricted to a single hemisphere, is information automatically copied over the intact commissures to the 'naive' hemisphere. Nevertheless human split-brain patients generally fail to show any gross disturbances of behavior, and subtle testing is needed to demonstrate mental disunity. Under such circumstances the subject is typically unable to report the content of information flashed to the LVF/RH, though its meaning or significance may be shown to have been understood, with the use of appropriate nonverbal pointing or selection responses. While the two hemispheres may appear unaware of what the other is perceiving, each appears able to operate in a thoroughly human fashion, albeit perhaps via different and idiosyncratic processing strategies. Exceptions to such a perceptual disunity have, however, been noted. In some cases this may be ascribed to utilization of ipsilateral sensory pathways, or to (often sophisticated, though unconscious) cross-cueing strategies. In other cases undivided midbrain commissures may permit the transfer of gross contextual information of a broad categorical nature, perhaps even at an unconscious level, while the forebrain commissures may be essential for the transfer of complex, detailed conscious information.

Similar questions have been raised concerning whether the two hemispheres possess independent processing capacities, such that two tasks may be simultaneously undertaken, one by each hemisphere. Traditionally it has been held that commissurotomy patients do not possess an increase (or doubling) of processing capacity, except perhaps in highly artificial circumstances, and even then they may not function as well as normal subjects do. However, recent evidence suggests that a commissurotomy patient may be able to break down a complex visual array into two smaller subsets, each manageable by one hemisphere, though again this reflects breakdown of information into more manageable subsystems, rather than a real increase in total capacity. Indeed there may be a constant quantity of resources available for information processing across the two hemispheres, with the commissurotomy operation merely happening under certain circumstances to aid the reallocation of such resources.

Do these patients likewise possess two separate streams of consciousness under certain artificial circumstances, and two separate systems of will? If so, must this also necessarily be true of the normal undivided brain? In one way, considerations concerning the modular nature of the human mind suggest a potential multiplicity of competing wills, whims and desires. On the other hand not only the commissures serve to bridge our two most obviously discrete processing systems; both hemispheres have also normally been exposed to the same environmental history of stimulation. Nor need we invoke only left/right distinctions, when the brain is also structured in an anterior–posterior and a cortical–subcortical direction. Several streams of consciousness may well co-exist at a potential level even in the normal brain, but we may normally only be aware of the one which currently happens to be tied to the output response system.

IMPORTANT READINGS

Bogen, J. E. The callosal syndromes. In K. M. Heilman and E. Valenstein (eds.), *Clinical Neuropsychology*. New York: Oxford University Press, 1985, pp. 295–338

Carroll, W. M., Jay, B. S., Mcdonald, W. and Halliday, A. M. Two distinctive patterns of visual evoked response asymmetry in human albinos. *Nature*, 1980, **286**, 604–6.

Cronin-Golomb, A. Subcortical transfer of cognitive information in subjects with complete forebrain commissurotomy. *Cortex*, 1986, **22**, 499–519.

Doty, R. W., Ringo, J. L. and Lewine, J. D. Interhemispheric mnemonic transfer in macaques. In F. Leporé, M. Ptito and H. H. Jasper (eds.), *Two Hemispheres, One Brain: Functions of the Corpus Callosum*. New York: A. R. Liss, 1986, pp. 269–79.

Gazzaniga, M. S. *The Social Brain*. New York: Basic Books, 1985.

Gazzaniga, M. S. Perceptual and attentional processes following callosal section in humans. *Neuropsychologia*, 1987, **25**, 119–34.

Johnson, L. E. Vocal responses to left visual stimuli following forebrain commissurotomy. *Neuropsychologia*, 1984a, **22**, 153–66.

Johnson, L. E. Bilateral visual cross integration by human forebrain commissurotomy subjects. *Neuropsychologia*, 1984b, **22**, 167–75.

Jones, E. G. Anatomy, development and physiology of the corpus callosum. In A. G. Reeves (ed.), *Epilepsy and the Corpus Callosum*. New York: Plenum Press, 1985, pp. 3–20

Kertesz, A., Polk, M., Howell, J. and Black, S. Cerebral dominance, sex and callosal size in MRI. *Neurology*, 1987, **37**, 1385–8.

Lindeboom, J. and Swinkels, J. A. Interhemispheric communication in a case of total visuo-verbal disconnection. *Neuropsychologia*, 1986, **24**, 781–92.

Myers, J. J. and Sperry, R.W. Interhemispheric communication after section of the forebrain commissures. *Cortex*, 1985, **21**, 249–60.

Puccetti, R. Experiencing two selves: The history of a mistake. *Behavioral and Brain Sciences*, 1985, **8**, 646–7.

Ramachandran, V. S., Cronin-Golomb, A. and Myers, J. J. Perception of apparent motion by commissurotomy patients. *Nature,* 1986, **320**, 358–9.

Sergent, J. Subcortical coordination of hemisphere activity in commissurotomized patients. *Brain*, 1986, **109**, 357–69.

Sergent, J. A new look at the human split brain. *Brain*, 1987, **110**, 1375–92.

Sergent, J. and Myers, J. J. Manual, blowing and verbal simple reactions to lateralized flashes of light in commissurotomized patients. *Perception and Psychophysics*, 1985, **37**, 571–8.

Sidtis, J. J.Bilateral language and commissurotomy: Interactions between the hemispheres with and without the corpus callosum. In A. Reeves (ed.), *Epilepsy and the Corpus Callosum*, New York: Plenum Press, 1985, pp. 369–80.

Sidtis, J. J. and Gazzaniga, M. S. Competence vs. performance after callosal section: Looks can be deceiving, In J. B. Hellige (ed.), *Cerebral Hemisphere Asymmetry: Method, Theory and Application*. New York: Praeger, 1983, pp. 153–76.

Sperry, R. W. Consciousness, personal identity and the divided brain. *Neuropsychologia*, 1984, **22**, 661–73.

Zaidel, E. Disconnection syndrome as a model for laterality effects in the normal brain. In J. B. Hellige (ed.), *Cerebral Hemisphere Asymmetry: Method, Theory and Application*. New York: Praeger, 1983, pp. 95–151.

4

Studies with normals

Studies with normals constitute the bulk of the experimental literature on human cerebral asymmetry, if only because of the ubiquity of the university student subject. While the findings are rarely as dramatic, or the procedures as heroic, as those employing commissurotomy patients, the literature typically integrates more easily with mainstream experimental psychology. Indeed experimental procedures overlap considerably with visual and auditory psychophysics, psycholinguistics, cognitive processes and human information processing. Often left–right differences are collected almost gratuitously; at other times confirmation is sought with normal subjects of findings or claims made with clinical or commissurotomy patients. More recently, questions have been asked about interhemispheric interaction, and the sharing (or otherwise) of processing resources. Most recently, clinical phenomena relating to unilateral neglect have been investigated, *mutatis mutandis*, in the normal context, and a radically new reappraisal may now be underway, in terms of possible asymmetries in the hemispatial distribution of attention. As yet it is unclear whether classical laterality findings may be subsumable within a wider theory relating to hemispatial phenomena. Nevertheless we shall see that the normative literature is replete with inconsistencies and contradictions, often stemming from inadequacies of experimental control or slight changes of procedure. Thus both state and process limiting variables fundamentally affect findings, especially in the visual and auditory modalities, and equally so for verbal and nonverbal tasks. While dichotic presentation has been the method of choice for auditory studies, a major controversy centers around the nature and extent of monaural asymmetries. This is because structural (anatomical) models, typically featuring absolute (rather than relative) hemispheric specialization and occlusion of ipsilateral by contralateral auditory pathways, have long enjoyed an ascendancy; it is only recently that the importance has again been recognized of certain attentional aspects, and the significance of the perceived directionality of stimulus origin in extracorporeal space. Despite the inherently unsatisfactory nature of much of the laterality literature with normals, it is interesting and important not least because of the way it represents the whole of experimental psychology as if in a microcosm—verbal and nonverbal, visual, auditory and tactual, sensory and motor, and in terms of the enormous available range of input and output variables. Without such normative laterality work, human experimental psychology would be the poorer, in terms of theory, methodology and general (nonlaterality) findings.

Since the commissures are intact in normal subjects, information is available to both hemispheres. The functional superiority of any one hemisphere for a particular task or processing operation may depend upon a set of variables whose effects summate or interact to determine the observable asymmetry (see Chapter 5). Thus at any one time some components may be associated with an asymmetry in one direction, and others with the opposite asymmetry (and see Moscovitch, 1986). Furthermore overall performance may be best when information goes directly to that hemisphere or processing module which is superior at processing the most difficult stage or operation in a task. Consequently studies with normals frequently generate contradictory findings, because of a diversity of often subtly varying procedures and tasks which differentially appeal to differentially lateralized components. We can present the same familiar faces, but the resultant asymmetries may depend upon whether the subject has to name them, or dichotomize them as male/female, or identify their owners' professions (e.g. actor, politician). Other important variables include use of reaction time (RT) or accuracy measures (where a speed–accuracy tradeoff may operate), go/no-go or target/nontarget discriminations, identity, similarity or category matches, perceptual matching of simultaneously presented stimuli versus the matching of test items to a memorized target. In the latter case there may be a variety of retention intervals, and one, many or constantly changing targets. Stimuli may be easily named or impossible to verbalize; they may be treatable as unitary wholes or as collections of discrete features or elements. The task (and stimuli) may be familiar or novel, easy or difficult, practised or unpractised, presented on its own or in company with another concurrent task; the latter may be easy or difficult, verbal or nonverbal. Even superficial changes in or interpretation of instructions may alter effects, as also may slight differences in methods of presentation or selection of subjects. (For a general consideration of the role of task factors in lateral asymmetries, see Hellige and Sergent, 1986.)

THE VISUAL MODALITY

Unless complex eye-tracking systems are employed linked to a computer-generated display, or a special corneal contact lens is applied (see below), exposure durations to the left or right periphery must not exceed 150 msec or even less for some individuals; this is the latency of a fixational eye movement, if presentations are to be initially lateralized to one or other hemisphere. This brief exposure and peripheral locus of stimulation is highly artificial, and greatly limits the complexity of available information (Bradshaw, 1989a; McKeever, 1986; Sergent and Hellige, 1986). There is moreover continuing debate about whether the boundary of an eye's left and right hemiretinae, which project to opposite hemispheres, is sharp or not at the vertical midline or meridian (Bradshaw, 1989a). Thus some argue that a narrow 1° strip straddling the vertical meridian may project to both hemispheres. Should this be true (and it is highly debatable), its only functional significance could be for the mediation of depth perception. Nevertheless it is usual to ensure that stimuli are presented no closer than 1.5° to the midline, and no further than 5°; beyond 5°, acuity drops off too rapidly. Likewise care should be taken with monocular viewing because of possible differences in the strengths of nasal (contralateral) and temporal (ipsilateral) retinal pathways.

Both speed and accuracy measures may be used with manual or vocal responses. However, it should be noted that with vocal responses, spurious RVF/LH superiorities may occur, especially perhaps with RT measures, due simply to the privileged access of the LH to the output channel for vocal responses. However, with very *difficult* tasks which may compete for limited processing resources, performance may possibly be superior when the hemisphere programming the response (LH) is *not* the same as the one processing the stimuli. Thus LVF superiorities have occasionally been reported for verbal tasks in the presence of other vocal responses. For latency measures, a low error rate is required, with relatively long exposures, while for accuracy measures a reasonable error rate is needed to avoid floor or ceiling effects. The continuously variable RT score tends to be more sensitive than the all-or-nothing accuracy measure, and with the latter we must contrast two possible sources of error—inaccuracies due to peripheral sensory factors (i.e. data limitations, e.g. brief exposure durations etc.), and inaccuracies due to *resource* limitations, processing load and so on. Floor and ceiling effects, guessing and speed–accuracy tradeoffs have to be considered with accuracy measures, especially perhaps where processing loads are high or concurrent tasks occur.

However the RT measure is not free of its share of problems. Is the 10 msec difference functionally the same when a 200 msec latency increases to 210 msec, as when an 800 msec latency increases to 810 msec? How do we allocate responses, e.g. in a same/different discrimination, between limbs (Hellige and Sergent, 1986)? Thus while a common paradigm is for one limb to respond 'same' and the other to respond 'different', spatial compatibility effects can often arise between responding limb (left or right) and side of stimulus presentation. It is therefore better if only one limb responds for a block of trials, with maybe the forefinger 'same' and middle finger 'different', as long as the limb lies on the midline and is turned so that the two response buttons also lie sagittally along the midline. However, since a given hand might have privileged access to its contralateral hemisphere, an even better solution is a bimanual response, as above, though with the two forefingers responding e.g. 'same' (the faster-responding finger stopping the clock) and likewise the two middle fingers responding 'different' (see Figure 1). In this way, with a bimanual response, it is possible to avoid hemispheric 'priming' by the contralateral limb. Half the subjects should respond with one finger-response configuration, and half with the other. A perennial problem, however, is what to do with long RTs. If possible the trial should be discarded and repeated without violating any random sequence of stimulus presentation. Otherwise such long RTs can be replaced with an arbitrary cut-off value, e.g. one or two standard deviations from the mean for all RTs exceeding that value. While a logarithmic transformation of the data may be employed to reduce the effect of extreme values, or the median instead of the mean may be used for similar reasons, this procedure may violate certain assumptions of additivity in the analysis of variance. On the other hand, very *short* RTs (< 100 msec) are usually anticipations, and reflect inadequate stimulus randomization, enabling the subject successfully to predict the next response upon the basis of prior sequencing, without having to discriminate the actual stimulus itself. Such short RTs should be dropped from further analysis. Since differences in visual laterality experiments are commonly of the order of 10 msec, an adequate number of trials is needed to attain statistical significance; from experience, for any limb of a comparison (e.g. LVF *vs* RVF for 'same') a minimum of 32 trials is probably needed, i.e. 64 presentations or 32 pairs.

Four main kinds of task may be distinguished: the subject may be required to detect the presence or absence of a stimulus, or to discriminate ('same'/'different', target *vs* test) between two simultaneously present stimuli, or to do the same with successively presented items (in effect a recognition task), or finally to identify a single stimulus. In this ascending hierarchy of cognitive complexity, different modes of lateralization may operate at each level, together with different levels of stringency in the decision process. Target ('same') judgements are typically faster and more lateralized than nontarget ('different') responses, especially if the latter occur by default, or if there is a tendency for the subject to recheck from *both* hemispheres before emitting the nonpreferred nontarget response.

Unilateral presentations (i.e. randomly to the LVF or RVF) are preferred in the visual modality; bilateral presentations (i.e. one to each visual field, *not* to each eye) were introduced by analogy with the dichotic (auditory) mode (see below). While stronger asymmetries may occur, this procedure may lead to weaker control of fixation, since the subject always knows exactly where stimulation will occur, i.e. one stimulus in each field. Placement of a fixation

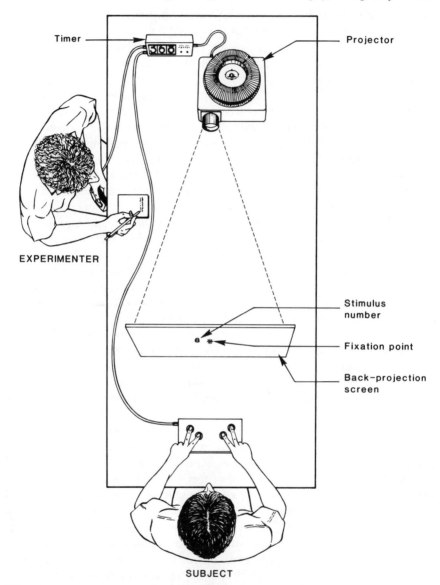

Fig. 1   The subject fixates a fixation point (e.g. a flashing light) in the centre of the back-projection screen. A digit may be flashed for e.g. 150 msec to one or other side of fixation by the projector. The subject performs a timed (see timer) discriminatory response by, for example, depressing the two buttons near him/her with the two forefingers if the digit is odd, and the two further buttons with the two middle fingers if it is even. The experimenter records the response (correct/incorrect) and its latency.

digit in the center for prior report, while controlling the direction of fixation, may favor a verbal mode of processing, or act as a further concurrent task, or lead to spurious RVF effects due to a rightwards scan from fixation. Intermixing of central (at fixation) trials with purely peripheral ones (in LVF or RVF alone) not only encourages central fixation, however, but also permits its calibration, by contrasting the (predicted) superior performance of central compared to peripheral presentations. Yet another and perhaps preferred strategy is to present a small arrow at fixation which must be processed for the subject to correctly report just the item in the field indicated by the arrow's point. In general, unilateral presentations may possibly permit us to assess the efficiency of interhemispheric communication so that the more specialized hemisphere can perform the task; on the other hand competitive bilateral presentations, by inhibiting such interhemispheric communication, may possibly enable us to assess each hemisphere's capacity individually to perform the task.

State-limiting variables

Certain factors directly affect sensory quality (Sergent and Hellige, 1986). With stimulus durations below about 50 msec, fine detail (for which the LH may be adapted) may be lost, with a resultant advantage to the LVF, via the RH's global processing strategy. Likewise stimulus eccentricity may directly affect acuity, and differentially influence the beginnings and ends of a word, themselves known to be of differential importance. Along with exposure duration (above), the (rarely reported) factor of stimulus luminance, which helps determine stimulus energy, may account for much of the conflict in the literature. Stimulus degradation, which of course enters into all the other state-limiting variables above, may favor the RH due to loss of the fine detail for which the LH may be adapted. Thus noise-masking of verbal stimuli may affect RVF performance more than that of the LVF. Finally, doubling the size of a stimulus halves the effective spatial frequencies inherent in a display, and reduces acuity problems; stimulus size must therefore be considered within the context of eccentricity, duration, luminance and spatial frequencies. Indeed the LVF advantage for the large, low-frequency components in large letters may possibly occur only with brief eccentric exposures. Such considerations have led to the spatial frequency hypothesis (Sergent and Hellige, 1986); for a regular grating its spatial frequency is defined as the number of light–dark sinusoidal changes (bars) per degree of visual angle. It has been proposed that the visual system may contain channels responding selectively to different spatial frequencies in a two-dimensional array, and that the output from these channels may compute, as if by Fourier analysis, the entire distribution of spatial frequencies. Fast exposures impair high spatial frequencies more than low, which tend to be available for information processing earlier than the high

Fig. 2   An example of a familiar face from which the relevant high-spatial-frequency information has been subtracted.

components. Thus contrast sensitivity (the resolution of the smallest pattern at the lowest contrast) at high frequencies benefits more from longer exposures or brighter stimuli than it does at lower spatial frequencies. Indeed exposure duration, eccentricity, size, spatial frequencies, contrast and luminance all interact, with high spatial frequencies the most vulnerable. The latter can be masked by overlay of an appropriate grid, or removed subtractively, or even replaced with spurious high spatial frequencies by averaging brightness within pixels on a television screen. Faces can still be recognized from which the relevant high frequency spectral components have been subtracted (see Figure 2); while the mid-frequency range may be the most useful for face recognition, the latter can be achieved by either high spatial frequencies alone (as in line drawings) or by exclusively low frequencies, where e.g. only the gross pattern of featural relationships remain (Sergent, 1989). Indeed the two hemispheres may be differentially sensitive to the outputs of spatial frequency channels, the RH to low ones and the LH to high ones. Consequently if stimulus degradation specifically impairs high spatial frequencies, then RVF/LH performance should suffer. In face identification tasks it has been claimed that a LVF advantage accrues with low-pass filtered faces, and the reverse superiorities with high. However, psychophysiological, behavioral and electrophysiological studies are far from unanimous that the two hemispheres are differentially sensitive to gratings of different spatial frequencies; nor is there unanimity on the exact frequency ranges for 'high' and 'low'. Moreover at least as far as faces are concerned, cycles per degree of visual angle may be less important than cycles per face width, and several studies employing filtered faces with normals, split-brain patients and prosopagnosics have failed to confirm the hypothesis (Bradshaw, 1989b). This hypothesis indeed may merely be a special case of the analytic–holistic processing dichotomy (i.e. low-frequency holistic, high-frequency analytic), perhaps at a more peripheral sensory level. If so, claims (see e.g. Moscovitch, 1986) that asymmetries are less likely to occur at peripheral sensory levels of processing would further predict stronger effects with true analytic–holistic processing strategies. Indeed by its very nature the spatial frequency hypothesis can only apply to *visual* stimuli, and we do require a deeper, more general hypothesis to cover all sensory modalities.

Process-limiting variables

Such factors are imposed by task requirements which include memory, personal involvement, motivation, familiarity, similarity and difficulty, and relate to the idea (see above) that early or superficial sensory processes may be less lateralized. Such claims, however, are disputed, as asymmetries at a sensory level certainly do occur, though they may increase as a function of memory, load or practice. Thus while difficulty necessarily interacts with familiarity (below), a LH superiority tends to occur with difficult face discriminations (where single features must be analyzed), and a RH superiority for easy ones. Both increasing memorization intervals and increasing practice may separately and independently increase asymmetries, and both will interact with difficulty and familiarity. Some claim that reliable asymmetries occur only with a limited range of amply repeated stimuli which become exhaustively familiar, as opposed to where new stimuli appear on each trial, though counter evidence is strong. It is of course possible that if a task can be efficiently processed by a single hemisphere, repetition will reduce asymmetries, as the other hemisphere learns to catch up, while if both hemispheres must substantially cooperate, repetition may increase hemispheric specialization. Thus we must not overlook the importance of strategies; matching letter pairs may be more efficiently carried out by the LVF/RH system if physical aspects are sufficient (e.g. AA, bb etc., matches), while if nominal identity (e.g. Aa, Bb) is important the RVF/LH system may predominate (see below for a more detailed discussion). Indeed apparent sex differences in lateralization may themselves stem from differences in strategic approach. Finally, imagery-based instructions may lead to LVF/RH advantages, while with verbal rehearsal the opposite asymmetries may appear.

Alternatives to tachistoscopic presentations in the periphery

The visual system did not of course evolve so as to recognize shapes by looking at objects briefly flashed up in the visual periphery, and indeed many lateral asymmetries may merely be an unwanted and trivial consequence of such degraded and abnormal viewing (see above). The pattern of results may itself be influenced by the need to expose for longer periods complex stimuli or changing or moving patterns, or when slow readers or clinical patients are employed. A simple way to obviate tachistoscopy is to oblige the subject to turn his/her eyes maximally to left (or right) and then to present stimuli for as long as is required a little further to the left (or right), with the head held facing forward; obviously the eyes cannot then fixate upon the peripheral signal. However, such a procedure is uncomfortable, and eye turn may itself interact with hemispatial or attentional modes of processing. Contact lenses have also been tried, e.g. opaque except for a small slit to occlude a hemifield; however, the procedure is difficult, uncomfortable and unreliable because of slippage and refraction. The 'Z' (Zaidel) lens is a modified version of the contact-lens system used to generate stabilized retinal images, now, however, stabilizing the occluder (mounted with a collimating lens on a stalk) rather than the stimulus. Good results have been reported with commissurotomy patients (see Chapter 6), though the procedure continues to be somewhat heroic. Perhaps the most promising systems are computer-based infra-red eye-movement sensors linked to displays, such that either the display itself or a superimposed electronic window can be made to move with the eye, thus simulating a scotoma. For a detailed discussion of proposed techniques for prolonged hemiretinal stimulation, see Bradshaw (1989a).

Verbal findings

A RVF/LH advantage occurs with single letter or number stimuli, using accuracy measures, or vocal naming latencies, or discriminatory manual RTs. Bigger effects appear with consonants than with vowels, and with stops than with continuants, just as in the auditory modality, suggesting a common LH mechanism for both modalities. Reduced or reversed effects occur with nonstandard typefaces, presumably due to the need to visuospatially pre-process the material. With pairs of simultaneously presented letters for matching same/different, physical identity (e.g. AA, bb) is associated with LVF/RH superiorities, while with nominal matching (e.g. Aa, Bb) the reverse occurs. When the relative numerical magnitudes of digits (i.e. 'greater'/'smaller') have to be determined, there may be a RH contribution from imaginal or analog processing. See Bradshaw (1989a) and McKeever (1986) for verbal and non-verbal findings.

With words, the resultant asymmetries are probably the culmination of many separate subprocessors, each perhaps differentially lateralized. Three major kinds of task have been employed (see e.g. Chiarello, 1988): lexical (word/nonword) decisions, semantic categorization (e.g. animal/plant), or naming (where the strongest RVF/LH advantage appears). Three kinds of information-processing operation also have been used: prelexical (visual–sensory), lexical access (lexical decisions) and post-lexical (post-retrieval). In the first of these, stimulus quality is important (see above), e.g. exposure duration, stimulus clarity, size, word length, all factors known to affect LVF/RH performance. With operations involving lexical access, word frequency and possibly also word class (abstract/concrete, though see Chapter 6) may be important, together with the kind of nonword distractor item employed (legal, e.g. 'goze', 'kife', or illegal e.g. 'gczd', 'knfr', or pseudohomophone, e.g. 'cote', 'brane'). Lexical decisions may even prove possible where exposures are too fast for positive identification of the stimulus; the resultant LVF/RH advantage shifts to a 'normal' RVF/LH superiority with slower presentations, when positive identification is possible.

With the technique known as semantic priming, a prime e.g. NURSE (centrally or laterally presented) is followed by e.g. DOCTOR (the laterally presented target, which is semantically related) or BREAD (unrelated), or a nonword, e.g. SLOVE. The second item presented is to be the subject of a lexical (word/nonword) decision. Two forms of priming have been distinguished, automatic and controlled. With the former, conditions prevent or discourage the subject from being able actively to use the prime word as an aid to lexical access, e.g. when prime words are pattern masked, when the prime–target interval is brief, or when only a small number of primes and targets are related in the experiment. The resulting priming facilitation may occur via spreading activation through the associative connections which exist in semantic memory. By contrast, controlled priming occurs when subjects are aware that the prime and target words are likely to be related, when prime words are clearly perceptible and are identified as clues, or where there is a relatively long prime–target interval. Primes can then serve as access clues to direct attention to a limited domain of related words, thus enhancing the processing of related, but not unrelated, targets. With automatic priming, and with orthographically similar stimuli (e.g. BEAK → BEAR), priming effects tend to be larger with LVF/RH presentations (Chiarello, 1985). With phonologically similar stimuli (e.g. JUICE → MOOSE), priming effects may increase with RVF/LH stimulation. When stimuli are semantically related (e.g. COW → BULL), the LVF/RH system may be slightly favored. With controlled priming, on the other hand, the clearly visible prime is not masked, and the subject knows that the two words are likely to be related. Effects may differ slightly from the automatic paradigm, but are perhaps less interesting if hemispheric effects are not automatic.

With post-lexical (post-retrieval) operations, the subject may name the stimulus, or make judgements about semantic categories. In the former instance a very strong RVF/LH superiority is typical, while with semantic-category judgements, the above asymmetry may weaken or even reverse, depending upon task or conditions.

Effect of report order, directional scanning and reading habits

English is of course read from left to right, while the reverse is the case with Arabic and Hebrew. In English the first (and most important) letter of a word lies adjacent to the fixation point with RVF but not with LVF presentations. Early studies with mirror-reversed English and normal Hebrew showed a LVF superiority, due, it was thought, to directional scanning. However, exposures were uncontrolled, there was no control over fixation, and large and poly-syllabic words were used, with letter-by-letter responses. Later improved studies showed normal RVF/LH advantages for normal and reverse-oriented English and Hebrew, and for horizontally and vertically presented English and Chinese (Bradshaw, 1989a). Indeed vertically oriented English, perhaps being unfamiliar, may even lead to reduced RVF/LH superiorities. These observations, together with findings that asymmetries are typically weaker with females and sinistrals (left handers), indicate that directional scanning is probably not a major source of artifact, and that asymmetries are largely hemispheric in origin. Indeed while the magnitude of the RVF superiority may increase with word length, the effect seems to operate via a decrease in LVF performance, with RVF performance remaining flat for words, though it is as sensitive as LVF performance to word length for nonwords or words in unusual formats.

Sundry other effects

The Stroop paradigm employs color words ('red', 'green', 'blue') appearing in colored dyes which the subject must name, ignoring the words themselves. Congruent color-word–dye relationships (e.g. 'red' in red) facilitate perfor-mance, while incongruent relationships (e.g. 'red' in blue) interfere. Greater interference typically occurs when incompatible color and word information falls in the RVF/LH system.

When pictures are presented for matching or categorizing, a LVF/RH advantage is usual; asymmetries reverse when such stimuli are to be named. Adding distractor words to pictures which are to be categorized may lead to greater interference (if incongruent) or facilitation (if congruent) with LVF/

RH presentations of the distractor word, suggesting a RH role for extracting meaning (see Chapter 6).

Nonverbal spatial processing

Studies with normals largely complement those reviewed above with clinical and split-brain patients (Bradshaw, 1989a; McKeever, 1986). Four major categories may be distinguished. Weak LVF/RH advantages may appear for the discrimination of such simple sensory aspects as color and brightness and the presence/absence of a dot; findings are ambiguous for stereopsis and depth perception. A LVF/RH superiority may appear for attempts to localize where, in e.g. an array of cells, a dot is located. A similar LVF/RH (and a left hand) superiority may occur for discriminating line (or rod) orientation or direction of movement; where verbal labels can easily apply (e.g. with such categorical orientations as horizontal or vertical), a RVF/LH advantage may result. Finally, with patterns and shapes, it should be noted that stimuli are more complex, multidimensional and unfamiliar than with words which typically consist of a finite set of overlearnt, high-spatial-frequency patterns. Such observations apply particularly to e.g. faces. With complex random polygons, asymmetries may depend upon retention intervals, complexity, familiarity and the nature of the judgement (same/different). Generally, a LVF/RH superiority occurs with intermediate levels of complexity, in the absence of verbal codability, and where there is a memory interval. Opposite effects may occur if the subject is simultaneously occupied with a verbal memory load. With hand signs for the deaf, asymmetries may depend upon meaningfulness, familiarity, and whether presentations are static or dynamic. Adults unable to read such signs show LVF/RH advantages, as might be expected, while skilled 'readers' viewing meaningful signs show opposite effects. Abnormal asymmetries have also been reported when acquiring new languages, scripts etc. (see Chapter 6).

Faces are of course complex configurations *par excellence*. They transmit information on personal identity, as well as emotional and verbal (lip-reading) data. They parallel language in complexity and both media may require special processors. The question is unresolved whether faces need a special processing mechanism over and above that needed for pattern processing and/or mediation of emotional signals (see Chapter 2, and Ellis and Young, 1989). Faces may of course only be special in terms of being the single most important visual configuration in our environment, and one which despite close constraints upon the limits of potential variability within and between the component features, nevertheless permits an almost infinite variety of individuals to be discriminated. Over a lifetime we can learn to recognize hundreds if not thousands of individuals by the face, often after only the briefest of encounters, and despite such changeable 'paraphernalia' as moustaches, beards, hats and spectacles, and despite the plastic changes associated with aging and different

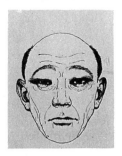

Fig. 3   Examples of Identikit faces used by the author in visual laterality experiments, whose features (hair, wrinkles, eyebrows, eyes, nose, mouth, chin) differ by specified amounts.

emotional expressions. A LVF/RH advantage, both by speed and accuracy, is securely established for processing photographed faces, cartoon drawings, Identikit constructions (see Figure 3) and schematic faces (Bradshaw, 1989a; Young, 1986). Typically a target face is learnt at leisure, and then a test face is flashed to one or other visual field for matching same/different (by manual RT); alternatively a single target face is laterally flashed, followed by a (lateralized, or central) test face for same/different judgements. The typical LVF/RH advantage appears for easy (holistic) discriminations (Figure 4, top row, and Figure 5), but may be lost or even reverse when e.g. only one feature differentiates between target and nontarget (i.e. difficult or analytic discriminations), or when a vocal response is required. The last observation indicates that hemisphere differences may be *relative* rather than *absolute* (see Chapter 5); if the latter, RVF presentations of a face would always be slower, as the information would require transcommissural transmission to the specialized RH, even were a vocal response to be made, which would in fact then simply operate as an extra constant factor. The finding that LVF/RH advantages may be lost with vocal responding indicates therefore that both hemispheres can

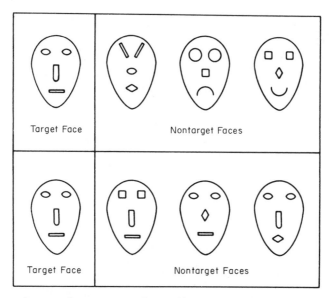

Fig. 4 Three features (eyes, nose and mouth) are relevant for discriminating these nontarget from target cartoon faces used by the author. In the top row, the easy discrimination resulting from the fact that all three features differ results in a left-field superiority. In the bottom row each nontarget differs from the target by only one (always different) feature. This difficult discrimination typically results in a right-field superiority.

participate in face processing (perhaps in different ways, see Chapters 2 and 5), and that both hemispheres can initiate stereotyped 'yes', 'no' or 'uh' responses, but that in both cases one hemisphere is 'better', and such superiorities mutually cancel.

Such LVF/RH effects appear independently and separately both for matching of emotions (irrespective of the 'carrier' faces), and for matching of faces (irrespective of the transient emotions). All effects may be weaker for females (though this is disputed) and sinistrals (see Chapters 8 and 9). The effects may be stronger with simultaneous bilateral presentations, when the subject has to process the face indicated by the fixation arrow (see above). When an individual whose face is presented has to be identified by name, or as a member of a defined category, e.g. a 'famous politician', such identification tends to promote RVF/LH superiorities. Of course we must distinguish between prolonged *personal* familiarity, obtained by encountering various instances of an individual in different contexts, and *stimulus* familiarity, where e.g. the same photograph may merely be repeated. Famous faces are of course both nameable and familiar, and these two (separable) effects *both* may lead to RVF/LH advantages, though there is some dispute about whether famous or familiar faces

STIMULI FOR HOLISTIC FACE TASK

TARGETS

NONTARGETS

Fig. 5   The eight nontargets (bottom two rows) differ from the eight targets (top two rows) in terms of the holistic pattern of spatial relationships (adjacency) between and independent of the actual feature shapes (eyes square or diamond, nose an upright or inverted triangle, mouth open or closed); a left-field superiority results. If, however, subjects have to ignore these holistic interrelationships and instead discriminate on the basis of the feature shapes, a right-field superiority may result.

always give RVF/LH superiorities. Indeed famous faces form a large indeterminate set, while familiar ones form a smaller more constrained one, thus perhaps accounting for the discrepancies. In fact LVF/RH effects may occur for familiar or famous faces if the subject knows exactly who might be presented, thus constraining the set.

Asymmetries may be bigger with deeper levels of processing, e.g. when matching sketched caricatures to photographs, or when two different poses of the same person are matched (Moscovitch, 1986). Is there a specialist processor for faces in the RH or is the RH merely generally better at differentiating between familiar classes of visuospatial stimuli in their canonical i.e. standard

STIMULI FOR HOLISTIC BUGS TASK

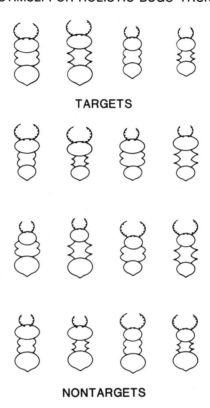

TARGETS

NONTARGETS

Fig. 6   The 12 nontarget bugs (bottom three rows) differ from the four targets (top row) in terms of the holistic pattern of spatial relationships (uniform or nonuniform relative sizes of antennae, head, thorax and abdomen), irrespective of whether the thorax is curved or spiky; a left-field superiority results. If, however, subjects have to ignore such holistic interrelationships and instead discriminate on the basis of the shape of the thorax, a right-field superiority typically results.

orientation? Note that face and emotion processing give independent LVF/RH advantages, which may even appear when bug-like stimuli are to be matched (see Figure 6), and the relationships are configurational rather than in terms of single isolable features. Infants can attend readily to faces, as compared to patterns consisting of their scrambled features; they can copy expressions, and produce them even if blind. Again this suggests a specialist faces processor which is prewired at birth, though doubt has been expressed about the resolving power of neonates' eyes, and in any case they seem also to prefer inspecting normal representations of cars and dogs, compared to scrambled versions. Thus they may be responding to symmetry and coherence, rather

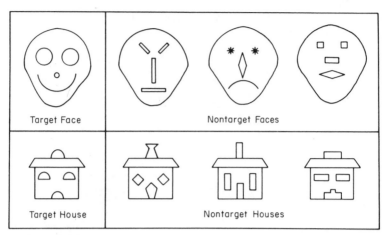

Fig. 7   Schematic drawings of target and nontarget faces, and houses, where targets and nontargets differ from each other in terms of all three 'features'.

than a facelike quality *per se*. Moreover their ability to copy gestures is not limited to facial expressions, but extends also to finger gestures, and their rapidly developing ability to recognize individuals by the face is matched by similar voice-recognition capacities. Face recognition may not therefore be unique, though both it and voice recognition may possibly share sites in the posterior RH. Configurational information may in fact be what makes faces seem somehow 'special', in that our expertise with this class of stimuli may depend upon our ability to use such configurational information. Inversion of course largely destroys such aspects, leading to loss of the expressive characteristics, and to difficulties in identification, categorization and remembering. Indeed recognition deficits following inversion are larger for faces than for any other class of mono-oriented stimuli, e.g. cars, houses (see Figure 7) and airplanes, except where the viewer is an expert therein. Thus dog fanciers are just as affected by inversion of dog profiles as the rest of us are by face inversion (Diamond and Carey, 1986). Perhaps as we gain familiarity with a class of stimuli, we rely more and more upon configurational (RH?) nonanalytic strategies and aspects. Thus a LVF/RH superiority for upright stimuli is not restricted to faces alone, and where such an advantage is found even for *inverted* faces, it is usually the case that highly schematic material or very brief exposures have been employed; these procedures are of course known otherwise to enhance RH involvement. Indeed children under ten years may be affected equally by inversion of faces and houses; thereafter, when the relational aspects come to predominate, faces are more affected by inversion. Moreover improvements in face recognition during childhood may stem from this developing ability to code configurational information with *unfamiliar* faces. Thus any improvement in the performance of children younger than ten years may be restricted to upright faces where configurational information is available, while performance on inverted faces, where such configurational information cannot be coded, may remain constant (see Chapter 10). Interestingly, at puberty there may be a brief dip in face- and voice-recognition ability, again indicating that there probably is nothing special about faces.

Visual imagery is one activity where a RH involvement might be predicted (and cf. left neglect of imagined street scenes as discussed in Chapter 2). However, according to Farah (in press), posterior regions of the LH instead are involved, as shown by loss of image generation ability after posterior LH injury, by electrophysiological (evoked potential) analysis, and by studies of changes in regional blood flow during visualization tasks. Moreover when mental images are used as templates to facilitate discrimination of laterally presented visual stimuli, effects may be greater with RVF (i.e. LH) presentations. Of course many computational processes are involved in imaging, perhaps differentially in the two hemispheres, e.g. storage and maintenance of visual memories from which images can be generated, their actual generation, and inspection of such images and matching to current visual input. Moreover the work of Kosslyn (1987) offers a further resolution of this conflict. LH specialization for image generation may occur only when the locations of image parts are specified precisely and categorically, with respect to other elements; a RH superiority may instead supervene when the loci of image parts are specified less precisely and with reference to an overall common frame. Kosslyn emphasizes the processing commonalities between veridical visual processing, and its subsitute visual imagery ('seeing without the actual sensory input') as in mental rotation and image scanning; imagery, he says, serves to simulate or model reality, and to permit navigation. The linguistic encoding of categorical relations may have served to attract similar, though nonlinguistic, processing operations, thus accounting for the LH's advantage in processing easily categorized (and named) shapes, line orientations (horizontal and vertical, while the RH is better with fine gradations, beyond such categorical anchor-points), and judgements of contact or not (while the RH is better at judgements of relative proximity). If the LH develops a catalogue of categorical representations, the RH, according to Kosslyn, encodes spatial relationships whether for determining the identity or location of objects, or for focussing and directing attention (cf. unilateral neglect). The virtue of such an approach is that just as we cannot claim that all aspects of language are mediated by the LH (see Chapter 6), or that all aspects of shape recognition are mediated by the RH (see Chapter 2 and this chapter), so too we cannot ask whether all aspects of imagery are mediated by a single hemisphere; the phenomenon decomposes into numerous sub-abilities, each differentially lateralized.

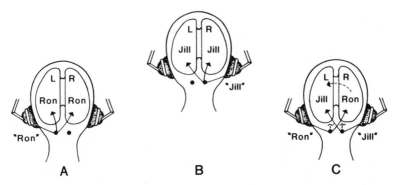

Fig. 8   According to Kimura's structural model, a word spoken in either the left (A) or right (B) ear is channelled to both hemispheres. If, however, two different words are simultaneously presented one in each ear (C) the ipsilateral ear-hemisphere pathways are occluded, and the left hemisphere can only receive left-ear input via the right hemisphere and commissures. Such ipsilateral input may then be further suppressed during transcommissural transmission to the left hemisphere, or in competition with direct, contralateral, right-ear input. (Figure redrawn and modified from S. P. Springer and G. Deutsch, *Left Brain, Right Brain*. San Francisco: Freeman, 1985.)

THE AUDITORY MODALITY

Human laterality studies have concentrated more on the visual and auditory modalities than the tactual. However, methodologies in the auditory and tactual modality have more in common than either has with vision, and have been approached from similar procedural and theoretical standpoints, e.g. with respect to report order, attentional biases, and use of simultaneous stimulation at the two ears (dichotic) or hands (dichhaptic). There is a long tradition of dichotic studies, starting with Broadbent's attentional investigations in the 1950s (Bradshaw, 1989a; Bradshaw, Burden and Nettleton, 1986; Bradshaw and Nettleton, 1988; Bryden, 1988; Porter and Hughes, 1983; Springer, 1986). Here, three pairs of temporally aligned digits were presented, one to each ear, at three pairs per second. Typically, the right ear was preferred for initial report except with slow presentations, and in any case proved superior (a right ear advantage, REA), whether only first ear or only second ear reports were compared. Since then the attentional and the laterality studies have diverged, independently, though recently the role of attention is again receiving emphasis in the context of lateral asymmetries. Although developed for the auditory modality (see Figure 8), the structural (anatomical) model attributed to Kimura is still preferred by many as a general explanation for lateral asymmetries in all other modalities. Thus the REA for dichotic report of verbal material is explained via four assumptions:

(1) one hemisphere, usually the LH, is specialized for speech and language (though see Chapter 6)

(2) auditory inputs are more strongly represented in the contralateral hemisphere; indeed the contralateral auditory pathway does generally have more fibres, and produces larger cortical activity

(3) dichotic stimulation initially lateralizes the input, as ipsilateral information is partially or completely suppressed by the contralateral input (we shall, however, see below that monotic stimulation, where there is competition at a *single* ear, and stimulation via a laterally placed loudspeaker which can thus reach *both* ears, can both under certain circumstances generate powerful REAs or right *side* advantages, RSAs)

(4) information from the nondominant ear/hemisphere is transferred transcallosally to the speech-dominant ear for processing, where it meets and perhaps competes with direct, contralateral, right ear (RE) inputs. Ear differences may thus reflect information loss during interhemispheric transfer to a solely and uniquely specialized hemisphere (as per the first postulate) or, alternatively, they may reflect the relative processing superiority of one hemisphere.

Some initial support appeared for the idea that nondominant ear/hemisphere inputs must be transcallosally despatched (the hypothesis of absolute hemispheric specialization, see Chapter 5), with evidence of a gross reduction in left ear (LE) scores in commissurotomy patients occurring only during dichotic but not monaural stimulation. However, a considerable LE improvement often appeared later, especially when attention was focussed on that ear. Moreover such patients may 'fuse' dissimilar dichotic inputs (e.g. 'back' + 'lack' → 'black'), and an ipsilateral signal necessary to complete something initiated by the RE may get through. We must therefore conclude that LE information is available during dichotic verbal stimulation, perhaps via the ipsilateral auditory pathways in the absence of the commissures. Indeed dichotic listening is similar to figure disembedding, i.e. disembedding LE from RE input; hence blend errors are commoner when the two channels cannot easily be separated, either because the same voice is used, or because they occupy the same locus. However, under appropriate competing monaural (i.e. monotic) conditions, enormous REAs may in fact be obtained.

Kinsbourne's dynamic activational model (see Chapter 5) was one of the first dissenters from the static Kimura account: levels of activation in the two hemispheres would normally be in a reciprocal balance, leading to a fixation straight ahead of both sensory receptors and the attentional focus. Eccentric stimulation, or where activation for whatever reason is endogenously generated in the contralateral hemisphere, perhaps because the subject expects to be presented with words rather than faces, or with stimuli in one rather than the other visual field, would lead to a number of consequences. These include

disturbances of the balanced equilibrium between the hemispheres, orientational biases, and biases in readiness to accept input, to process it, or to emit
responses in the direction contralateral to the activated hemisphere. Verbal
processes activate the LH, visuospatial processes the RH, and bias attention
and the orientation of receptors contralaterally. Thus asymmetries are seen as
due not to Kimura's structural determinants, but rather to attentional and
activational biases. However, there have been several criticisms of this
viewpoint:

(1) appropriate, opposite, asymmetries may occur with the simultaneous
     presentation of verbal and nonverbal stimuli
(2) asymmetries are not necessarily largest when the subject knows in
     advance the verbal/nonverbal nature of the upcoming signal
(3) nor are they necessarily largest when the subject cannot predict which
     side will be stimulated. (Advance information should allow the con-
     tralateral hemisphere to build up activation, and so 'wash out' task-
     related asymmetries.)

Nevertheless the way attention is distributed may indeed somehow be involved
in the relationship between dichotic REAs and cerebral language lateralization; thus people with language in the RH may be more likely to attend to the
LE in a free choice situation, and, likewise, the preferred direction of attention
could even be linked to handedness, irrespective of language lateralization.
Indeed response or attentional biases are common in the traditional dichotic
procedure, though the verbal REA is nevertheless remarkably robust, despite
any attentional or report-order constraints. Bryden describes how to score only
trials where all items from one ear are reported before all those from the other,
splitting them by which ear is reported first, and computing separate means for
each ear, and each report order by ear. We can thus calculate how subjects
would have performed had they always employed an ear order of report. The
procedure is cumbersome and wasteful, and assumes (not necessarily correctly) that subjects attend as much to the LE when they spontaneously
commence with a LE item, as they do to the RE when starting on the right;
nevertheless it provides a relatively pure measure of laterality, free of memory
factors and starting or attentional biases. Indeed indices of lateralization
continue to be subject to dispute. A simple difference score between correct
right (R_c) and left (L_c) will be greatly influenced by the overall score correct
($R_c + L_c$). While the resultant ratio, $(R_c - L_c)/(R_c + L_c)$, is a satisfactory
compromise where the task is not subject to floor or ceiling effects, the ratio
with a 10% accuracy level can be as big as 1.00 (e.g. $(10 - 0)/(10 + 0)$), but
with a 90% accuracy level it cannot exceed 0.11 (e.g. $(50 - 40)/(50 + 40)$).
Various mathematical transformations have been proposed, none of which
completely resolve the problem of a correlation with total accuracy.

Backwards speech has also been shown to generate REAs, though meaningless sequences may require normal syntactic ordering and intonation, especially the latter. Shankweiler and Studdert-Kennedy poineered use of single dichotic pairs of consonant–vowel–consonant (CVC) nonsense syllables, which systematically differed in one or other phoneme, thus eliminating the effects of attention and memory. Subjects attend to both ears, and report both items, the one they are most sure of first. Stop consonants are typically used (b, d, g, p, t, k), though others have also been studied, which are artificially synthesized, with exact onset alignment. Thus there is minimal memory and semantic involvement. The biggest REAs appear with stops, with small or reverse effects with minimally encoded vowels; fricatives, affricates and liquids appear intermediate. However, vowels may generate REAs if embedded in noise, or shortened, or if the listener is unsure of the effective vocal trace size or voice pitch of the speaker.

While target-detection procedures (d' or discriminability, but especially RT) often give robust and reliable REAs, as do vocal shadowing latencies, the magnitude and incidence of typical dichotic REAs is often less than that shown by 'objective' measures of lateralization. These include unilateral ECT or amobarbital, see Chapter 2; 95% of dextrals thereby appear LH dominant. However, dichotic report may access less-lateralized perceptual asymmetries compared to the motor ones tapped by the so-called 'objective' techniques. Indeed good correlations have been reported between the magnitudes of dichotic verbal REAs (obtained when terminally ill cancer patients were alive) and post-mortem morphological assessments of posterior (planum temporale) brain asymmetries (the *receptive* speech zones), but not so far of anterior (motor, Wada-assessed) areas (Witelson, personal communication and see also Witelson, 1983). Indeed while anterior asymmetries may need to be sharper, perhaps to avoid competition for articulatory output, it is also possible for the posterior and anterior language areas sometimes to reside in opposite hemispheres. In any case, we can also ask whether ear asymmetries might be influenced by possible asymmetries of an idiosyncratic nature in subcortical auditory pathways, which could lead to large verbal asymmetries and small or reversed nonverbal asymmetries in one individual, and the opposite perhaps in another. We need therefore a 'neutral' task to detect such subcortical biases. Everyone should then show similar *absolute* differences between ear-superiority magnitudes for verbal and nonverbal tasks, even if for some individuals both tasks generate REAs (i.e. with enormous verbal and small nonverbal REAs) or LEAs. Conversely, according to the 'noncomplementarity' hypothesis (Chapter 5), the normal asymmetries for verbal and nonverbal tasks may be relatively independent of each other for any given individual; averaging *across* several individuals is needed to give the usual picture of a LH-verbal, RH-nonverbal specialization. However, since sinistrals show weaker REAs than dextrals (64% *vs* 89%), and females than males, hemispheric asymmetries, not just subcortical pathways, must in fact play a major role.

Sussman developed a pursuit auditory tracking task, whereby a subject hears two simultaneous tones, one in each ear, the target in one and the cursor in the other (Sussman and Westbury, 1978). The frequency of the randomly varying target tone is to be tracked with the cursor, via unidimensional movements of the tongue, jaw, lips or hand. Better performance is reported with the target tone to the LE and the cursor to the RE, and asymmetries are weaker with respiratory or hand-movement control, suggesting that the speech musculature proper is important. However, the fact that significant asymmetries appear with right-hand tracking suggests that a RE/LH superiority operates for cursor control, rather than a LE/RH superiority for target-tone analysis. We can conclude that a LH specialization operates for the sensorimotor integration of speech-related movements and their auditory concomitants, and for complex sequential programming of changing orofacial configurations from one target position to another, and for all fine coordinated movements.

Nonverbal dichotic studies

LEAs occur for the report of environmental sounds (e.g. a motor starting, a toilet flushing, a cock crowing or a bell ringing), nonverbal vocalizations (a cry, sigh, laugh, shriek, cough), the emotional tone of speech, and intonation patterns (Bradshaw, 1989a; Bradshaw, Burden and Nettleton, 1986). However, Thai speakers still show REAs when discriminating Thai words which differ only in pitch; pitch, in Thai, conveys phonological information. In the musical context, LEAs occur for report of single notes, synthetic musical tones, melodies on solo instruments, and hummed melodies. Of course dichotic melodies in the traditional paradigm involve two dichotic target items, plus four binaural test passages, two new and two old; such a lengthy presentation imposes an even bigger memory load than is the case with verbal studies, making direct comparisons difficult. According to Sidtis (1984), such LEAs reflect a RH superiority in processing steady-state harmonic information, and extraction of pitch information from complex periodic sounds. Thus a note from a musical instrument consists of a fundamental frequency together with a series of partials or overtones, which are integer multiples (i.e. a harmonic series) of the fundamental. These overtones produce the instrument's characteristic timbre. The fundamental can be removed experimentally by frequency filtering, leaving only the overtones; the subject still 'hears' the missing fundamental, a phenomenon which underlies the perception of timbre and melody, and may be the province of the RH. Thus the magnitude of the LEA is proportional to the number of overtones present—the tone's complexity. It is probably such complex harmonic information about timbre which underlies demonstrations of LEAs in recognition of target instruments when the same note is presented as played on different musical instruments; presumably the RH acts upon the Fourier analysis performed by the auditory system upon the acoustic input of melodies, music, and speech prosody.

However, not all aspects of music are RH. A REA appears for the discrimination of temporal order when a sequence is presented of brief tones, and for the recognition of rhythm. We can therefore ask whether the fundamental superiority of the LH, underlying its mediation of speech, is the ability to process rapidly changing acoustic information. Alternatively perhaps, is the LH better at processing such rapidly changing temporal aspects simply *because* of its facility with speech? Whatever the answer (and see Chapter 7), the sequential aspects of music which often appeal to the LH indicate that music is not an exclusive province of the RH; music, like speech, consists of many different components, each with their own characteristic mode of lateralization. We must therefore conclude that laterality is a *processing-specific* rather than a *material-specific* phenomenon, and that some aspects of language belong to the RH, just as some aspects of music (especially rhythm and the temporal aspects) are mediated by the LH, while the melodic aspects are more truly the province of the RH.

There is a curious tone illusion which Deutsch (see Bradshaw, 1989a) has thoroughly investigated. It consists of a two-tone sequence, whose members are one octave apart, and which are repeatedly presented in alternation. Thus an effectively identical sequence goes to both ears simultaneously, except that when the RE receives the high tone, the LE gets the low, and vice versa. Consequently the listener *receives* a single, continuous two-tone chord, with ear of input for each component repeatedly alternating; however, what is *heard* is a single tone switching from ear to ear, whose pitch simultaneously alternates from high to low, i.e. a single high tone in one ear alternating with a single low tone in the other. With dextrals, a high tone is usually heard in the RE and a low tone in the LE. A similar effect occurs even with the use of loudspeakers instead of earphones, indicating that the illusion does not occur along pathways conveying ear information, but rather with respect to the representation of the two sides of auditory space. Thus *what* is heard is determined partly by *where* in space the signals appear to come from. Such findings agree with those relating to the phenomenon of unilateral neglect (see Chapter 2), i.e. the brain maps the location of events in extracorporeal space no less than where they impinge upon the body's proximal receptor surface. Indeed a new generation (see Bradshaw, Pierson-Savage and Nettleton, 1988, and below) of laterality research with normal subjects is now demonstrating asymmetries as a function of where e.g. the hands are located with respect to the midline, and where (e.g. by visual ventriloquistic capture of an ambiguous sound source) a sound *seems* to come from.

Before leaving the topic of dichotic stimulation, we should note that, in theory, a verbal signal which arrives at the LE may be delayed during transcallosal transfer, with an earlier-arriving RE signal occupying the language processor. Consequently, making the LE lead should cancel the REA; however, the REA *increases* if the LE leads by between 15 and 60 msec, due perhaps to a backwards masking effect. Indeed exact onset alignment may be less important than alignment of the words' perceptual centers, though the dichotic REA is robust over a range of asynchronies and intensity differences: at least a 10 dB increase on the LE is needed to cancel the verbal REA. Moreover recent evidence (see below) indicates that *monotic* stimulation (i.e. competition between signals at a single ear) or use of a loudspeaker (competition between two laterally located sound sources, or at a single loudspeaker on one or other side) can generate robust asymmetries.

Monaural asymmetries

A crucial test of the structural or anatomical (Kimura) model, especially of the third postulate (which claims suppression of ipsilateral signals by simultaneous contralateral activity), is whether ear asymmetries can be obtained with monaural stimulation (Bradshaw and Nettleton, 1988). This is the situation where one message, maybe only one of the normal two dichotic channels, goes to a single ear. Of course *processing load* is decreased under such circumstances. Monaural stimulation is not to be confused with the *monotic* paradigm, where two competing messages both go to a single ear, or with *binaural* stimulation, where one message goes to *both* ears. As we shall see, under certain circumstances all procedures (dichotic, monotic, monaural and binaural) can generate asymmetries. These effects, however, depend upon a number of factors: the nature of the task (verbal or nonverbal), the measure (threshold, speed, accuracy or preference), the nature of any simultaneous input (nothing, continuous contralateral white noise, competing monaural, i.e. monotic stimulation), ear uncertainty (i.e. whether or not the subject can focus attention on one ear or side, or has to divide it between ears/sides), and finally such subject variables as handedness, sex, practice and expertise. We should also note that random or unpredictable alternation of signal(s) between ears does not necessarily lead to ear uncertainty if (as with phrases rather than isolated words) sequences of more than one or two seconds are presented to a given ear; this may be long enough to switch attention to that ear and focus upon it. Moreover extra (competitive) input on the same (or opposite) ear may affect asymmetries purely on the basis of task load, task difficulty, disembedding of signals etc. Finally, there are always the biases in the literature of reporting only the results which are significant, positive or interesting.

With verbal tasks presented monaurally, there is some suggestion that thresholds are lower for RE inputs, and for LE inputs with certain nonverbal forms of stimulation. Speech may be preferentially listened to via the RE (and music via the LE). Recall of short verbal materials (digits, words) may show weak REAs, though many other studies only obtain asymmetries under the 'control' dichotic conditions. The best evidence for such monaural REAs

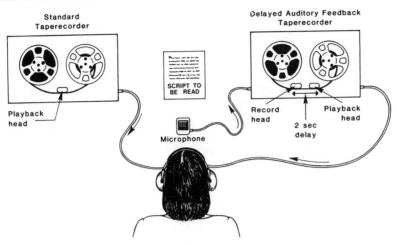

Fig. 9   When a subject hears his/her own speech delayed via a delay loop on a taperecorder by about 200 msec, stuttering or hesitations typically ensue. Effects are worse if the delayed signal reaches the right ear and something else is played to the left ear, than if the ear/earphone relationships are left/right reversed.

comes with conditions of ear uncertainty or high load. When recall of longer verbal materials (phrases etc.) is called for, ear uncertainty is of course impossible. However, REAs have been reported, often without the need for any kind of competition on the other ear, even continuous 'babble' or cocktail party noises. With probed recall (i.e. of an item which in an original list followed the current test probe), REAs may appear without the need for ear uncertainty or contralateral stimulation of any sort. When RTs to designated targets are obtained, or discriminatory RTs or vocal naming latencies, again REAs are often reported without the need for ear uncertainty or competing input, and effects are often bigger with harder discriminations. Many such experiments, however, can be faulted on the basis of improper control of hand used for responding; spatial compatibility effects, moreover, between side of stimulation and responding can obscure laterality effects of interest. When a word is repeatedly re-presented it undergoes an apparent change in quality (the 'verbal transformation effect') due to a form of central saturation; more such transformations are reported with RE than with LE inputs. When two tones, one high and one low, are presented along with two words 'high' and 'low' (or, alternatively, the two words are spoken in either a high or a low voice), with RE inputs there is greater facilitation of pitch judgements (when pitch/tone and word agree) and greater interference (when they disagree); this is of course the Stroop effect.

We can measure the effect of performance disruption when delayed auditory feedback (DAF), or noncontingent masking, is fed to one ear during a variety

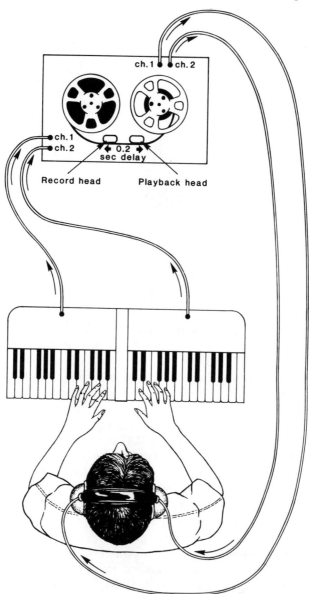

Fig. 10   In a musical performance task with an electronic organ, as used by the author, performance is more disrupted when the left ear receives the left hand's signal, delayed, and the right ear receives the right hand's signal, delayed, than when the ear–hand relationships are reversed.

of speech, tapping or musical performance tasks; these, by their extended nature, do not of course permit of ear uncertainty. Greater speech disruption occurs when DAF is channelled to the RE (see Figure 9), or when a continuous 'babble' is fed to the RE, with opposite asymmetries for musical performance tasks. Lower DAF intensities at the RE suffice to disrupt verbal performance, and again the asymmetries reverse for musical tasks. Effects may be bigger with some kind of contralateral input; indeed use of a completely muted electronic-organ keyboard permits study of *pure* monaural stimulation, a situation which with bone-conducted feedback is obviously unobtainable for speech. Again it seems that some form of competitive stimulation is necessary. Musical effects may be complicated by differing levels of expertise (i.e. strategies), and by interactions between ear of input (or feedback) and operating hand in these performance tasks. Thus DAF disrupts performance more when the LE receives the left hand's signal, and the RE that of the right hand, than when ear–hand relationships are reversed (see Figure 10).

Emotional aspects of monaurally presented verbal materials also seem to appeal to the LE/RH systems (Bradshaw and Nettleton, 1988). In most cases some form of competition (e.g. contralateral 'babble') has been used, and the length of the material precludes ear uncertainty. Typical tasks have included judging the emotional content of sentences read monaurally in an angry, bored, happy or depressed fashion, or recognition of a speaker's voice; often a double dissociation has been reported, i.e. a REA for report of the verbal content along with a LEA for the nonverbal aspects. A LEA has also been reported for identification of isolated second-format transitions; these are rapidly changing bands of acoustic energy which code the information necessary for perceiving stop consonants, and which if heard in isolation may sound like chirps. Thus rapid temporal transitions may be insufficient *per se* to produce REAs, unless perhaps they are heard in a speech context, or the discrimination is difficult.

A LEA appears in monaurally presented tonal tasks, where buzzer sequences are to be recalled, or where matching-to-sample or oddity-detection is employed in three-tone sequences. The same is true with intensity and frequency judgements, RTs to target notes, recognition of musical excerpts, or judgements of emotional appeal of musical sequences. Often the effects require the presence of some form of competition, though the extended nature of the material obviously precludes ear uncertainty.

In conclusion, therefore, competitive noise ('white', or 'babble') may sometimes increase the magnitude or probability of monaural asymmetries, preferably when it is synchronous with the target material rather than merely operating continuously; indeed this may be especially the case with simple or easy tasks. However, such contralateral competition is not essential; it may act merely by increasing the level of task difficulty. Nor is ear uncertainty (i.e. divided attention, which may again perhaps merely act to increase processing load) essential for the demonstration of monaural asymmetries. We do not therefore need to employ the traditional dichotic paradigm, or to invoke Kimura's structural/anatomical model. In both dichotic and monaural presentations, ear of entry and a sound's spatial location are systematically confounded; we now know (see Bradshaw, Pierson-Savage and Nettleton, 1988) that the latter (spatial location) may be no less important than ear of entry as a determinant of asymmetries. Thus loudspeakers instead of headphones may be used in a diotic analog of dichotic listening, with both ears able to receive both laterally located signals, to generate a verbal right-side advantage (RSA) equal in magnitude to a true dichotic REA. Indeed we showed that competing stimulation over a single unilaterally placed loudspeaker may generate powerful verbal RSAs, indicating that spatial competition between messages is unnecessary. Moreover ventriloquistic capture of the apparent origin of a sound by the sight of a fictitious source in an auditory reaction time task demonstrates that it is the perceived position of a sound source, rather than its actual position, or ear of entry, which determines behavioral asymmetries. Thus sounds apparently coming from the right side of space may have a stronger representation in the primary auditory cortex of the LH, than sounds apparently coming from the left. All this suggests that the brain maps the distal locus of events occurring in extracorporeal space, and not merely their proximal locus upon the body's receptor surfaces.

THE TACTUAL OR HAPTIC MODALITY

While largely synonymous, the term 'haptic' is preferred for active palpation, and 'tactile' for passive stimulation. This modality has been less studied (see Bradshaw, 1989a), even though the sensory pathways are strongly contralateral, perhaps due to the special problems associated with stimulus construction, presentation and control. The left side of the body may have a lower pressure-sensitivity threshold, and the left hand seems to be superior for discriminating line slant. There is currently dispute over hand asymmetries in Braille, but (and cf. sign language for the deaf) its degree of language relatedness varies with the user's familiarity; laterality effects may depend upon use of one or both hands simultaneously. Usually a tactile (dichhaptic) analog of the dichotic procedure is employed; the subject feels pairs of raised letters simultaneously presented one to each hand, each for 2 sec, with a 1 sec inter-stimulus interval. While sex differences may appear, typically there is a right hand superiority for reporting letters and the opposite for nonsense shapes. This active dichhaptic exploration gives more accurate responses than the alternative, passive touch; however, it needs longer presentation times and results in problems similar to the dichotic technique. These include memory load, difficulty of ensuring equal allocation of attention, division of attention

Fig. 11   In this vibrotactile reaction-time task, one hand receives the signal and the other initiates a button-press response. Either or both hands can lie to left or right of the body, with one or both arms in ipsilateral or contralateral (across the body) hemispace. Performance is faster when the *responding* hand (left or right) lies to the right compared to the left of the body.

(compared to alternation) and report-order effects. Again asymmetries tend to be bigger with the hand reported second (cf. second-ear reports), and again with good control a double dissociation may appear, a left hand superiority for shapes and a right hand one for letters. Effects such as these occur both with active palpation and passive experience of stimuli traced by the experimenter upon the subject's fingers. A (monohaptic) right hand superiority may occur in reporting or reproducing sequential patterns of finger stimulation, and a left hand effect for static patterns of finger spacing, though the locus (to left or right of the midline) may be just as important as the actual hand involved.

Vibrotactile RTs with a hand (left or right) held in various positions with respect to the body midline have shown that performance is slower when the hand lies in left hemispace, especially 45° or more to the left of the midline and thus out of the preferred processing space or territory of the dominant right hand (see Bradshaw *et al.*, 1988). These effects appear to involve the preparation of motor responses, rather than the detection of sensory (vibrotactile) events (see Figure 11), and only occur when attention can be fully deployed for blocks of trials to one or other side; under conditions of uncertainty, hemispace asymmetries are replaced by hand effects. Thus when subjects cannot predict which hand or side will be stimulated and have to respond on any given trial, covert attention (i.e. directed attention which is independent of the current orientation of head and gaze) cannot be directed to a particular side. The best strategy may then be to concentrate upon the preferred hand. Thus in such a choice task, hemispatial asymmetries are lost, and are replaced with a right hand advantage and spatial compatibility effects, i.e. faster performance when a given hand responds within its own ipsilateral hemispace. These effects give way to a right side advantage with simple reaction times, when only one hand/ side is stimulated and responds for a block of trials, and covert attention cannot therefore be directed to that side. In fact it might be preferable to use the term 'left side disadvantage' instead of right side advantage, as performance only deteriorates when *either* hand lies more than 60° to the left of the midline. Thus dextrals may have difficulty in focussing covert attention towards far left space, in the region *outside* that wherein the preferred hand normally operates. Experiments which have dissociated overt attention (i.e. the locus of directed gaze) and covert attention (i.e. irrespective of the latter) indicate that the former is only important under conditions of unpredictability, or when 90° head turns result in postures which dissociate head and body coordinates of extracorporeal space. Then, or when a horizontal posture upon one or other side dissociates corporeal and gravitational coordinates, hemispace asymmetries are lost. Indeed clinical hemineglect may also be greatly modified under such circumstances (see Chapter 2). Attention towards events which occur in extracorporeal space may be just as important as the proximal locus of receptor stimulation, in determining performance asymmetries. We should, however, perhaps at this point distinguish between three kinds of asymmetries: classical laterality effects (visual field and ear asymmetries), true hemispace asymmetries (e.g. superior performance in shadowing verbal material presented via a single laterally located loudspeaker when it lies to the right), and vibrotactile RT effects. The second group may in fact subsume the first as a special case. However, vibrotactile RT effects are probably independent of any prior *hemispheric* specialization, and the obtained right side advantage may merely reflect the easier focussing of covert attention by dextrals to regions wherein the preferred hand normally operates, when the locus of stimulation and response is predictable. Kinsbourne's attentional account (see Chapter 5) of classical laterality effects presupposes prior or existing hemispheric specializations, and in addition invokes an activational component. Thus LH activation with verbal tasks results in a shift of covert attention to the right side of space, with a consequent facilitation of processing for events occurring there, as indeed also happens with an overt rightwards shift of attention. However (and again see Chapter 5), his predictions are not met with respect to the effects of prior knowledge of side of stimulation, or verbal/nonverbal nature of the stimulus, upon lateral asymmetries. Thus while classical laterality effects may be subsumable under 'true' hemispace asymmetries (see above), and attentional processes may or may not play a role, any such role is unlikely to be that envisaged by Kinsbourne. Conversely the vibrotactile RT paradigm probably taps overt and covert attentional processes, though not of the sort envisaged by Kinsbourne, and underlying cerebral asymmetries make a negligible contribution, except in so far as the subject's preferred hand is concerned.

DOUBLE TASK PERFORMANCE

Apart from employing speed and accuracy, we may measure performance in terms of the processing load it indirectly imposes upon another concurrently measured task. Thus a vehicle driver is likely to be able to correctly perform more mental-arithmetic computations while driving along a deserted road, compared to when it is choked with traffic and pedestrians. While this secondary or concurrent-task measure is useful when it is undesirable or impossible directly to intervene in a primary task, nevertheless the presence of a secondary task can itself affect performance of the primary task, as well as vice versa. It is possible that easy secondary tasks may facilitate or 'prime' a hemisphere to perform another related task normally performed by that hemisphere. This may perhaps only occur if the secondary task draws enough resource effort to activate structures in the same hemisphere, but not so much as to deprive the other task of resources (cf. Chapter 5). If both tasks require attention, or compete for common resources, then interference may result. The problem with such a formulation is that it is *ad hoc*, and can predict effects in either direction; it also derives from Kinsbourne's attentional/activational account, against which objections have been raised on other grounds (see above and also Chapter 5).

Nevertheless effects with this procedure do seem robust (Hiscock, 1986). In an early demonstration, subjects balanced a dowel rod on the index finger of the left or right hand, while simultaneously repeating sentences aloud; under these conditions, right hand (LH) performance dropped more than that of the opposite hand/hemisphere system. Thus performance was better when opposite hemispheres mediated the two concurrent tasks, due to reduced interference.

More recently, tapping (with one, two or all four fingers of either hand, in simple or patterned configurations) has been studied, while the subject performs a (nonlateralized) verbal or spatial task, e.g. counting backwards in threes. Separate tapping scores must be obtained for each hand with and without the concurrent (verbal or spatial) task—and of course the primary task (tapping) may itself interfere in an interesting and relevant way with the secondary (e.g. counting) task. A common metric is

$$\frac{\text{performance without concurrent task MINUS performance with it}}{\text{performance without it}} \times 100$$

Typically, with a verbal concurrent task, the right hand performance is decremented more than the left; a verbal task suffers more with right than with left hand tapping; the opposite occurs with spatial tasks. However, these ideal results rarely appear fully. Primary tasks include dowel balancing (see above), single, dual or four-button tapping with one or more fingers. Secondary verbal tasks include backwards counting, recitation, listing, verbal or arithmetic problem solving, reading aloud or memorization; secondary nonverbal tasks (i.e. typically resulting in a left-hand decrement) include finding hidden figures, performing the Progressive Matrices, the Wechsler Block Design, and a running memory span for faces. Note, however, some recent suggestions that the dominant hand, *regardless* of handedness, may suffer greater tapping interference with a concurrent verbal task; if true, then the task cannot be said to assess hemispheric language dominance.

CONJUGATE LATERAL EYE MOVEMENTS

Conjugate lateral eye movements (cLEMs) are said to be a component of a contralateral orienting response or overflow of cognitive neural activity into the orientation control system within the same hemisphere (Hiscock, 1986). The direction of eye movements on interrogation is said to remain fairly consistent for a given individual, and may index cognitive style (see Chapter 11). Thus right movers are said to be better at verbal tasks. Such claims are hotly disputed, and there has been little success at correlating overall cognitive performance with any measure of lateral asymmetry. More importantly, and less radically, the direction of cLEMs is said to reflect current verbal/nonverbal processing; however, it is difficult to see how one measure can assess both long-term aspects (cognitive style, above) and short-term processing modes as here. Moreover many attempted replications have been unsuccessful, and there are problems in how we should interpret eye movements (Bradshaw, 1989a). Thus what should be counted as a cLEM? Any movement, however small? The first—or longest—movement? The total number over (what?) duration? Should the eyes be 'zeroed' before each task? An alternative possibility is that lateral deviation of the gaze may facilitate the skills of the contralateral hemisphere, with perhaps rightwards looking an aid to verbal processing. Similar ideas of an activational overflow come with claims that during speech, dextrals make freer hand movements with the right as compared to the left hand, while self-touching movements occur equally often with either hand, due to an overflow of activation from cognitive to motor areas. However, there is no evidence of differential effects with nonverbal activity, and the whole idea of activational overflow and balances is open to some dispute.

SUMMARY AND CONCLUSIONS

Asymmetries with normals may depend upon the aggregate of several differently lateralized component processes, the perceived nature of the task, a whole range of stimulus factors and dependent variables, and subject expectancy, expertise and strategies. Even the artificial nature of stimulus presentation needed to lateralize the input may bias the findings. In the visual modality, duration, contrast, luminance, size, eccentricity and degradation all interact and partly determine spatial frequencies; the LH may be particularly sensitive to high spatial frequencies and the RH to low. Since written material and faces differ with respect to spatial frequencies, this may partly account for their associated patterns of lateralization, though it is not yet clear how the spatial-frequency hypothesis may relate to e.g. the analytic–holistic processing dichotomy, and a more general account is needed to cover nonvisual modalities. Verbal materials are typically associated with RVF superiorities or REAs, except where materials are unfamiliar, degraded or need pre-processing. Phonological and lexical aspects may be more lateralized to the LH than e.g. purely semantic aspects. Nonverbal and spatial asymmetries typically associated with RH superiorities (visual and auditory) tend to be weaker, as well as lacking the easily definable qualities of verbal materials. Yet faces provide some of the strongest visual effects, and, as stimuli comparable in complexity to verbal materials, may be subjected to more experimental manipulations than any other class of nonverbal stimulus. While LH superiorities may appear if face judgements are difficult or depend upon feature analysis, typical RH advantages occur both for the global recognition of facial identity, and for emotions portrayed. It is not yet clear whether there is a specialized processor in the RH dedicated to processing faces (and maybe other mono-orientational stimuli, complex configurations and emotions), analogous to a LH language procesor.

It may be unnecessary to invoke Kimura's structural/anatomical model to explain auditory asymmetries. Nor even may competition (between or within ears) be essential to generate them, though difficulty in 'stimulus disembedding' may play a role. While directional attention is an important variable, coding in terms of the perceived origin (left or right) of a sound source may suffice. The less encoded an auditory stimulus, the less likely it is to appeal to exclusively LH processors. By their nature, tachistoscopic and auditory techniques assess the probably less lateralized perceptual aspects of cerebral asymmetry (though cf. Sussman's auditory tracking task and DAF studies), partly accounting thus for inconsistencies in the literature. Not all aspects of music appeal to RH mechanisms, any more than all aspects of language appeal to the LH. Tactual asymmetries, especially with the dichhaptic paradigm, generally follow the parent example of dichotic listening. While double or concurrent task performance has provided a further useful technique, unfortunately the same cannot be said for cLEMs.

IMPORTANT READINGS

Bradshaw, J. L. Methods in studying human laterality. In A. Boulton, G. Baker and M. Hiscock (eds.), *Neuromethods*, Vol. 15. Clifton, N.J.: Humana Press, 1989a, in press.

Bradshaw, J. L. Spatial frequencies and the cerebral hemispheres. In A. W. Young and H. D. Ellis (eds.), *Handbook of Research on Face Processing*. Amsterdam: North Holland Publishing Company, 1989b, pp. 93–100.

Bradshaw, J. L., Burden, V. and Nettleton, N. C. Dichotic and dichhaptic techniques. *Neuropsychologia*, 1986, **24**, 79–91.

Bradshaw, J. L. and Nettleton, N. C. Monaural asymmetries. In K. Hugdahl (ed.), *Handbook of Dichotic Listening: Theory, Methods & Research*. New York: Wiley, 1988, pp. 45–69.

Bradshaw, J. L., Pierson-Savage, J. M. and Nettleton, N. C. Hemispace asymmetries. In H. Whitaker (ed.), *Contemporary Reviews in Neuropsychology*. New York: Springer, 1988, pp. 1–35.

Bryden, M. P. An overview of the dichotic listening procedure and its relation to cerebral organization. In K. Hugdahl (ed.), *Handbook of Dichotic Listening*. New York: Wiley, 1988, pp. 1–43.

Chiarello, C. Hemisphere dynamics in lexical access: Automatic and controlled priming. *Brain and Language*, 1985, **26**, 146–72.

Chiarello, C. Lateralization of lexical processes in the normal brain: A review of visual half-field research. In H. A. Whitaker (ed.), *Contemporary Reviews in Neuropsychology*. New York: Springer, 1988, pp. 36–76.

Diamond, R. and Carey, S. Why faces are and are not special: An effect of expertise. *Journal of Experimental Psychology: General*, 1986, **115**, 107–17.

Ellis, H. D. and Young, A. W. Are faces special? In A. W. Young and H. D. Ellis (eds.), *Handbook of Research on Face Processing*. Amsterdam: North Holland Publishing Company, 1989, pp. 1–26.

Farah, M. J. The lateralization of mental image generation: Evaluating data, and arguments on the localization of cognitive processes. *Journal of Experimental Psychology: Human Perception and Performance*, in press.

Hellige, J. B. and Sergent, J. Role of task factors in visual-field asymmetries. *Brain and Cognition*, 1986, **5**, 200–23.

Hiscock, M. Lateral eyemovements and dual-task performance. In H. J. Hannay (ed.), *Experimental Techniques in Human Neuropsychology*. New York: Oxford University Press, 1986, pp. 264–308.

Kosslyn, S. M. Seeing and imagining in the cerebral hemispheres: A computational approach. *Psychological Review*, 1987, **94**, 148–75.

McKeever, W. F. Tachistoscopic methods in neuropsychology. In H. J. Hannay (ed.), *Experimental Techniques in Human Neuropsychology*. New York: Oxford University Press, 1986, pp. 167–211.

Moscovitch, M. Afferent and efferent models of visual perceptual asymmetries: Theoretical and empirical implications. *Neuropsychologia*, 1986, **24**, 91–114.

Porter, R. J. and Hughes, L. F. Dichotic listening to CVs: Method, interpretation and application. In J. B. Hellige (ed.), *Cerebral Hemisphere Asymmetry: Method, Theory and Application*. New York: Praeger, 1983, pp. 177–218.

Sergent, J. Structural processing of faces. In A. W. Young and H. D. Ellis (eds.), *Handbook of Research on Face Processing*. Amsterdam: North Holland Publishing Company, 1989, pp. 57–91.

Sergent, J. and Hellige, J. B. Role of input factors in visual-field asymmetries. *Brain and Cognition*, 1986, **5**, 174–99.

Sidtis, J. J. Music, pitch perception and the mechanisms of cortical hearing. In M. S. Gazzaniga (ed.), *Handbook of Cognitive Neuroscience*, New York: Plenum Press, 1984, pp. 91–114.

Springer, S. P. Dichotic listening. In H. J. Hannay (ed.), *Experimental Techniques in Human Neuropsychology*. New York: Oxford University Press, 1986, pp. 138–66.

Sussman, H. M. and Westbury, J. R. A laterality effect in isometric and isotonic labial tracking. *Journal of Speech and Hearing Research,* 1978, **21**, 563–79.

Witelson, S. F. Bumps on the brain: Right-left anatomic asymmetry as a key to functional lateralization. In S. J. Segalowitz (ed.), *Language Functions and Brain Organization*. New York: Academic Press, 1983, pp. 117–44.

Young, A. W. Subject characteristics in lateral differences for face processing by normals: Age. In R. Bruyer (ed.), *The Neuropsychology of Face Perception and Facial Expression*. Hillsdale, N.J.: Erlbaum, 1986, pp. 167–200.

5

Models of hemispheric interaction

It is one thing to note that there is normal, clinical or commissurotomy evidence for human cerebral asymmetry. However, such often disconnected observations only become meaningful if they can be integrated into a theoretical account of the nature of interhemispheric interaction—an interaction which is necessarily largely lacking in cases of commissural section. Evidence from such commissurotomy cases has generally been interpreted in support of relative rather than absolute hemispheric specialization. Thus such authors argue that hemispheric differences are quantitative and ones of degree, rather than qualitative or differences of kind. On the other hand, clinicians note that unilateral injury may often produce devastating effects upon certain higher cognitive functions, and stress the absolute or qualitative nature of hemispheric specialization. Paradoxically, this means that clinical evidence emphasizes the role of the cerebral commissures in transferring information from incompetent to uniquely specialized regions for processing. As so often is the case with such controversies, a compromise may be proposed, e.g. the so-called 'horse-race model'. We shall see moreover that it is probably mistaken to view a hemisphere as being specialized for a particular task; even apart from the considerable individual differences apparent in these respects, tasks are inevitably composed of varying mixtures of component processing requirements. Each of these is perhaps variously lateralized in direction and extent, and each is subject to the effects of load, practice, experience and adopted strategy. Moreover, even if a function, task or processing stage is more or less lateralized to one hemisphere, we can ask whether this will necessitate the 'complementary' lateralization of opposite functions in the other hemisphere. Indeed, what *are* such opposite or complementary functions? Verbal/visuospatial? Analytic/holistic? Because we have two sides to our brain, should we be forced into dichotomizing all aspects of mental life? What is the role here of the cerebral commissures anyway? Interhemispheric transfer of information, inhibitory control of levels of activation, the allocation of resources, or the integration of complementary modes of processing? Satisfactory answers to such questions as are raised in the following chapter will provide more than just a useful account of hemispheric specialization and interaction; they will be a springboard to a wider understanding of brain function generally.

Behavioral asymmetries stem from two sources. The first of these is the structural and functional differences between the two hemispheres, whether verbal versus spatial, or sequential/analytic versus global/holistic (see Chapter 7). We shall, however, argue (and see also Chapter 4) that the ultimate observed asymmetry will be the algebraic sum of individual subprocessor asymmetries, which for different tasks, strategies or levels of practice will not all be lateralized the same way. Note also that just because the LH may be dominant for language in a given individual, the RH may not necessarily be equally dominant for some other opposite or contrary function. The second source of behavioral asymmetries stems from the contributions of the interhemispheric commissures, excitatory and inhibitory, and the connections between the hemispheres and the receptor surfaces of hand, ear and visual field, and between hemispheres and motor outflow; in the case of such central–peripheral connections, they will usually be predominantly, though perhaps not exclusively, contralateral.

An important issue is whether the dominance relationship between the two hemispheres is one of causal or statistical complementarity (Bryden, 1986). According to the viewpoint of causal complementarity, the RH may take on certain roles because the LH is engaged upon opposite functions, e.g. RH spatial processing occurs by default, since the LH has assumed language control (and see Corballis, 1983). The viewpoint of statistical complementarity, however, proposes that while one set of factors may e.g. bias the LH for language, a quite different set may predispose the RH for visuospatial processing; thus there are two sets of determinants and two sets of effects, which are causally independent of each other and only statistically associated across the population at large. To take an example: if the likelihood, overall, of LH language is 95%, and that of visuospatial processing being mediated by the RH is 80%, their joint probability (i.e. that an individual will demonstrate 'standard' lateralization) will be 95% × 80% = 76%. Indeed there often fails to be a good negative correlation between laterality effects for verbal and spatial processing; frequently the same (e.g. left) hemisphere seems to subserve both functions. When this occurs it is not always the case that the *verbal* functions are more strongly lateralized to the LH than the spatial processes, or, conversely, that the *spatial* processes are more strongly lateralized than verbal processes to the RH. Indeed, in sinistrals, while RH language is commoner than in dextrals, this is not necessarily the case for LH visuospatial processing. Another observation contrary to the idea of causal complementarity is that aphasic sinistrals are more likely to show visuospatial deficits than nonaphasics, suggesting that sinistrals may have one or both of language and visuospatial functions bilaterally represented. Moreover, language and motor skill (cf. apraxia after LH damage) are probably two fairly independent LH abilities, which are not causally interconnected. Finally, of course, it is by no means certain that all aspects of language (phonology, semantics, reading, speaking . . .) are always lateralized to the same hemisphere.

There are two major ways of looking at hemispheric asymmetry in terms of functional specialization: the idea of absolute, qualitative or unilateral specialization, and the idea of relative specialization ('relative efficiency' or 'direct access'), see Allen (1983) and Zaidel (1983). The first approach is suggested by clinical studies, in the light of major dysfunctions after unilateral injury, and assumes the need for transcallosal transmission from an incompetent to a competent hemisphere; however, in the same light it should be noted that the clinical incapacity after unilateral damage, which is so much greater than that evident when the 'nondominant' hemisphere is interrogated in a split-brain patient, could itself stem from callosal inhibition. The latter phenomenon is of course necessarily absent after the commissurotomy operation. Indeed commissurotomy and normal studies both support the second ('relative specialization') approach, as apparent specializations often seem far from absolute, and the ultimate observable asymmetries seem to represent the algebraic sum of the outputs from the differently specialized subprocessors; the latter may vary for different tasks, strategies, levels of practice and subjects. We shall now examine both approaches in some depth.

ABSOLUTE, QUALITATIVE SPECIALIZATION AND CALLOSAL RELAY

For a given task, at least one of its processing components will be exclusively represented in only one hemisphere, which alone will be competent to operate. Thus information initially reaching the incompetent hemisphere must be transferred across the commissures to the specialized hemisphere, with either or both of two consequences, interhemispheric signal degradation, or processing delay due to interhemispheric transmission time. Signal degradation assumes a low-fidelity transfer of information; however, split-brain patients usually *can* perform some language functions with the RH (though perhaps *not* the *phonological* or *articulatory* components which may be uniquely lateralized subprocesses), unless of course this is merely due to abnormal brain reorganization after long-standing epilepsy. Comparison of performance for lateralized tasks with separate left and right hand responses (and cf. Moscovitch, 1986a, 1986b), should in theory resolve the second alternative—interhemispheric transmission time. The absolute specialization model predicts constant RVF

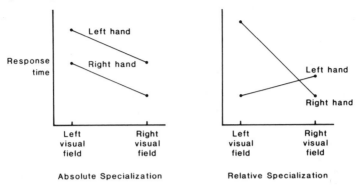

Fig. 1   The effects upon response time for left and right field presentations, with left and right hand responses, according to two models of hemispheric specialization, absolute and relative.

superiorities to verbal stimuli, irrespective of button-press responses by the left or right hand. Thus there should be a main effect of visual field (e.g. a RVF superiority) and maybe one for hand (e.g. right hand superiority), but with no interaction, as there will always be one more callosal crossing for a word in the LVF/RH, *whichever* hand responds. Conversely according to the relative specialization model, the hand used will modify verbal/nonverbal asymmetries, resulting in a statistical interaction (see Figure 1). Thus the effects of a word in a (poor) LVF/RH will cancel the possible advantage of a (good, fast) right hand/LH response. However, the exact effects may be difficult to predict, depending upon the costs of the combination of a wrong hemisphere and hand (e.g. a possible 3 msec callosal crossing for hand motor control) versus e.g. an estimated difference in hemispheric processing time of 15 msec for certain cognitive tasks. Nevertheless a verbal response in a face-discrimination task may destroy LVF/RH superiorities previously found with manual responses; thus the RH may be rather better at processing faces, and the LH at (simple) verbal responses, the two effects cancelling. There are some other problems with the absolute-specialization model as it stands: some aspects of processing may indeed be more or less exclusive to the LH (e.g. phonology, articulation), while others may in fact be relative, or differentially distributed, e.g. semantics (cf. Chapter 6). Secondly, the way stimuli are processed may be more important than their verbal/nonverbal nature; thus the effects of context, practice and strategies all suggest the second model, the relative specialization approach.

RELATIVE HEMISPHERIC SPECIALIZATION

According to this general idea, either hemisphere can perform a task, or its various substages, though to different levels of efficiency and in different ways;

moreover different strategies, task demands and parameters may influence the different stages. There are several versions of this general approach.

(1) Cooperative positive interaction

Here, both hemispheres cooperate, though one may lead or predominate. It accounts nicely for the reported findings of weaker asymmetries with females and sinistrals (see Chapters 8 and 9) if they have less specialized and more redundant cerebral organization. However, this implies a less efficient use of cerebral information processing space, and the approach lacks the sophistication of the 'subprocessor' version (below); here relative specialization and cooperation is at a hemispheric level, with (at an *intra*hemispheric level) absolute specialization of subprocessors which are differentially distributed between the two hemispheres.

(2) Parallel processing by the two hemispheres

This approach goes beyond the first (above) by dropping the idea of cooperation; thus both hemispheres do exactly the same thing, in parallel—an even more redundant and inefficient approach—or alternatively they are specialized for different components of a task. In this case we are in effect left with the subprocessor version (below).

(3) Allocation version

While both hemispheres in principle are capable of doing everything, in practice a task is normally allocated to one hemisphere on the basis of preanalysis, attention, strategies, etc. In effect this reduces to the absolute specialization account (above), unless we view allocation as occurring only *after* unilateral injury; this would be an adaptive solution, accounting nicely for e.g. functional recovery, though in health it would again be redundant, as, without allocation to one or other hemisphere, it would reduce to the parallel-processing version. Consequently the allocation model would only be viable in the (evolutionarily unnatural) context of survival after unilateral injury.

(4) Negative (inhibitory) interaction

Thus for example the LH suppresses original RH speech capacity, perhaps later in development. It accounts for early plastic takeover by the RH if the LH is damaged in infancy (see Chapter 10); it also accounts for the greater apparent degree of aphasia in unilaterally damaged patients with intact commissures, compared to split-brain patients, when in both cases we assess putative RH language (see Chapter 6). There are several versions of this influential approach. According to Kinsbourne (1975), the two hemispheres are in a state of mutual inhibitory balance for attention, orientation and language; behavioral asymmetries are only indirectly due to hemispheric specialization, and more directly to expectations concerning the nature of the material to be processed. Thus if verbal material is expected, the LH is activated and such verbal material then receives correspondingly better processing. The commissures are conceived of as *inhibitory* channels between the hemispheres. However, asymmetries do not seem to vary as a function of expectancies—indeed a simultaneous double dissociation can even occur with corresponding (and opposite) asymmetries appearing at the same time for both verbal and nonverbal material. Moreover commissurotomy does not reduce inhibition, and therefore asymmetry, as according to the model it should.

Moscovitch's (1986a, 1986b) version of the idea of negative (inhibitory) interaction suggests that resources and attention are differentially allocated to one or other hemisphere, to activate it in a mode consistent with its cognitive capacities when so primed. While deriving from aspects of Kinsbourne's model (above), it is perhaps best considered separately in the context of the resources model (below).

Yet another approach asks whether the corpus callosum is important for controlling the development of cerebral organization. We could thus account for the unusual (bilateral) organization in congenital acallosals, and for recent claims (now disputed, see Chapter 3) that the corpus callosum differs morphologically between the two sex and handedness groups. The callosum is thus seen as a cause of differences in cerebral organization. However, as observed, not everyone agrees with the above claims about callosal morphology, and nowadays the idea that lateralization develops is largely rejected (see Chapter 10). Nevertheless the callosum may well transmit inhibitory information—not general inhibition to regulate activation, as proposed by Kinsbourne (above), but complementary signals, somewhat analogous to the informational relationship between a photographic negative and a positive. Thus Cook (1986) observes that the callosum is our biggest and fastest evolving transcortical tract; it connects largely homotopic regions in the association (not primary) cortex on each side. The most useful kind of hemispheric specialization would involve complementarity, analogous to patterns of surround inhibition which occurs in e.g. the primary visual cortex. Thus the concept of inhibitory callosal interconnectivity of homotopic association cortex would ensure that activation of a point in e.g. the LH would lead to inhibition of the corresponding locus in the RH, with excitation of the immediately surrounding areas, due to release from surround inhibition. Mirror-image-negative relationships can thus be generated between corresponding LH and RH regions, analogous to figure–ground relationships in visual perception. Thus if an area is dominant for a specific function in the LH (e.g. phonology), the homotopic area in the RH would

LEFT   RIGHT

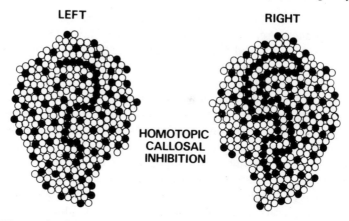

HOMOTOPIC
CALLOSAL
INHIBITION

Fig. 2   The mechanism proposed by N. D. Cook (*The Brain Code: Mechanisms of Information Transfer and the Role of the Corpus Callosum*. London: Methuen, 1986) for interhemispheric communication. On the left is shown an arbitrary configuration of active cortical columns. On the right is the cortical consequence of topographical callosal inhibition which produces a double inversion of the pattern on the left. (Figure reproduced with permission.)

generate complementary aspects, e.g. context. Similar ideas apply to the idea of a LH : denotative, RH : connotative opposition. This approach avoids redundant duplication in favor of complementarity (see Figure 2). However, this model need not fall foul of our objections (earlier) to the concept of causal complementarity, since that concept related to gross macro aspects, e.g. language versus spatial skills, not, as here, to the microstructure of all kinds of information processing. Thus the present account sees both hemispheres contributing to language, and to spatial processing, and indeed operating in a cooperative fashion for any such processing task. Nor is it incompatible with the next approach (5).

(5) Subprocessors version of the idea of relative specialization

A finite number of specialized subprocessors may be differentially distributed to either hemisphere for different aspects of a task. Thus there may be absolute specialization at the subprocessor level, but because all these subprocessors are differentially distributed left and right for different aspects of a task, the appearance is gained of relative hemispheric specialization at the macro level; this occurs via the algebraic sum of such subprocessor activity, with the interhemispheric transcallosal traffic of outputs from one subprocessor in one hemisphere to act as input to another subprocessor in the other. Indeed electrostimulation of the cortex and PET scan studies (see Chapter 2) show differential localization of e.g. the phonological, syntactic, semantic and visual aspects of language, and their differential activation during an ongoing verbal task. While it is not immediately clear how these subprocessors are to be sequenced or allocated, the model is potentially very flexible, and is supported by experiments employing the double or concurrent task paradigm (see Chapter 4).

(6) Resources model

In some ways this is a hybrid between the Kinsbourne version of negative (inhibitory) interaction, and the subprocessors version. It postulates that each hemisphere is a separate processing system, each with its own component subprocessors, some unique and some common to both—the crux of this 'resources' version. Thus each hemisphere has its own limited set of attentional or cognitive resources. A second postulate is that the component processes involved in executing a hemisphere-specific concurrent task will draw primarily upon resources of the hemisphere in which they are represented; this will result in fewer resources in that hemisphere for the primary task, so that now the other hemisphere will predominate and asymmetries will *reverse*. Thirdly, with low demands and ample resources, a secondary task may then prime a hemisphere, thus increasing both its efficiency and asymmetries for the primary task (i.e. an effect opposite to the situation above where resources are strained). Finally, if asymmetries in a primary task are due to hemisphere differences in processing efficiency, then a concurrent task should alter asymmetries by affecting any information-processing stage. If, however, asymmetries are due to absolute specialization, with callosal transfer to a uniquely specialized local component, then changes in asymmetry should only occur if the concurrent task can alter resource allocation to that component, or to those preceding it. This 'resources' version of the relative-specialization account assumes that only higher levels of processing are lateralized (and see Moscovitch, 1986a), with largely unlateralized initial sensory processing. Nevertheless there is considerable evidence of asymmetries at a sensory level (e.g. brightness, color, depth . . . see Chapter 4), a conclusion which is also implicit in the idea that the LH is specialized for processing high spatial frequencies, and the RH for low ones (see Chapter 4).

The following general points can be made. We must obviously reject the idea of absolute hemispheric specialization on its own. However, the derived view is attractive, that there are sets of uniquely specialized subprocessors, each contributing different mixes of *resources* to the two hemispheres, with different tasks, strategies or experiences calling upon different mixes of such specialized subprocessors. Such a view is not necessarily incompatible with the further suggestion that there is homotopic mirror-image-negative connectivity between the hemispheres, permitting them to interact, at the microprocessing level, in a complementary fashion. Resources need therefore not be restricted to individual hemispheres, but at all levels may be shared between hemispheres. Secondly, we can perhaps combine both models, absolute and relative specialization, via a 'horse-race' model. Thus a hemisphere which happens currently to be overall somewhat inferior in a given task may yet attempt it, while simultaneously sending information over to the notionally superior one, with a 'horse-race' occurring between these two effects, signal transmission and attempted processing by the weaker hemisphere. Interhemispheric transfer (which rarely exceeds a few milliseconds) will usually be completed before the notionally weaker hemisphere has overcome its handicap, especially for easy simple processes; however, if the stronger or more specialized hemisphere is loaded up with a concurrent task, the other relatively unspecialized hemisphere may then overcome its handicap and win the horse-race. There appears to be some good experimental evidence for this general kind of model (Umiltà *et al.*, 1985) which also makes good biological sense.

SUMMARY AND CONCLUSIONS

Behavioral asymmetries result both from intrinsic hemispheric differences, and from their mutually excitatory and inhibitory interaction transmitted via the commissures. Conventionally, RH superiorities complement those of the LH, and may even arise by default of that hemisphere's prior specialization. However, such complementarity may be a statistical artifact from averaging *across* individuals, and it may not necessarily be present at an individual level. While clinical studies seem to suggest absolute or qualitative specialization of the hemispheres, other studies indicate that this may result from inhibitory processes, and that asymmetries are instead relative, quantitative and a matter of degree. While information may be transmitted across the commissures to a specialized processor, and suffer either loss of fidelity or delay, it is likely that except for e.g. articulatory control, the 'inferior' hemisphere or its component subprocessors will also attempt to process the information. A 'horse-race' may decide which wins out—the 'inferior' hemisphere perhaps employing its own strategies, or instead transcommissural transmission to a 'dominant' hemisphere. In any case for most *complex* tasks resultant asymmetries will be the sum total of separate asymmetries each associated with individual subprocessing mechanisms, themselves differentially lateralized.

There are several versions of the idea of relative hemispheric specialization. One of the most influential sees the activation levels of the two hemispheres kept, via the commissures, in a state of mutually inhibitory balance. A variant which avoids certain problems associated with this approach, and has greater explanatory power, sees the commissures transmitting 'mirror-image-negative' complementary information. This would permit complementary hemispheric specialization, similar to figure–ground relationships perhaps at a point-to-point level; activation of a point in the LH would lead to inhibition of the corresponding locus in the RH, with excitation of the immediately surrounding areas, due to release from surround inhibition. This account is not incompatible with causal noncomplementarity of verbal and spatial processes at the level of an individual subject, as it deals with the microstructure of processing. Nor is it incompatible with a 'resources' account, as the latter need not be restricted to individual hemispheres, but at all levels of processing may be shared between them. Thus for all tasks except possibly gross articulatory control, processing may occur via subprocessors which are distributed as resources between the hemispheres, perhaps in different ways for different individuals; each of these subprocessors *themselves* may also operate *between* the hemispheres, in a mirror-image-complementary fashion, though perhaps with major responsibility ('figure') lying with one hemisphere, and the context or 'ground' with the other.

Viewed this way it may no longer even be appropriate to ask whether hemispheric superiorities are relative or absolute. For most tasks the resources of a hemisphere are perhaps governed by the operation of interhemispherically acting subprocessors. While the latter *may* in some cases be uniquely lateralized, even then their activation in different mixes during different tasks will generally result in the manifestation of relative hemispheric asymmetries, except perhaps where actual speech is involved.

IMPORTANT READINGS

Allen, M. Models of hemispheric specialization. *Psychological Bulletin*, 1983, **93**, 73–104.

Bryden, M. P. The nature of complementary specialization. In F. Leporé, M. Ptito and H. H. Jasper (eds.), *Two Hemispheres—One Brain*. New York: Alan R. Liss, 1986, pp. 464–9.

Cook, N. D. *The Brain Code: Mechanisms of Information Transfer and the Role of the Corpus Callosum*. London: Methuen, 1986.

Corballis, M. C. *Human Laterality*. New York: Academic Press, 1983.

Kinsbourne, M. The mechanism of hemispheric control of the lateral gradient of attention. In P. M. A. Rabbitt and S. Dornic (eds.), *Attention and Performance V*. New York: Academic Press, 1975, pp. 81–97.

Moscovitch, M. Hemispheric specialization, interhemispheric codes and transmission times: Inferences from visual masking studies in normal people. In F. Leporé, M. Ptito and H. H. Jasper (eds.), *Two Hemispheres—One Brain*. New York: Alan R. Liss, 1986a, pp. 483–510.

Moscovitch, M. Afferent and efferent models of visual perceptual asymmetries: Theoretical and empirical implications. *Neuropsychologia*, 1986b, **24**, 91–114.

Umiltà, C., Rizzolatti, G., Anzola, G., Luppino, G. and Porro, C. Evidence of interhemispheric transmission in laterality effects. *Neuropsychologia*, 1985, **23**, 203–13.

Zaidel, E. Disconnection syndrome as a model for laterality effects in the normal brain. In J. B. Hellige (ed.), *Cerebral Hemisphere Asymmetry: Method, Theory and Application*. New York: Praeger, 1983, pp. 95–151.

6

Language and the right hemisphere

Injury can occur at any age, though the younger the patient the more likely he or she is to enjoy the benefits of functional recovery with a still developing and 'plastic' nervous system. Thus damage in infancy, especially the extreme case of removal of one hemisphere, can tell us something about the limits of plastic takeover of function, and particularly how language and hand use can develop under such circumstances. Conversely, such damage in the adult can provide useful information about the extent of major and minor hemispheric involvement in a given function in the normal mature brain. Indeed the unique syndrome of acquired deep dyslexia in a previously normal reader may possibly be interpreted in terms of a RH role in developing connotative meaning and associations. In fact a major controversy has arisen concerning the reading skills of deep dyslexics, and those of the directly interrogated RHs of commissurotomy patients. Of course neither subject group may be at all representative of what happens in the normal RH. Comparatively little is known, moreover, about the effects of RH trauma, and deficits in prosody and in the comprehension of metaphor, humor and connotative meaning are only recently being appreciated. Normal studies have emphasized emotionality, imagery and concreteness, often with somewhat unsatisfactory experimental designs; however, in the long term the most significant advances in the study of a RH contribution to language will perhaps come from investigating bilingualism and the effects of illiteracy, deafness and such 'soft' neurological conditions as stuttering and developmental dyslexia. In this context, Geschwind's 'testosterone' theory is perhaps the most controversial and exciting.

It is almost axiomatic that the LH is dominant for most language functions. However, this statement is perhaps strictly true only for a limited subset of the population—right-handed males (see Chapters 8 and 9)—and for certain aspects of languages, i.e. the phonological and articulatory aspects (and see Searleman, 1983). Evidence for these conclusions comes from the same three sources we have already considered in other contexts—studies with clinical patients (Chapter 2) who have sustained unilateral lesions early or late in life, recently or in the distant past, commissurotomy patients (see Chapter 3), and normal intact subjects (Chapter 4). Of course we cannot expect language performance by the RH to be the same whether operating with a damaged LH, or in the absence of a LH due to left hemispherectomy, or when separated from its fellow by commissurotomy, or in its presence in the fully normal brain. Disagreements in the literature can be attributed, at least in part, to such paradigm differences.

CLINICAL STUDIES

We have already seen (Chapter 2) that with unilateral injection of sodium amytal to the LH via the left carotid artery, speech is temporarily abolished (the Wada amytal test), though not the comprehension of simple spoken commands which may be correctly executed; some speech clichés and automatisms may be preserved, together with the capacity to sing along. A recovered aphasic who had earlier sustained LH trauma and who now again experiences speech loss after RH amytal suppression may possibly have come to rely upon alternative RH mechanisms, though many believe that the LH is normally the source of much if not most recovered aphasic speech (and see Lambert, 1982a). However, the above amytal findings, reversed asymmetries in cortical evoked potentials and in rCBF, and relapse after new RH lesions do all seem to indicate the possibility of increased RH involvement during language restitution, while recovering from aphasia induced by earlier LH trauma (Papanicolaou *et al.*, 1988). We are therefore left with a series of important general questions: do the surviving language capacities of LH patients reflect functioning islands of undestroyed tissue in the LH, or do they reflect the operation, by takeover, of RH structures, with or without interference from the LH? Furthermore, if the RH can take over LH functions in this manner, does it do so more successfully in very young immature individuals (see Chapter 10)? Does it play a role in *normal* speech and reading? If in the clinical patient surviving LH structures act as a possible source of inhibition or interference, impeding RH takeover, is it perhaps better to remove such residual damaged regions? Similarly, do any language difficulties after RH injury reflect deficits in that hemisphere's normal contribution to language, or do they instead reflect noise or inhibition reaching the LH from the right? Other considerations include the possibility of a 'cognitive crowding' effect, if the RH takes over language functions from a LH perhaps injured in early infancy (Chapter 10), to the detriment of the RH's normal capacities for spatial processing.

Damage in infancy

The effects of LH or RH injury on language strongly depend upon age: age when injured, age when deficits appear, age when any corrective surgery may be undertaken, and age at testing or assessment; other important factors include the effects of drug management, personality, education, ability and cooperation. The general opinion is that both residual hemispheres can handle basic language and spatial functions, especially with very early damage, though sophisticated testing, many years later, of adults who as infants had sustained LH injury may reveal deficits. While hemispheric equipotentiality has been claimed traditionally in the event of unilateral decortication before puberty (or, by other authorities, by one, two or five years), it does seem that LH injury at or even before birth will result in some language deficits.

Satz (Satz *et al.*, 1985; Orsini and Satz, 1986) claims that prenatal and early postnatal damage to the LH is most likely to lead to strong sinistrality and/or bilateral or RH language, and therefore, *relatively (though not completely) intact* language because of successful early reorganization of cerebral structures. Indeed, the greater the sinistrality, perhaps the better the language. Note that this argument does not reject the idea of pathological sinistrality leading to language deficits (Chapter 8). Satz goes on to argue that early lesions which do not modify early hand preference tend not to shift language lateralization; thus the LH tends to remain language dominant, especially for speech production, less so maybe for speech perception, and hand preferences may be less stable than language lateralization after early LH trauma. He also claims that language deficits characterize LH trauma incurred even at the youngest developmental age, so infants do not exhibit early bilaterality for language, just extreme plasticity. Damage to the LH after the first few years, when dextrality and language are firmly established, is more likely to lead to ambidextrality, weak sinistrality, language deficits and inadequate cerebral reorganization with language remaining in the damaged hemisphere. Satz argues that there is little or no relationship between severity of early LH trauma and sinistrality; age at injury, not severity of lesion, is he says the important factor.

How then does language develop and recover after early LH insult? There are three possibilities: by substitution, whereby other neural substrates, probably in the LH, may employ alternative mechanisms towards the same end; by equipotentiality, whereby redundancy in the LH permits remaining structures to carry out near-normal functioning; and by vicarious functioning, where there is takeover by neural substrates not yet functionally employed, and whose normal functions may thereby be sacrificed. An example of the latter is spatial areas in the RH taking over language functions to the detriment of their own specializations. Indeed, after LH injury in the *adult*, we can similarly ask whether the resultant aphasia stems from decremented LH function, or from a gradual takeover of linguistic capacities by the RH, perhaps no longer subject to inhibitory influences from the (now nonfunctional) LH. Should aphasia, after an initial recovery, recur with suppression of the RH by sodium amytal, or with further (now RH) brain injury, one might conclude that the RH can and has taken over language functions, perhaps in terms of its pre-existing and now residual capacities, such that it becomes the source of aphasic speech. Alternatively, RH *cognitive* modes with their specializations *complementary* to language may now play an increasing role. Yet again, the RH may actually take over language functions themselves, more or less successfully. Depending upon the nature and extent of the injury, the lapse of time, and the educational and other history of the patient, the actual outcome may vary. However, any RH takeover is likely not only to be incomplete, but to be *qualitatively* different from 'normal' LH language function. Even so, aphasics, young or old, can and often do recover, and indeed it would be strange if a system potentially capable of some language function (the RH) was unable to take over to any extent, due e.g. to inhibitory processes. Good evidence for RH language under such circumstances would come from individuals subjected to left hemispherectomy or extensive left decortication as adults. Of course such left hemispherectomies performed in adulthood are necessarily rare; they reveal severe expressive deficits with very little propositional speech, though with gradual regaining of considerable auditory comprehension. The RH is said in this context to behave like an intelligent nominal aphasic, with perhaps retention of the ability to utter some expletives and automatisms. This is an essentially similar profile to that demonstrated when the isolated RH of commissurotomy patients is interrogated. However, there is currently debate on how such isolated RHs, after LH removal in adulthood, compare to 'normal' aphasia after partial LH trauma; no one aphasic profile seems to be matched.

To return again to the issue of *infantile* left hemispherectomy, with later testing when adulthood is reached; such extensive hemidecortication is theoretically the cleanest source of evidence of unilateral functioning and potential, though available subjects are few, and not everyone accepts Dennis' findings (see below) at face value (Bishop, 1983a, 1988). Generally, however, it appears that some syntactic and phonological deficits always remain, though with relatively unimpaired semantic representation (Goodman and Whitaker, 1985). Complex syntax, e.g. passive negatives and 'clefted' sentences, may suffer most. Does the RH use different or less efficient strategies, e.g. direct lexical access (Coltheart, 1983, 1985), rather than operating via phonological recording? This would explain observed difficulties in reading legal nonwords, e.g. 'gife', 'zobe' etc. While Bishop objects that the alleged impairments in syntactic and phonological capacities in such left hemidecorticates is actually within the normal range, and may simply reflect difficult tests, it would surely be strange if there were not some residual deficits, and if the two hemispheres were totally equipotential in early life (see Chapter 10); any such difficulties might be expected to manifest themselves where complex phonology or syntax is encountered.

Of course the often very considerable subsequent recovery of language abilities after left hemispherectomy performed in infancy may be less due to the relatively greater neural plasticity believed to be present in infancy (see Chapter 10), than to the lengthy interval before testing as an adult; thus the (extremely rare) *adult* left hemispherectomies who survive for any length of time may apparently recover a surprising amount of function. However, even they always comprehend spoken material better than written, and have very little expressive capacity. Any evidence of RH language after left hemispherectomy must therefore be considered in the context of age when the original pathology commenced, age at operation, the interval between these two events, and the interval between operation and testing. Consequently hemispherectomy studies may reflect gradual functional reorganization rather than initial capacities of the RH. Nor do we know how much help is available from residual *subcortical* structures in the LH.

Subtotal damage to the LH in adults

The appearance of LEAs and LVF advantages with dichotic and tachistoscopic studies of such patients (Lambert, 1982a; Searleman, 1983) may suggest RH takeover. Of course some of these effects could instead merely reflect the loss of the usual contralateral RE route, leaving only the ipsilateral LE-to-LH pathway, with continuing LH (not RH) mediation. It is in fact difficult to interpret dichotic findings in aphasia, due to a confounding between the *dominance* effect (the superiority of the ear contralateral to a specialized, processing hemisphere) and the *lesion* effect (the superiority of the ear ipsilateral to a damaged hemisphere). A better indication of gradual takeover of functions by the RH in adults suffering subtotal damage to the LH would be fixed RE or RVF scores, with gradually improving LE or LVF scores, or alternatively, LEAs or LVF advantages for certain types of language task only (e.g. where semantic aspects are emphasized), with very poor scores perhaps on phonological aspects.

Another issue is the problem of deep dyslexia (see Chapter 2), a disability acquired in adults who previously had normal reading capacities. (Of course we must assume, though this assumption may not in fact always be correct, that the continuing function of the damaged brain reflects at least part of its previous cognitive arrangement, and is not the result of complete reorganization. Thus at least some modules presumably continue much as before, in the face of damage to others. Nevertheless while such modular function may be dissociable in pathology, as we shall see below some critics claim that this may not necessarily be true in health.) Similarities have been noted between acquired deep dyslexia in adults, and developmental dyslexia in children; in both cases there may be preserved ability to read irregular words (e.g. 'yacht', 'sword'), but not legal nonwords ('grife', 'crobe'), while the opposite is true for surface dyslexia. (With the latter syndrome, there appears to be an overreliance upon the phonological system in reading; legal nonwords may be read, as also may be words with regular spelling-to-sound patterns, unlike irregular items which may be incorrectly regularized, e.g. 'sweat' → 'sweet', and 'pint' which may be read to rhyme with 'lint'.) In deep dyslexia, certain symptoms may be considered obligatory (Temple, 1987): impaired ability to convert graphemes to phonemes, semantic paralexias, and (perhaps) better reading of concrete than of abstract words. With respect to the first of these, the patients cannot read legal nonsense words (see above), or say if two words rhyme ('sail'/'sale'), though on the basis of visual similarity they will happily claim that 'sew' and 'few' *do* rhyme! Nor can they say if pseudohomophones (e.g. 'brane', 'gote') sound like real words. Semantic paralexias may appear on reading aloud, e.g. 'rock' for 'stone', 'dagger' for 'sword'. Function words (e.g. 'be') may be lost, but not so similar substantives, e.g. 'bee'. Such semantic paralexias may be most apparent with concrete imageable words. Given the country name 'Holland', such a patient may respond 'It's a country; not Europe, not Germany . . . it's small . . . it was captured . . . Belgium . . . that's it!' This 'intelligent guessing' is reminiscent of the apparent spread of semantic activation when the LHs of commissurotomy patients are interrogated about what was presented to the RH, or vice versa (see Chapter 3).

All three phenomena (impaired ability in grapheme–phoneme conversion, semantic paralexias, and better reading of concrete than of abstract words) can be demonstrated without the need for actual speech; indeed when the isolated RHs of commissurotomy patients are appropriately interrogated, similar effects occur to the above demonstrations with clinical patients. However, the RHs of commissurotomy patients typically tend to perform more poorly than do deep dyslexics, suggesting that in deep dyslexia there may be some residual assistance from the LH, especially of course in reading aloud; however, LVF advantages sometimes shown by such patients in lexical decision tasks suggest a RH involvement in their reading (though see the analogous argument above concerning the possible destruction of contralateral routes from the right ear). Indeed when deep dyslexics try to read aloud such laterally exposed words, their rate of semantic paralexias tends to increase with LVF presentations, indicating that the RH may have had to take over some semantic processing. Interestingly, normal subjects may also give some semantic paralexias with briefly flashed materials, particularly if concrete and/or if flashed to the LVF, though there is currently some dispute about how to correct for guessing, and to score, in such experiments.

There is a strong body of opinion (e.g. Coltheart, 1983, 1985) that deep dyslexia reflects the operation of the RH, rather than of surviving LH functions, that lexical access via the LH's phonological mechanisms is lost, that the RH has a directly accessible lexicon via a nonphonological route, and that semantic information passes from the RH to the LH, where a semantic paralexic oral response is initiated (see Figure 1). Cook (see Chapter 5) has

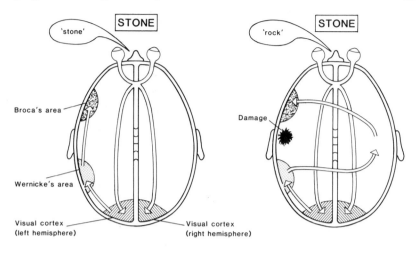

NORMAL BRAIN   **BRAIN OF DEEP DYSLEXIC**

Fig. 1 When a normal reader sees the written word 'stone', the signal, initially projected to the occipital visual cortex, is transmitted forwards to Wernicke's area in the left hemisphere (probably via the angular gyrus) and on to Broca's frontal speech area, when 'stone' may be spoken. In the case of a deep dyslexic, a break between Wernicke's and Broca's areas may require a bypass via connotative language areas in the right hemisphere, with the result that the left hemisphere eventually utters the semantic paralexic response 'rock'.

recently taken these ideas yet further, suggesting that the corpus callosum transmits inhibitory patterns of information between the hemispheres to generate 'mirror-image-negative' relationships of a complementary, contextual, figure–ground nature. Thus e.g. activation of 'farm' in the LH (and its resultant articulation) will lead to its suppression in the RH, with, instead, activation of its surrounding network of associations, which will have been released from inhibition. Conversely, were 'farm' to be activated in the RH, its corresponding locus in the LH would be suppressed, while its LH associates would be released from inhibition, leading to production of semantic paralexias (see Figure 2).

Others (e.g. Patterson and Besner, 1984a, 1984b), however, believe that reading by deep dyslexics reflects more than just RH performance, given the extremely sophisticated nature of many of their paralexic errors, e.g. 'hermit' → 'recluse', 'oblivion' → 'infinity', 'lunatic' → 'moon-man', 'muddy' → 'quagmire'. Moreover deep dyslexics can read far better than can the isolated RHs of split-brain patients; however, direct comparisons are difficult since the latter patients have generally had a long pre- and postoperative history, while deep dyslexics have intact commissures and some remaining LH tissue with which to speak. So are some LH mechanisms preserved, which assist RH

Left Hemisphere

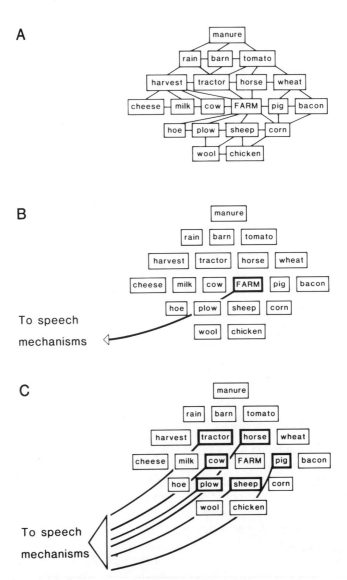

Fig. 2   A bilateral portion of a possible 'agricultural' semantic network (A). When FARM is activated on the left, a direct articulatory output can occur (B). When FARM is activated on the right, however (C), translation into speech will require transcallosal transfer, which, if inhibitory, will result in suppression of the perceived word FARM and activation (for speech) of close semantic associations. (Figure reproduced from N. D. Cook, *The Brain Code: Mechanisms of Information Transfer and the Role of the Corpus Callosum.* London: Methuen, 1986, with permission.)

Right Hemisphere

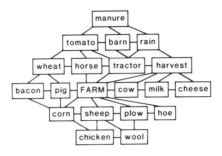

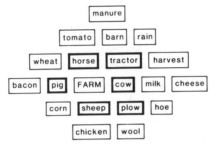

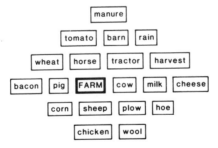

functions? There is also the problem of pure alexics who can write but not read due to callosal damage and LH lesions which restrict verbal information to the (intact) RH; why do not pure alexics read as well as, and similarly to, deep dyslexics? Pure alexics typically show painful letter-by-letter reading, perhaps because their LH damage inhibits the reading ability of the RH. Indeed some pure alexics can correctly point to pictures of objects whose names are flashed too fast for letter-by-letter spelling out (see Zaidel and Schweiger, 1984). Another solution to the problem of pure alexia (and see Coltheart, 1983) is to invoke two kinds or levels of information processing as relevant to reading: uncategorized, veridical, visual information, and categorized, semantically recoded information, with both kinds of information transmissable between hemispheres. The deep dyslexic may be unable to process either mode in the LH, but can semantically process (i.e. at the second level) in the RH, which then signals the LH to give an associated verbal output. However, the pure alexic who can only read letter-by-letter has such LH damage that the LH cannot receive (from the RH) information from the second (semantic) level, but can only receive uncategorized veridical information. Because the RH cannot generate a response, and due to damage the LH may not be able directly to access the lexicon, but may only do so indirectly and phonologically, this would be the route upon which the pure alexic is forced to rely. This may be the case even though the RH may have successfully categorized the material semantically, while remaining unable to communicate this to the LH.

Another possibility is that the RH normally has very little reading ability, except in a very few people, and it is these *rarae aves* who become deep dyslexic if they happen to experience appropriate LH injury. However, a recent single-case study (Roeltgen, 1987) goes against the idea that the residual reading capacity of deep dyslexics relies upon RH structures; thus a deep dyslexic after an initial LH stroke suffered a second, also to the LH, and lost his residual reading abilities. This suggests that *LH* structures mediate the residual reading of deep dyslexics. While arguments from the single case are intrinsically dangerous, in many ways all the conflicting phenomena described above represent, generally, a large number of idiosyncratic single-case reports. Perhaps the best evidence for the RH theory is the finding that LH lesions are usually very large in deep dyslexics, and the bigger the affected area, the higher the incidence of deep dyslexia. Thus on this basis semantic paralexias could even represent the release of RH functions from LH control.

Right hemisphere damage and language

There is increasing evidence that while the LH mediates the propositional aspects of language, and phonology and syntax, the RH is concerned with prosody (Ross, 1985)—the melody of speech, its pauses, intonations, stresses and accents (see Chapter 2). This may serve to enhance the propositional meanings proferred by the LH, and even to replace them, e.g. during infancy when propositional speech has not yet unfolded. There may be four aspects to prosody: paralinguistic aspects (grunts, sighs), the emotional (to indicate happiness, sadness, anger, surprise, disinterest), the intellectual (e.g. for emphasis, sarcasm etc.), and the intrinsic. The last may reflect dialectical and idiosyncratic differences in speech, together with linguistic uses, e.g. raised inflection to signal query, and the stress alternation between noun and verb usage as in cónvict/convíct, cóntest/contést. Thus RH damage may lead to dysprosody, as well as to anomalies of facial expression, while LH damage may result in propositional deficits and anomalies of gesture. Ross claims close parallels between RH aprosodia (in terms of loci and deficits) and LH aphasia, both at receptive and expressive levels.

Traditionally, RH damage was thought to have only subtle linguistic effects, e.g. dysprosody (see above), deficits in vocabulary, verbal dysfluency, perseverations, hesitations, naming difficulties, possible problems with clichés and automatic phrases, and with verbal creativity and abstract words and ideas. However, Gardner and his group (e.g. Gardner *et al.*, 1983) have also described such problems as missing the point in looking at cartoon drawings and jokes, with a predominance of inappropriately concrete or literal interpretations, an inability to see the humorous context or to choose correct endings or punchlines in verbal jokes, problems in understanding metaphor and connotation, problems in detecting absurdities, interpreting aphorisms and mapping figurative language on to appropriate situations, with a resultant tendency to confabulate and interject irrelevancies. Indeed Bihrle, Brownell and Gardner (1988) have recently summarized their work on deficits in the perception of humor in RH patients. As they observe, humor depends upon alteration of expectancies, recognition of surprise, and the resolution of incongruity. Patients with RH damage have particular difficulty with the last, even though they appreciate the role of surprise in humor, and know the difference between humorous and nonhumorous statements. The RH seems important in appreciating the relationship between the body of a joke and its punchline. Difficulties in resolving the incongruity of humor and integrating the elements into a coherent whole may stem from a rigidity in interpretation, a literalness in interpreting information in terms of denotative rather than connotative meaning, and an insensitivity in figuring out relevant details. The problem of interpretational rigidity leads to an unwillingness to revise an initial interpretation. Perhaps for these reasons the speech of such patients may be marked by the frequent injection of personalizations, insignificant details, tangential and inappropriate comments, irrelevant jocularities and frank confabulations. This all leads to inappropriate interactions with others, and may extend to other types of speech acts, e.g. sarcasm and hyperbole that are important in natural interactions. Such considerations suggest lost of context, which of course in a sense is also the basis of yet another RH syndrome, unilateral neglect (see Chapter 2). There is some evidence of similar deficits in commissurotomy patients (see below), whose speaking LHs are now disconnected from their RHs. Before discussing this, however, we should note that the only disorder directly and overtly affecting the comprehension of *writing* after RH damage is neglect dyslexia; the left side of the page, or initial leftmost letters, are ignored. In the latter instance they are often incorrectly replaced, e.g. 'mown' → 'down', 'hint' → 'pint'; thus the correct vowel sound of the *new* word is formulated, indicating that the deficit arises at an early stage.

COMMISSUROTOMY STUDIES

As we have already seen (Chapter 3), the traditional view was that split-brain patients had a modest receptive vocabulary, as long as it was possible to signal responses nonverbally; the RH could obey simple commands and instructions. Later, however, claims that the RH could not cope with verbs, tenses, complex syntax etc., were disproved, though admittedly the RH is still generally regarded as poorer in these areas (and see Sidtis, 1985). In the 1970s, development of Zaidel's 'Z' lens system (Chapter 3) permitted prolonged lateral stimulation with nonverbal (pointing) responses. The isolated RH was found to possess a large auditory vocabulary and a smaller visual one. Words appeared to be represented more in terms of an auditory than a phonological representation; they could not therefore be coded by reference to the articulatory apparatus. The RH proved deficient at matching auditorily presented consonant–vowel nonsense syllables (e.g. ba, da, ga, etc.), with probe consonants (e.g. b, d, g, etc.) presented in the visual periphery. The RH was found to have a shorter duration for short-term verbal memory (around three items) than the LH (around seven); it could not match a printed word with a picture of a homonym of that word (e.g. 'sale' and a picture of a yacht's sail), nor could it match two printed words that rhymed ('rough' and 'cuff') or two similarly rhyming nonwords 'loat' and 'sote'), or two pictures whose names sounded alike but meant different things (polysemous words, e.g. finger *nail* and carpenter's *nail*), though occasional exceptions have been reported. Generally, while the RH may be able to cope with transforming orthography to picture naming, or picture naming to word sound, it has problems in going directly across more than one stage, e.g. from orthography to word sound.

Nevertheless the RHs of split-brain patients do seem able to cope with antonymy, synonymy, homonymy (as long as the phonological aspects are not too important); and with episodic and semantic information. In fact they seem to behave in an appropriate, linguistically human fashion at all times, even though they may perform more poorly and in a more labile fashion, use different strategies, and show irritation when the LH confabulates when trying to take over from a slower and less successful RH. An extreme and dissenting viewpoint is that of Gazzaniga (see e.g. Gazzaniga and Smylie, 1984) who denies that the RHs of such patients normally have any language abilities, except for a few cases with very early LH injury and cerebral reorganization; he even goes as far as to say that the RHs of split-brain patients have cognitive skills inferior to a chimpanzee's, and can only perform simple nonverbal, matching-to-sample tasks. He adds that in most cases all linguistic information processing has been deferred to the LH during development, like a foolish schoolchild allowing a friend to solve all scholastic problems for him. Instead of adopting such an extreme position, we might instead ask why the verbal performance of commissurotomy patients' RHs often differs so markedly from that of many aphasics with LH damage. Two factors could account for this: split-brain patients have often had a long period for cerebral reorganization to occur, and the damaged LH of aphasics may inhibit the RH via intact commissures. Indeed much of the disagreement about RH capacities for language in split-brain patients stems from differences in the conduct of the operation (total or subtotal callosal section, and sometimes also section of the anterior commissure, which may be carried out simultaneously or in a staged operation), differences in age at onset of original pathology, interval to the operation, interval to testing, etc. Moreover any damage to the RH occurring during commissurotomy could even lead to an *underestimation* of its linguistic potential. In conclusion, it is probably more important to establish patterns of performance similarity between commissurotomies, aphasics and deep dyslexics, than absolute or relative levels of ability.

Does the ability level of the RHs of commissurotomy patients correspond to any developmental age in normal children? We shall see (Chapter 10) that according to Lenneberg the RH is linguistically arrested at a developmental age of around 10 years; however, even were this to be so, we need not assume that similar strategies would necessarily be used. In any case Zaidel (1978) reports nonuniformity in corresponding ages for different functions, with the RH exhibiting a rich auditory vocabulary and a poor grammar. Thus the RH may *generally* approximate the linguistic skills of three to six year olds, though with total suppression of articulatory output, and with further development of lexical and semantic comprehension. Just as in aphasia, therefore, we cannot point to any single corresponding developmental stage. Nor, probably, is it safe to generalize from such patients to the RHs of normal adults. Thus if the isolated RH can read, move cut-out letters around etc., this does not necesarily mean that the RHs of normals usually participate in a similar fashion in reading (Coltheart, 1983, 1985), even though the RHs of deep dyslexics may possibly take over in this fashion. However, it might be objected that the RH must surely have a function during reading in normality as well as pathology, and may well contribute to comprehending the extrapropositional aspects of humor, context and metaphor (see above).

NORMAL STUDIES

Imaging using rCBF and PET techniques (see Chapter 2) usually reveals greater LH (than RH) activation during language tasks, though details may conflict with the tachistoscopic data (below), and may indicate considerable apparent involvement of the RH. However, such RH involvement may primarily occur at an initial sensory level (e.g. preprocessing, or for low-level prosodic aspects while speaking). Of course activation of the RH could possibly reflect a linguistically deficient RH endeavoring to compensate for its intrinsic inadequacies. Nevertheless, while electrophysiological measures indicate the expected LH involvement in discrimination of consonants by place of articulation (/b/vs/g/vs/k/ etc.), voice onset time, the interval between laryngeal pulsing and onset of release, which cues the distinction between voiced and unvoiced stop consonants (e.g. /b/vs/p/, /d/vs/t/), indicates involvement of RH temporal regions. Clinical evidence supports such a role.

Visual-field asymmetries may reflect either relative or absolute specialization of the hemispheres (see Chapter 5), and if the specialization is relative, we can again ask whether LVF advantages reflect early stages in perceptual processing or preprocessing. As discussed in Chapter 4, there is much evidence of a LVF/RH advantage for new, unfamiliar, degraded or florid stimuli, and of a RVF/LH advantage only appearing with practised subjects and familiar stimuli. Different language components may be differentially lateralized to different degrees, e.g. phonology versus semantics. The RH can perhaps rapidly and directly access a relatively small lexicon of simple concrete words, maybe without knowing all aspects of denotative meaning. Where particular linguistic functions are bilaterally represented, this may reflect either duplication, with performance of similar computations in both hemispheres, or complementary processing. If language is less lateralized for perceptual than for expressive speech, then tachistoscopic studies should reveal strong evidence of RH involvement.

Deep dyslexics often reveal deficient oral reading and comprehension of abstract words; while this could be a characteristic of RH processing, it could also reflect LH differences in reading different kinds of material. Studies with normals often (but not always, see e.g. Lambert, 1982b; McMullen and Bryden, 1987) demonstrate similar effects, with a RH bias towards concrete imageable stimuli. Indeed brief degraded inputs may be needed to demonstrate such effects, or alternatively priming techniques (Chiarello, Senehi and Nuding, 1987), rather than conventional lexical decisions.

Japanese possesses two kinds of script, *Kana* (phonological) and *Kanji* (ideographic). A major dissociation often occurs between them in the clinical context, with loss of the ability to read one or the other, though as yet there is no clinical evidence of a *double* dissociation. Nevertheless such a phenomenon (a RVF/LH superiority for *Kana* and abstract *Kanji*, and the opposite asymmetry for single Kanji characters) has been reported with normal studies. However, according to Jones and Aoki (1988) and Tzeng and Hung (1988) the evidence for a RH involvement in normals when processing Kanji or Chinese logographs (from which Kanji is derived and to which it is closely related) is very shaky; it occurs perhaps only with material which is concrete, familiar or highly 'hieroglyphic' (i.e. pictorially resembling closely its referent), and where exposure durations are *short*, which as we saw in Chapter 4, can result in strong LVF advantages. Otherwise even Kanji can be associated with RVF advantages. Even the *clinical* evidence of a selective impairment of one or other script does not necessarily imply RH mediation of Kanji; both processes, Kana and Kanji, may be differentially localized in the LH. Indeed LH, not RH, patients fare worse in writing Chinese logographs. It is not therefore a matter of hemispheric lateralization *per se*; there is probably more than one mechanism in both hemispheres, with the current direction of asymmetry depending upon the requisite nature of the processing, rather than just the form of the script.

Bilingualism, like sinistrality and callosal agenesis, is a natural experiment for the neurologist. Acquisition of a second language is often difficult—and the manner different—after puberty. Thus certain children who for one reason or another were kept in isolation during the years when the first language is naturally acquired, and who were only exposed to it in their teens, never properly acquired it, and gave dichotic evidence of abnormal patterns of cerebral lateralization (see Chapter 10). Indeed when any of us acquire a second language later in life, we probably employ different strategies. We can therefore ask whether all languages in polyglots are mediated by common neuropsychological mechanisms, and the extent to which age at acquisition, familiarity etc., may possible affect their cerebral representation (Obler, 1984). Dissociations have been reported between languages after polyglots have sustained unilateral damage. Thus the ability to read one language may be better retained, and likewise the capacity to speak another, when previously both were read and spoken at similar levels. Similar dissociations may occur between reading, writing, comprehension and translation, and between various kinds of alexia, due sometimes to differences in orthography or regularity. Antagonistic modes of recovery may occur, with one language regressing while another recovers, or with leap-frogging. Alternatively, while recovery occurs at a manifestly equivalent level for all the languages, one or more may 'feel' harder. Any differential contribution of the RH may relate to acquisition of second or later languages, especially in early stages, or for formulaic (rather than propositional) utterances, for clichés and automatisms, for pragmatic rather than syntactic information, for prosodic rather than phonetic features, for informal acquisition rather than by rule. The RH may be involved in reading (direct lexical access) rather than in articulation and phonology, and when acquiring new languages later in life. It is probably safe to conclude that hemispheric processing in bilinguals who acquired their second language early in life is like that of monolinguals, though later or incomplete acquisition may differentially engage the hemispheres. Clinical data indicate that true bilinguals tend to show impairment and recovery of both languages in parallel, though it may depend upon modality, mode of testing, educational background and competence. However, most studies have proved incomplete or defective, with inadequate neurological and psycholinguistic information, lack of control of sex and handedness, reporting of single-case studies and behavioural measures (tachistoscopic and dichotic) of doubtful validity.

Illiteracy is in some ways the other side of the coin to bilingualism. Does literacy contribute to the development of language dominance in the LH? Indeed does language dominance develop at all (see Chapter 10)? Does experience with written language aid language lateralization? Is language more bilateral in illiterates, and do they have less severe aphasia after LH lesions? Despite earlier claims to the contrary, it is probably safe to conclude that the frequency of aphasia after LH injury is about the same in literates and illiterates; moreover with normals, if task difficulty and performance levels are controlled, illiterates probably demonstrate REAs as big as those of literates (Castro and Morais, 1987). However, Lecours *et al.* (1988) note that the maturational realization of the genetic program which determines language could be subject to individual postnatal variations stemming from exposure to a particular linguistic environment. Illiterates typically find segmentation of speech sounds more difficult at the phonemic than at the syllabic level; expertise at the former may depend upon the formal acquisition of reading skills, and not just general maturation. Given the phonological nature of many dichotic listening tasks, apparent differences between literates and illiterates in auditory laterality could result. In this sense literacy could enhance lateralization, even though illiterates are still LH language dominant.

If illiteracy is unimportant, does experience with *spoken* language aid language lateralization? (Again, such a question assumes, not necessarily correctly, that lateralization develops.) It is often claimed that the deaf show abnormal visual or tactual lateralization. However, they are likely anyway to be poor readers, so that LEAs and LVF advantages may stem from unfamiliarity or task difficulty; moreover the deaf are likely to have had prolonged experience with manual signing. Indeed there is evidence of LVF advantages in the deaf for *meaningless* signs, and of the opposite asymmetries with meaningful ones (and see Poizner, Klima and Bellugi, 1987). Sign language has largely similar morphology, syntax and semantics to oral languages, and LH lesions tend to result in parallel deficits in signing for the truly deaf as in speech for the nondeaf. There is even evidence of electrostimulation of speech-related regions in the LH resulting in disruption of finger spelling by the deaf. The best evidence that deafness may be associated with atypical lateralization comes from a study using the dual task paradigm (see Chapter 4) to engage the more lateralized motor rather than purely perceptual processes

(Marcotte and La Barba, 1987). The congenitally deaf, and those with deafness acquired before two years, showed atypical lateralization for speech production; the later the onset of hearing loss, the more probable that a normal LH pattern of lateralization would emerge. Note that such findings do not necessarily imply that lateralization (which is known to be present at birth, see Chapters 1 and 10) develops; it is possible to argue that continued exposure to a linguistic environment is necessary to *maintain* LH specialization as speech unfolds in increasing complexity. (For a further consideration of these issues, see Chapter 10, and cf. the children described above who had experienced extreme social deprivation and who demonstrated abnormal patterns of lateralization). Thus in the absence of a linguistic environment, only the simplest (maybe phonological) aspects may be lateralized to the LH, and not so the unfolding syntax and semantics. In this sense, therefore, the first two years may be critical; if there is an abnormal linguistic environment, the initial LH bias which is present in infancy may be distorted or disappear.

Stuttering is another form of pathology, motor now rather than sensory, which has been associated with abnormal patterns of lateralization. There are of course many forms of stuttering, and, probably, a multiplicity of possible causes. However, a strong family pedigree is often present (though there is some dispute), and the same is true (including the controversy!) concerning crossed dominance (i.e. LH language with left handedness, or RH language with right handedness) and LEAs with dichotically presented verbal stimuli. Indeed an exactly similar controversy arises in the context of developmental dyslexia (below). Stuttering is of course a classic deficit of LH praxic sequencing, and one wonders whether bilateral language representation could result in a maladaptive competition for the articulators. (While females may tend to exhibit bilateral language representation, see Chapter 9, they typically show a much smaller incidence of stuttering than males, a paradox which may be resolved by recognizing that bilateral language in females is almost certainly receptive, and not expressive or motor.) Amytal suppression of either hemisphere by the Wada technique (see Chapter 2) may lead to language loss in stutterers, while surgical removal of one hemisphere (for other, unrelated reasons), or unilateral trauma, may relieve stuttering. (Of course one would therefore expect that Wada suppression of one hemisphere should lead to loss of *stuttering*, and not to loss of *speech*.) The pursuit-auditory-tracking task pioneered by Sussman (see Chapter 4) may be the strongest evidence for bilaterality of speech in stutterers, as it indexes productive (expressive or motor) rather than receptive speech; the subject hears two simultaneous tones, a target to one ear and the cursor to the other. The frequency of the randomly varying target must be tracked via the cursor, by means of jaw movements. While normal speakers are typically better with the input of the adjustable cursor to the RE, and the target to the LE, with stutterers there may be no ear difference (Sussman and McNeilage, 1975).

Developmental dyslexia is the archetypal condition which in the past has been associated with abnormal or reversed language dominance. Learning to speak is a largely automatic (though none the less impressive) phenomenon, and one which is often achieved against great odds; it is an evolutionary 'old' phenomenon (see Chapter 7). On the other hand learning to read is a recently acquired capacity, and one which is effortful and requires deliberate training. There are of course many different kinds of scripts which have evolved thoughout the world, and perhaps for this reason the incidence of dyslexia differs in different cultures, and children who are dyslexic in one language may possibly learn to read scripts which rely less upon phonology and more upon direct ideographic symbolism. Indeed in a historical sense scripts evolved from deepest levels (coding for meaning) first, and only recently have alphabets been invented which code for surface phonology, an efficiency which has been achieved at the cost of sacrificing a direct grapheme-to-meaning link, and interposing a phonetic one. The earliest pictures upon walls, in caves and on muddy or sandy surfaces were ambiguous both in terms of referents and directionality (i.e. do we read time from left to right or vice versa?); also, how do we deal with abstracts? Symbols such as Chinese logographs, Egyptian hieroglyphs, pictograms and ideograms (including many modern road signs) were the next stage, though they continued basically to be stylized pictures. Phonograms followed, with two elements, the semantic referent (as above) together with some phonetic information, i.e. a cue how to say it. Modern Chinese follows this tradition, though the problem remains of an enormous multiplicity of necessary characters, imposing a huge memory load and requiring slow coding. Syllabaries such as the cuneiform of ancient Babylon, and Japanese *Kana* were an economical solution, as now the unit of spoken and written language (the syllable) could be made to coincide; how, however, do we deal with homophones, e.g. 'bear' and 'bare'? The Indo-European development (perhaps from the Phoenicians) of the alphabet provided for the greatest economy of all, mapping as it does on to language at the level of the phoneme, which is smaller than the syllable but larger than the ('invisible') articulatory feature (e.g. voicing, nasality, place of articulation). The homophone problem is solved by simultaneously indicating the etymological derivation (e.g. sign/signature) at the cost of exceptions to spelling rules. The child has to parse input in terms both of syllables and morphemes. Thus the evolution of writing systems (Tzeng and Hung, 1988) has inexorably led to a decrease in the number of symbols, an increase in the abstractness of the relationship between script and meaning, and a stronger link between graphemes and phonemes. This pattern of development parallels the general trend of cognitive development in children, and may have important implications for readers acquiring different orthographies. Patterns of reading disorders, moreover, may depend not only upon the locus of brain damage, but also upon the orthography. Lexical access of words written in alphabetic or logographic scripts may be accomplished by different neurolinguistic pathways, which are probably differentially repre-sented in the two hemispheres. A stroke patient therefore may experience differential loss or preservation of different scripts (*Kana* vs *Kanji*), and there may be differential incidences of developmental dyslexia in children from different cultures.

There are many names for developmental dyslexia, and much controversy, e.g. concerning whether there is more than one syndrome, concerning the multitude of theories and treatments all of which claim some success, and concerning the question whether there is a continuum of reading (dis)ability or whether developmental dyslexia is separate from generally poor reading performance. The condition is really defined by exclusion: a relatively normal full-scale IQ and peripheral sensory functions, with no obvious neurological or phonological disability or significant social or emotional problems, no socio-economic disadvantage, adequate opportunity to learn to read, and so on. The condition is up to four times more frequent in boys, like all other language-related disorders, e.g. stuttering, autism, congenital dysphasia and even hyperplexia. There is often a family pedigree and association with anomalous lateralization (Bryden and Saxby, 1986; Ellis, 1985; Gordon, 1984; Harris, 1985). Many of the propositi are what Annett (see Chapter 8) would classify as *rs*−, or lacking in a right shift factor.

In the 1930s, Orton noted an increase, among developmental dyslexics, of sinistrality and mirror reversals while reading and writing. He assumed that the dominant (usually left) hemisphere records letters and words in the correct orientation, while the opposite (nondominant) one records them in the reverse orientation, due to homotopic interhemispheric connections via the com-missures. This situation, according to Orton, would result in the formation of mirror-symmetrical engrams in the opposite hemispheres, unless the nondomi-nant one is 'elided' to avoid confusion (see Figure 3). Incompletely developed dominance, he believed, would result in the inability of the dominant hemi-sphere to perform this 'elision'. This situation would be manifested in mixed motor dominance, with inconsistent hand preferences, or noncorrelation between hand, foot, eye and ear preference; such a concept relies upon the highly dubious assumption that just as a hand is controlled by its contralateral hemisphere, so also is an eye. Orton suggested remediation to enhance dominance, though his cautious approach has not been followed by modern zealots who advocate training in lateralization (Harris, 1985). Nevertheless apart from the question of unihemispheric control of the contralateral eye, Orton was wrong on a number of points (and see also Bishop, 1983b).

(1) Sinistrals do not usually possess language in the RH (see Chapter 8).
(2) Dominance almost certainly does not progressively develop (see Chapter 10).
(3) The minor hemisphere does not record *percepts* in a mirror-reversed

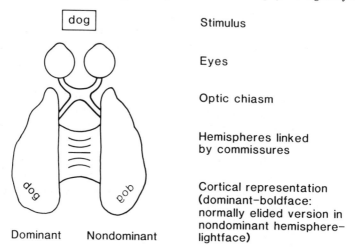

Stimulus

Eyes

Optic chiasm

Hemispheres linked
by commissures

Cortical representation
(dominant–boldface:
normally elided version in
nondominant hemisphere–
lightface)

Fig. 3   According to Orton, the dominant left hemisphere records words in the correct orientation, while the right records them in the reverse (mirror) orientation due to homotopic commissural connectivity, unless they are 'elided'. (Figure modified and redrawn from M. C. Corballis, The left–right problem in psychology. *Canadian Psychologist,* 1974, **15**, 16–33.)

form; *memory* transfer could possibly lead to interhemispheric mirror reversal, such that Orton's hypothesis could only work if information were first stored on one side, then copied to and accessed from the other hemisphere.

(4)   There is no evidence that poor readers perceive visual stimuli mirror reversed.

(5)   There is dispute whether bd, pq confusions are commoner in developmental dyslexics; they occur in normals while learning to read, and maybe dyslexics are still learning.

(6)   There is dispute whether dyslexics or sinistrals can mirror read or write (when so required) better than normals. Moreover RH language might make reading Western scripts from right to left (i.e. reversed) easier, as the next word then would fall into the dominant RH (LVF), just as people with normal LH lateralization should find a left-to-right scan easier (as the next word similarly falls into the dominant RVF/LH). Nevertheless Arabs and Israelis who *normally* read from right to left should then either be dyslexic or have reversed dominance. Neither of these situations obtains.

(7)   Why should hemispheric dominance have any relation to eye dominance? There is normally a poor correlation between hand, eye and language dominance, and mixed or incomplete motor dominance is not related simply or directly to either cerebral dominance or reading disability.

Nevertheless crossed hand/eye dominance could just possibly reflect weak lateralization (see below), and abnormal lateralization does seem to have a higher incidence in developmental dyslexia.

We should, however, note the following points: *symmetrical* organisms should have difficulty with left-to-right, or right-to-left directional scripts (see Chapter 1) and there does seem to be less developmental dyslexia with nondirectional Chinese and Japanese. Secondly, oculomotor and fixational difficulties, and regressive eye movements, are commoner in dyslexia, though it is unclear whether this phenomenon operates in a causative capacity, or as an effect, e.g. go back for a 'retake' if you do not initially comprehend. In the third place, reduced or reversed field or ear asymmetries may be due to difficulty, unfamiliarity, floor/ceiling effects (performance which is overall so bad, or so good, that laterality differences have no room to manifest), or abnormal strategies. Finally, we are left with a dilemma: we can embrace the developmental-lag hypothesis, whereby dyslexia is due to the faulty development of language lateralization, which in principle could possibly be cured—except that all the evidence points against the idea that lateralization develops (see Chapter 10); alternatively, according to the hypotheses of abnormal cerebral organization, dyslexia is due to genetic defects or early developmental events (see Chapter 8). In the latter case the condition cannot be treated, except possibly in terms of ameliorating strategies, whether lateralization is normal but the language processor is inefficient, or lateralization is abnormal. If, however, the apparent anomalies of lateralization are merely due to abnormal attentional biases or inability to direct attention, then, in principle, treatment is possible.

There is much evidence in support of a LH deficit underlying developmental dyslexia (Gordon, 1984). There are persistent claims that, in dyslexics, performance IQ outscores verbal IQ, with deficits in sequential processing and often abnormally *good* performance in (RH) spatial processing. This may be the case even when all appropriate precautions are observed such as excluding all those with abnormally low IQs, physical handicaps, 'hard' neurological signs, defective learning opportunities or environmental backgrounds etc. (Geschwind, 1984). There is even evidence that close family relatives of developmental dyslexics, who themselves are normal readers, often have abnormally high spatial (RH) scores. It is therefore possible that dyslexics may be obliged to employ inappropriate RH strategies in reading, though it must be noted that, on current evidence, lateralization of language mechanisms to the LH is as characteristic of many dyslexics as it is of normal readers, despite possibly inferior processing strategies or processing mechanisms therein.

Geschwind has frequently reported structural anomalies in the LHs of developmental dyslexics, together with a high incidence of immune dysfunction (see Chapter 8). He proposed that high levels of fetal testosterone may adversely affect the development of the LH, leading to a slowed rate of maturation of certain structures together with an enhanced development (as a consequence of contralateral retardation) of corresponding structures in the RH; this will all lead to poor language and superior RH functions, especially in boys because of their contribution to fetal testosterone levels. He cites further evidence of testosterone excess leading to specific patterns of immune dysfunction and allergies, which appear to be genetically linked and correlated with sex, handedness, language disorders and mathematical excellence. The hypothesis, which is not without both its critics and growing statistical support from some surprising quarters, accounts nicely for a number of phenomena. These include the male preponderance in language disabilities (stuttering, dyslexia, autism) and in mathematics and spatial excellence, sex differences in immune disorders, the increased incidence of sinistrality in males and those with dysfunctions of language, and the long recorded history of abnormal lateralization in developmental dyslexia. Finally, yet another independently developed yet compatible hypothesis is that of Lovegrove (see e.g. Lovegrove, Martin and Slaghuis, 1986); he presents evidence to indicate a low-level visual deficit in many specifically disabled readers. Such individuals, he argues, suffer from a deficient transient, but not sustained, subsystem. (Neural activity in the transient channel is initiated by eye movements, and lasts for a very much shorter duration than the sustained activity, which lasts several hundred milliseconds, and normally occurs during fixations.) Thus he finds that according to measures of visible-persistence duration as a function of spatial frequency, disabled readers have a different pattern of temporal processing across spatial frequencies. Such readers are also less sensitive than controls on measures of pattern-contrast sensitivity at low but not at high spatial frequencies, where they may even excel. On measures of temporal contrast sensitivity, he finds that specifically disabled readers are less sensitive than controls at all flicker rates, but especially at the higher temporal frequencies.

However, can we neatly fit all developmental dyslexics into a single category? Several authorities (e.g. Boder, and Pirozzolo, see Pirozzolo, Rayner and Hynd, 1983) have independently distinguished between two major groups: in the dysphonetic (or audiolinguistic) group, words can only be read (as above) via direct access, a situation which of course is reminiscent of the (later discovered) syndrome of *deep* dyslexia. This situation would correspond to LH dysfunction with sparing or RH mechanisms, and reduced or reversed asymmetries for language; Japanese *Kanji* and Chinese should be read comparatively easily. The second (minority) group, the dyseidetic or those suffering from a visuospatial deficit, would only be able to read by sounding out. In this regard they would resemble *surface* dyslexics, and would exhibit normal lateral asymmetries. We should, however, end upon a note of caution. It is perhaps dangerous to correlate normal hemispheric asymmetries with two routes to reading, direct word recognition (via the RH) and grapheme–phoneme translation (via the LH), as both surface dyslexia (involving impairment of the first route) and deep or phonological dyslexia (impairment of the second route) require LH damage (Ellis, 1985). While the RH may indeed possess a limited capacity for directly accessing the lexicon, this is probably secondary to the dominant LH system, and the actual existence of such a capacity is still open to dispute.

SUMMARY AND CONCLUSIONS

Females and sinistrals may engage the RH during language tasks more than other groups, though the articulatory mechanisms are perhaps the most securely lateralized to the LH, except where very early damage has destroyed those centers. Even then, plastic takeover of function by the RH is rarely total, as evidenced by syntactic deficits with adult testing. However, lesions which are insufficiently severe or early to modify the less stable hand preferences may not shift language lateralization. An early language shift to the RH under such circumstances may nevertheless be a better prognosis, while damage to the LH after the first few years, when dextrality and language are firmly established, may lead to language deficits and inadequate cerebral reorganization. However, such reorganization may be to the detriment of other e.g. spatial functions ('crowding'). The characteristic reading profile of deep dyslexics suggests RH mediation without the benefit of phonology, though other evidence may indicate that the associated semantic paralexias are still mediated by the LH. In any case debate continues on the possible extent to which the RH may or may not contribute to reading in the normal situation. Nevertheless it does seem from clinical studies to be concerned with prosodic and emotional aspects. Indeed RH damage may result in an inability to see the point in jokes, to detect absurdities, or to interpret figurative speech. The isolated RHs of split-brain patients, when appropriately interrogated, exhibit linguistic competence which, while certainly not negligible, is still far below that of an adult; however, there is no developmental age to which it can be said to correspond.

Laterality studies suggest a RH involvement with novel, unfamiliar or degraded verbal material, with concrete words or ideographic representations, or when first learning a new language (bilingualism). Debate continues about its possibly greater involvement in cases of illiteracy or deafness, or where there is a history of a reduced linguistic environment. Two pathologies, stuttering and developmental dyslexia, have also been associated with RH mediation. Indeed a family pedigree which also includes sinistrality may be prominent with developmental reading disability. While Orton's hypothesis can probably be discounted, there is persistent evidence of both a LH deficit and abnormally developed RH functions in this condition, and Geschwind's fetal testosterone hypothesis may ultimately, in some form, provide an explanation. Nevertheless this may only apply to one form of developmental dyslexia, the dysphonetic (or audiolinguistic) subgroup.

In conclusion, some aspects of language may be better handled than others by the RH, which may even employ substantially different strategies from those of the LH; indeed its performance may be different from rather than worse than its partner. Alternatively, it may normally not play much of a role, except perhaps in the event of its partner's injury. Its language abilities may develop with relative ease early in life, and then gradually fall behind those of the developing LH. If it does normally play only a superficial or initial role in e.g. reading, even this may merely have developed from always accompanying the LH in such contexts. We certainly cannot conclude that all speech and language functions are limited to the LH, with a mute aphasic RH playing no role at all. In fact Van Lancker (1987) sees a continuum between a LH which via a generative grammar can synthesize new propositions according to combinatorial or syntactic rules at the level of phoneme, morpheme, word and phrase, and, on the other side, a RH which processes more at the level of complex integrative patterns. Thus information on age, sex, mood, personality, personal identity and dialect origin which is conveyed across the whole utterance, is not easily analyzable into subunits and is independent of propositional content. Automatic phrases, clichés, formulaic utterances, metaphors, expletives, idioms, greetings, proverbs, rhymes, conventional and overlearnt expressions, serial lists (numbers, days of the week, months of the year), quotations all fall into this potential RH category. The intermediate position, she argues, is occupied by bilaterally represented material of varying levels of familiarity, automaticity or spontaneity of initiation. It is unclear whether the actual articulation of such RH material must necessarily occur through LH mechanisms; however, there is evidence of considerable RH powers of articulation. This evidence includes preservation of singing and speech automatisms after massive LH insult or Wada amytal suppression, and the fact that motor sources for phonation and articulation appear to be bilaterally represented in precentral Rolandic and supplementary motor cortex. Indeed such evidence counts against the frequently proposed argument that speech must be lateralized to one side to avoid competition for access to the articulators, and perhaps stuttering; thus many individuals are incompletely lateralized, and the articulatory complexities of formulaic utterances and song approach that of novel propositional speech.

IMPORTANT READINGS

Bihrle, A. M., Brownell, H. H. and Gardner, H. Humor and the right hemisphere: A narrative perspective. In H. A. Whitaker (ed.), *Contemporary Reviews in Neuropsychology*. New York: Springer, 1988, pp. 109–26.

Bishop, D. V. M. Linguistic impairment after left hemidecortication for infantile hemiplegia? A reappraisal. *Quarterly Journal of Experimental Psychology*, 1983a, **35A**, 199–208.

Bishop, D. V. M. How sinister is sinistrality? *Journal of the Royal College of Physicians of London*, 1983b, **17**, 161–72.

Bishop, D. V. M. Can the right hemisphere mediate language as well as the left? A critical review of recent research. *Cognitive Neuropsychology*, 1988, **5**, 353–67.

Bryden, M. P. and Saxby, L. Developmental aspects of cerebral lateralization. In J. E. Obrzut and G. W. Hynd (eds.), *Child Neuropsychology*, Vol. 1. New York: Academic Press, 1986, pp. 73–94.

Castro, S. L. and Morais, J. Ear differences in illiterates. *Neuropsychologia*, 1987, **25**, 409–18.

Chiarello, C., Senehi, J. and Nuding, S. Semantic priming with abstract and concrete words: Differential asymmetry may be postlexical. *Brain and Cognition*, 1987, **31**, 43–60.

Code, C. *Language, Aphasia and the Right Hemisphere*. Chichester: Wiley, 1987.

Coltheart, M. The right hemisphere and disorders of reading. In A. W. Young (ed.), *Functions of the Right Cerebral Hemisphere*. New York: Academic Press, 1983, pp. 172–201.

Coltheart, M. Right hemisphere reading revisited. *The Behavioral and Brain Sciences*, 1985, **8**, 363–5.

Ellis, A. W. The cognitive neuropsychology of developmental (and acquired) dyslexia: A critical survey. *Cognitive Neuropsychology*, 1985, **2**, 169–205.

Gardner, H., Brownell, H. H., Wapner, W. and Michelow, D. Missing the point: The role of the right hemisphere in the processing of complex linguistic materials. In E. Perecman (ed.), *Cognitive Processing in the Right Hemisphere*. New York: Academic Press, 1983, pp. 169–91.

Gazzaniga, M. S. and Smylie, C. S. What does language do for a right hemisphere? In M. S. Gazzaniga (ed.), *Handbook of Cognitive Neuroscience*. New York: Plenum Press, 1984, pp. 199–209.

Geschwind, N. Cerebral dominance in biological perspective. *Neuropsychologia*, 1984, **22**, 675–83.

Goodman, R. A. and Whitaker, H. A. Hemispherectomy: A review (1928–1981) with special reference to the linguistic abilities and disabilities of the residual right hemisphere. In C. T. Best (ed.), *Hemispheric Function and Collaboration in the Child*. New York: Academic Press, 1985, pp. 121–55.

Gordon, H. W. Dyslexia. In R. E. Tarter and G. Goldstein (eds.), *Advances in Clinical Neuropsychology*, Vol. 2. New York: Plenum Press, 1984, pp. 181–205.

Harris, L. J. Teaching the right brain: Historical perspective on a contemporary educational fad. In C. T. Best (ed.), *Hemispheric Function and Collaboration in the Child*. New York: Academic Press, 1985, pp. 231–74.

Jones, E. A. and Aoki, C. The processing of Japanese Kana and Kanji characters. In D. de Kerckhove and C. J. Lumsden (eds.), *The Alphabet and the Brain: The Lateralization of Writing*. New York: Springer, 1988, pp. 301–20.

Lambert, A. J. Right hemisphere language ability: 1. Clinical evidence. *Current Psychological Reviews*, 1982a, **2**, 77–94.

Lambert, A. J. Right hemisphere language ability: 2. Evidence from normal subjects. *Current Psychological Reviews*, 1982b, **2**, 139–52.

Lecours, A. R., Mehler, J., Parente, M. A. and Vadeboncoeur, A. Literacy and the brain. In D. de Kerckhove and C. J. Lumsden (eds.), *The Alphabet and the Brain*. New York: Springer, 1988, pp. 291–300.

Lovegrove, W. L., Martin, F. and Slaghuis, W. A theoretical and experimental case for a visual deficit in specific reading disability. *Cognitive Neuropsychology*, 1986, **3**, 225–67.

McMullen, P. A. and Bryden, M. P. The effects of word imageability and frequency on hemispheric asymmetry in lexical decisions. *Brain and Language*, 1987, **31**, 11–25.

Marcotte, A. C. and La Barba, R. C. The effects of linguistic experience on cerebral lateralization for speech production in normal hearing and deaf adolescents. *Brain and Language*, 1987, **31**, 276–300.

Obler, L.K. Dyslexia in bilinguals. In R. N. Malatesha and H. A. Whitaker (eds.), *Dyslexia: A Global Issue*. The Hague: Martinus Nijhoff, 1984, pp. 476–96.

Orsini, D. L. and Satz, P. A syndrome of pathological left-handedness: Correlates of early left hemisphere injury. *Archives of Neurology*, 1986, **43**, 333–7.

Papanicolaou, A. C., Moore, B. D., Deutsch, G., Levin, H. S. and Eisenberg, H. M. Evidence for right hemisphere involvement in recovery from aphasia. *Archives of Neurology*, 1988, **45**, 1025–9.

Patterson, K. and Besner, D. Is the right hemisphere literate? *Cognitive Neuropsychology*, 1984a, **1**, 315–41.

Patterson, K. and Besner, D. Reading from the left: A reply to Rabinowicz and Moscovitch and to Zaidel and Schweiger. *Cognitive Neuropsychology*, 1984b, **1**, 365–80.

Pirozzolo, F. J., Rayner, K. and Hynd, G. W. The measurement of hemispheric asymmetries in children with developmental reading disabilities. In J. B. Hellige (ed.), *Cerebral Hemisphere Asymmetries: Method, Theory and Application*. New York: Praeger, 1983, pp. 498–515.

Poizner, H., Klima, E. and Bellugi, U. *What the Hands Reveal about the Brain*. Cambridge, Mass.: MIT Press, 1987.

Roeltgen, D. P. Loss of deep dyslexic reading ability from a second left-hemispheric lesion. *Archives of Neurology*, 1987, **44**, 346–8.

Ross, E. D. Modulation of affect and nonverbal communication by the right hemisphere. In M.-M. Mesulam (ed.), *Principles of Behavioral Neurology*. Philadelphia: F. A. Davis, 1985, pp. 239–58.

Satz, P., Orsini, D. L., Saslow, E. and Henry, R. Early brain injury and pathological left handedness: Clues to a syndrome. In D. F. Benson and E. Zaidel (eds.), *The Dual Brain: Hemispheric Specialization in Humans*. New York: Guilford, 1985, pp. 117–25.

Searleman, A. Language capabilities and the right hemisphere. In A. W. Young (ed.), *Functions of the Right Cerebral Hemisphere*. New York: Academic Press, 1983, pp. 87–111.

Sidtis, J. Bilateral language and commissurotomy. In A. Reeves (ed.), *Epilepsy and the Corpus Callosum*. New York: Plenum Press, 1985, pp. 369–80.

Sussman, H. M. and MacNeilage, P. F. Hemispheric specialization for speech production and perception in stutterers. *Neuropsychologia*, 1975, **13**, 19–26.

Temple, C. M. The alexias. In J. R. Beech and A. M. Colley (eds.), *Cognitive Approaches to Reading*. New York: Wiley, 1987, pp. 271–95.

Tzeng, O. J. L. and Hung, D. L. Orthography, reading and cerebral functions. In D. de Kerckhove and C. J. Lumsden (eds.), *The Alphabet and the Brain: The Lateralization of Writing*. New York: Springer, 1988, pp. 273–90.

Van Lancker, D. Nonpropositional speech: Neurolinguistic studies. In A. W. Ellis (ed.), *Progress in the Psychology of Language*, Vol. 3. Hillsdale, N. J.: Erlbaum, 1987, pp. 49–118.

Young, A. W. Cerebral hemisphere differences in reading. In J. R. Beech and A. M. Colley (eds.), *Cognitive Approaches to Reading*. New York: Wiley, 1987, pp. 140–68.

Zaidel, E. Auditory language comprehension in the right hemisphere following commissurotomy and hemispherectomy: A comparison with child language and aphasia. In A. Caramazza and E. B. Zurif (eds.), *Language Acquisition and Language Breakdown: Parallels and Divergencies*. Baltimore: Johns Hopkins University Press, 1978, pp. 229–75.

Zaidel, E. and Schweiger, A. On wrong hypotheses about the right hemisphere: Commentary on K. Patterson and D. Besner, 'Is the right hemisphere literate?' *Cognitive Neuropsychology*, 1984, **1**, 351–64.

7

Evolutionary aspects of language and tool use

Along with questions about the nature and origin of the universe and of life, our own place in prehistory and in primate evolution has been a major source of fascination. The origins of Man, and of language, have been debated at least from the days of the classical Greek historian Herodotus, who recounts the results of the Egyptian Pharoah's ultimate experiment—the isolation from birth and observation of a group of children to ascertain what language they apparently began to speak, without external human influence. (It is not clear why the oldest or 'original' language would necessarily emerge under such circumstances.) As we have seen, language and handedness *seem* somehow to be interrelated, not least in terms of asymmetric cerebral representation, though it is unclear how closely the two phenomena are tied to each other. However, language and hand use are two ways whereby we qualitatively differ from other primates. (Tools of course may leave a fossil trace, while language and praxic functions on their own obviously cannot.) How have language and praxis co-evolved? Speculative debate about the origin of language was so popular in nineteenth century Europe that it was twice banned from discussion by the Société Linguistique de Paris; however, fossil evidence for human origins and early tool use has expanded so enormously during the last two decades, particularly in eastern and southern Africa, but also in Asia, the Levant and continental Europe, that some kind of consensus is beginning to emerge. One such finding is the extreme antiquity of hominid dextrality. In this chapter we discuss the evolutionary sequence of and relationship between an upright bipedal posture, tool use, gesture, language and consciousness, and ask whether human language is continuous with early primate call systems.

There is considerable disagreement about the details and chronology of hominid evolution and lineage (Andrews, 1986; Lovejoy, 1981). Tobias (1985) claims that *Sivapithecus*, the beginning of the Asiatic orangoid lineage, split from the African hominoids sixteen to ten million years ago (mya). In Africa, hominids (on the line leading to ourselves) and pongids (the lines leading to *Pan*—chimpanzee—and *Gorilla*) split between 9 and 5 mya. There is, however, some debate about comparative chromosome analyses and the relative speeds of the molecular clock in *Homo* and other primates. Nevertheless in terms of genetics (DNA sequencing and hybridization techniques) and evolutionary time, we are probably closer to chimpanzees than are the latter to gorillas, despite the fact that chimpanzees and gorillas look more alike; both are hairy, walk on all fours, knuckle walk, have short legs and long arms, brachiate, are less manually dextrous than ourselves, have smaller brains and larger canine teeth with thin enamel. Thus apparent chimpanzee–gorilla similarities do not necessarily reflect closeness of kinship, or convergent evolution, so much perhaps as retention of ancestral traits which we have lost. Our own physical differences from chimpanzees, despite the close genetic similarity, probably stem from the fact that much of our joint genetic make-up is in fact largely nonfunctional in both species without impact upon morphology, thus even permitting it to be used as a clock for genetic change or drift uninfluenced by selective pressures. The African hominids are said to have split about 2.3 mya into gracile (*A. africanus*) and robust (*A. boesei*) australopithecines, though again there is dispute about the place of *A. afarensis* at the bifurcation, and alternative scenarios have been proposed. The oldest known manuport (a pretty, red jasperite pebble, thought to have been carried around because of its intrinsic attractiveness) was found with the 3 mya remains of *Australopithecus* (Oakley, 1981). The first undisputed stone-cultural remains (*H. habilis*, of the Oldowan culture) occur between 2.5 and 2 mya. To judge from analysis of the pattern of successive flaking from stone cores (Toth, 1985), *H. habilis* was habitually dextral. Thus dextrals typically hold cores in the more passive left hand, and rotate them clockwise, leaving a sequential trace of characteristically superimposed scars (see Figure 1). *H. habilis* was the first hominid with an enlarged cranium (600 to 800 cm^3), and while resembling *Australopithecus* in face, jaws and teeth, was like later types of *Homo* in skeleton. It developed into *H. erectus* (Java, Peking Man) about 1.5 mya, which had a larger brain (800 to 1200 cm^3), more advanced tools and perhaps fire. (In the Swartkrans cave of South Africa, burnt bones have been found, heated to a range consistent with campfires; they have been dated to between 1 and 1.5 mya. While only the remains of *A. robustus* were found in association, *H. erectus* may well also have been present.) *H. erectus* (1.5 mya) moreover seems to have been interested in red ochre, and constructed flint hand axes around spectacular fossils which were preserved in a prominent central position, to serve as a personal blazon according to Oakley (see Figures 2 and 3). At this point *Australopithecus* seems to have become extinct, perhaps as a result of competition, climatic changes or both. Archaic *H. sapiens* at 0.5 mya was also African as perhaps also was

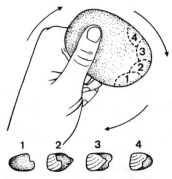

Fig. 1 According to analyses of the pattern of successive flaking from stone cores, the earliest tool-using hominids may have been dextral. Dextrals hold cores in the more passive left hand, and rotate them clockwise, leaving a sequential trace of characteristically superimposed scars. (Figure redrawn from N. Toth, Archaeological evidence for preferential right-handedness in the lower and middle Pleistocene, and its possible implications. *Journal of Human Evolution*, 1985, **14**, 607–614, with publisher's permission.)

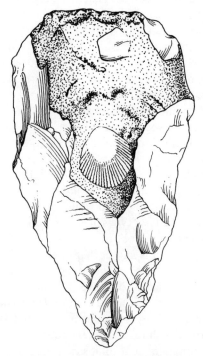

Fig. 2 Pointed Acheulian flint hand axe constructed around Cretaceous fossil which has been preserved in a prominent and aesthetically pleasing location. (Figure reproduced from K.P. Oakley, Emergence of higher thought, 3.0–0.2 Ma B.P. *Philosophical Transactions of the Royal Society of London B,* 1981, **292**, 205–211, with permission.)

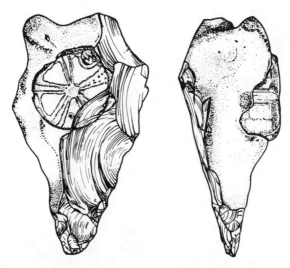

Fig. 3   As in Figure 2. View from side and above. (Figure reproduced with permission.)

modern *H. sapiens* at about 100 000 years ago, though just such a date is now appearing for its arrival in the Levant. Neanderthals, who were probably not closely related phylogenetically to modern *H. sapiens*, though their tools were quite sophisticated and they employed ritual burying, may have subsequently arrived there in south-west Asia at a relatively late date from Europe, where they may have emerged around 300 000 years ago; they became extinct around 35 000 years ago, again perhaps due to competition. Analysis of striated wear patterns on the anterior teeth of Middle and Upper Pleistocene antenean-derthals from Spain suggests that they habitually held meat between their front teeth, and cut it with stone tools held by the right hand (see Figure 4).

Modern man is of course characterized by language, tools and an upright bipedal posture, characteristics of which none are totally unique to ourselves (Passingham, 1982). Thus there is currently a vigorous debate (see e.g. Premack, 1986) about whether the communication systems (signing, use of keyboards or plastic tokens), which can be taught to higher apes, really qualify as true language, in terms of novelty of sequences, capacity to prevaricate etc. Likewise many species employ sophisticatedly modified tools of one sort or another, and while only Man is habitually bipedal, chimpanzees do sometimes adopt this posture, and other nonprimates can be taught to do so. These and the following issues are reviewed in detail by Bradshaw (1988).

The morphological asymmetries in brain regions which in ourselves mediate speech also occur, though perhaps less prominently, in other primates. Thus (and see Chapter 1) such lateral asymmetries are present in homologous regions of the monkey brain, e.g. the expansion of the parietal cortex over the caudal ends of the Sylvian and superior temporal sulci of the LH, and the

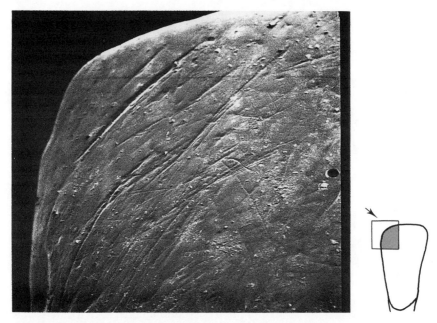

Fig. 4   A scanning electron micrograph of a lower central incisor of an antenean-derthal from Spain. The striated wear patterns on such anterior teeth are thought to be comparable with abductive cutting, by a stone tool wielded by the right hand, of meat held in the front of the mouth. (Reproduced with permission from material kindly supplied by T. G. Bromage.)

greater inferior-parietal growth of the LH, with lowering of the distal end of the Sylvian fissure on that side (Falk, 1978; Holloway and de la Coste-Lareymon-die, 1982; LeMay, 1985; Steklis, 1985). There is also much evidence of a similar counterclockwise torque (left posterior and right anterior regions each respectively longer and wider than those on the opposite side) in monkeys and apes, as in ourselves, though not all species show all of the asymmetries.

  H. habilis had an indisputably upright bipedal posture and locomotion, a mosaic of primitive and derived skeletal features, and could fabricate tools while still probably continuing to climb trees. (There is currently a debate concerning whether prior *A. afarensis* was also fully bipedal; according to a very recent analysis of pelvis and femur the 3 mya australopithecine female Lucy was even *better* designed for bipedalism than ourselves, but only because the resultant constriction in her birth canal was tolerable because she predated the dramatic expansion in fetal head size at birth. Secondly, *A. robustus*, a descendent of earlier australopithecines, at 1.8 mya possessed a hand adapted for precision grasping, and has been found associated with stone tools, though the latter could instead have come from *H. erectus*.) Upright walking may have been preadapted for by tree climbing (i.e. arboreal refuge), as the same muscle systems are involved. An alternative hypothesis developed by Morgan (1984), from an earlier proposal by Hardy, invokes an aquatic phase with massive flooding between 8 mya and 4 mya; this would have led to loss of body hair, the presence of subcutaneous fat, face-to-face copulation (as in all aquatic mammals), the characteristic position of fetal hair, weeping (salt excretion), the diving reflex (apnea, bradycardia), and bipedalism. Again the same muscle systems are involved and swimming would have been a good preadaptor for bipedalism on return to the land; moreover a hairless mother would have had to carry her offspring, who would have had no pelt to cling on to. Unfortunately there is absolutely no paleoclimatic evidence for such an attractive hypothesis. Moreover other explanations can account for our nude skin, e.g. the dissipation of excess metabolic heat during temporary exertion, such as fleeing predators, or opportunistically pursuing small savannah prey. Indeed a new ecological niche would be opened for hominids were they to do the latter during noonday heat. Furthermore, bipedalism is itself a thermoregulatory advance, removing much of the body from close proximity to the heated ground, and exposing less skin to the sun's rays. Such a thermoregulatory advance, together with a massive increase in sweat glands (themselves of course useless in water) would remove a barrier to further brain growth. A large brain is itself also a considerable source of metabolic heat, as well as being particularly vulnerable to its effects.

Other factors which favor bipedalism, and ultimately dextrality, include missile throwing (Calvin, 1983) and tool use (Frost, 1980). The latter factor really subsumes the former. While manual specialization may result in one hand holding a store of missiles, and the other throwing, or one hand holding and steadying an object, while the other works on it, *population*-level asymmetries require further factors. One such possibility is imitative learning; thus two dextrals (or two sinistrals, i.e. two individuals of the *same* handedness) learn more efficiently from each other how to tie knots. However, as discussed above, *H. habilis* may already have been dextral, and in any case tools, until maybe the advent of *H. erectus*, were hardly of sufficient complexity that interactive or imitative learning would benefit from homogeneity of handedness. Thus dextrality appeared either much *earlier*, for other reasons, or much *later*. Presumably sinistrality is not entirely maladaptive; such individuals can use their *nonpreferred* hand more efficiently than dextrals, and may possess certain more highly developed spatial skills (see Chapter 8).

A common viewpoint is that an upright posture led to tool use, which led on to gesture and language. However, gesture appears too late in this sequence, given the commonality of gesture between chimps and modern Man. Moreover tool use might have hampered gesture, thus favoring the emergence of auditory–vocal communication. (So also would the need to communicate in the dark, at a distance or among vegetation.) Indeed the fact that human infants learn to speak before gesture emerges is a further indication that gesture is probably not phylogenetically prior. The fact that tool development progressed remarkably slowly, until well into the time of *H. erectus*, despite huge increases in brain size, suggests that tool use was not such an important factor in brain development. Language may therefore have developed, along with specialized modes of thought, as a comcomitant of brain and cortical increases in size, due to survival needs in a new ecological niche. This might have been occasioned by a climatic change, or a move to the savannah, and been accompanied by the appearance of socially cooperative hunting and butchering. Indeed bipedalism may even have originally been a foraging adaptation (Cartmill, Pilbeam and Isaac, 1986), together of course with brachiation and thermoregualtion, and would have freed up the hands for tool use.

With increasing fetal head sizes, either obstetric or walking problems would have occurred with respect to the maternal pelvis. A solution would have been a shift to a prolonged postnatal development, involving extended parenting, learning, socialization and family bonding (Lovejoy, 1981). Foraging for a family of at least three, presumably by the father, would be a consequence, probably for meat rather than plant food, to provide sufficient protein. While early hominid teeth suggest wear patterns indicative more of vegetable consumption than of carnivory (and see McHenry, 1982), it may be remembered that the predominantly vegetarian chimpanzee is an opportunistic carnivore. The idea of a division of labor between the sexes (spatially oriented hunting and foraging by the male parent, the fostering of the offsprings' social and communicative skills by the female parent) are reminiscent of two claims; on the one side that males may be slightly superior to females with respect to spatial abilities, and correspondingly inferior verbally, and on the other that in females there is a more focal and anterior representation of speech and manual praxis (see Chapter 9).

So was language continuous with earlier primate vocalization? Jerison (1982) believes this is not the case, and that language began in small-brained hominids as an auditory–vocal marker system to replace olfactory markers as used in the cognitive world of social carnivores like wolves, which hominids ecologically resembled, despite their loss of olfaction. He claims that the system was used to create a cognitive spatial map in which others could share, e.g. replacing an inflexible alarm call (corresponding to 'danger'!) with a statement like 'there is a predator behind the large rock'. According to tradition, the calls of other species are involuntary, nonreferential, nonpropositional, nonsymbolic and of limbic rather than cortical origin. Steklis (1985), however, has shown recently how rich monkey calls really are, providing information on sex, personal identity, group membership, social relationships and several kinds of predator. The latter can be inferred by the range of looking and searching behaviors elicited by taped calls. Indeed not only may cortical structures be involved, but *human* speech *also* relies heavily on *noncortical* regions, e.g. thalamus and basal ganglia (see Chapter 2). There is

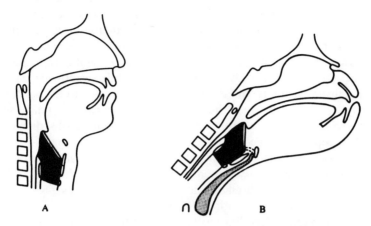

Fig. 5   As a result of the descent of the larynx in humans (A), shown here in sagittal section, the epiglottis no longer interacts with the soft palate to allow the oral cavity to be closed off while breathing through the nose. The epiglottis, which is high and wider in its upper portion in the chimpanzee (B), is capable of sealing off the inlet to the larynx while swallowing. This is no longer possible with humans. The black region is the laryngeal cavity and the dotted area is the laryngeal sac. (Figure from W. O. Dingwall, The evolution of human communicative behavior. In F. J. Newmeyer (Ed.), *Linguistics, The Cambridge Survey, Vol. III: Language, Psychological and Biological Aspects.* Cambridge: Cambridge University Press, 1988, pp. 274–313. Reproduced with permission.)

therefore the possibility of a direct evolutionary descent of language from primate call systems involving the LH (see Chapter 1).

Lieberman (1985) also stresses such a continuity, and argues that syntactic and phonological skills evolved from other complex sequences of skilled automatized behavior which also involved the hands. Pre-existing capacities for complex orofacial movements and a developing laryngeal tract would act as additional adaptatory factors. Certainly, language appears unique to our species, and permits enormously fast acoustic transmission of information. Of course, we possess neural and laryngeal specializations for language; there are, universally, critical periods for language acquisition, as shown by the tragic cases of children held in extreme social deprivation (see Chapter 10), and the relative difficulty we have as adults acquiring new languages fluently and with correct accenting. However, in infancy, language is acquired often against enormous odds, and it can only be taught, in highly modified form, and with great difficulty if at all, to other species. Other indications of our relatively unique species-specific capacity for language include the existence of linguistic universals, the heritability of certain language dysfunctions (see e.g. Chapters 6 and 8), and the fact that even neonates possess language lateralization (see Chapter 10), and move in synchrony with the rhythms of speech. Other species lack our complex neural and articulatory apparatus, especially the supralaryngeal tract which has been lowered at the expense of other nonspeech functions like breathing and swallowing (see Figure 5). The human neonate can breathe while drinking; it does not choke since the epiglottis can connect the larynx directly to the nasal cavity, sealing it off while swallowing. However, during the first year the larynx is lowered and develops into the adult human form. While it has been argued that Neanderthal man could not have spoken, on the basis of soft-tissue vocal-tract reconstruction from fossil skull bases, not everyone accepts such reconstructions. Moreover human partial laryngectomies can communicate well with remaining structures, and parrots with a grossly different articulatory system can closely mimic the sounds of our speech. It could even be argued that cerebral mechanisms preadapted for speech evolved *before* the evolution of a modern vocal-tract morphology, since our capacity for rapidly decoding written letters is far higher than for producing or following spoken speech.

In contrast to the view being proposed here, that there is a direct evolutionary continuity between human speech and earlier call systems, we should perhaps note the nativist account of Chomsky. This proposes that our language ability derives from an innate, language-specific neural mechanism, with no prior evolutionary history, no prior adapting counterparts in earlier species, and no precedent. (Compared to this 'creationist' viewpoint, the corollary idea, that there is a common deep structure to all languages and grammars which is independent of meaning, is less controversial.) However, there is abundant evidence for the evolutionary utilization and adaptation of pre-existing structures for new functions; the swim bladders of lung fish became lungs, the airway between lungs and mouth was adapted for phonation, and many other peripheral and control structures have been adapted for speech.

There are even claims that tool use *presupposes* a pre-existing language, though, as Jaynes (1977) observes, even *modern* language cannot usefully describe to a novice how to operate tools. Nevertheless language may have potentiated the cognitive strategies necessary for successful tool manufacture and use, and evidence of speech in modern microcephalic dwarves (with a brain comparable in size to a chimpanzee) suggests that even the australopithecine brain might have supported some form of speech. By contrast, Jaynes (1977) argues that language (and consciousness) appeared suddenly, 50 000 years ago, on the basis of a sudden change in the nature of art and artifacts; moreover (see Ruhlen, 1987), glottochronological studies of modern language point to a convergence about then. Alternatively, a 'critical mass' phenomenon in terms of technology, society and communication could have brought about such changes without involving anything 'biological' or to do with the 'emergence of consciousness'.

SUMMARY AND CONCLUSIONS

There seems to be a continuity with earlier species for our two most obvious asymmetries, language lateralization, and movement control and sequencing by either hand. Recent evidence of lateral asymmetries in nonhuman species suggests the probability of an ancestral LH specialization for sensory and motor discrimination learning. Perhaps by default (see Chapter 5), spatial and emotional functions were relegated to the RH. (It could be argued, against the default claim, that hemispheric specializations for language are independent rather than complementary; however, while this may currently be true at the level of the individual, it may well not necessarily have been true earlier in evolution, perhaps at a *population* level.) Inhibitory control processes involving higher learning in the LH would tend to take over language and communication, together with manipulative and motor sequencing capacities; hence the close cortical proximity of our centers for articulation and eye/hand control. A right hand preference for manipulation, possibly of considerable ancestry and maybe even related to turning biases in the rat, would stem from LH control of motor sequencing. The two basic LH functions, communication and manipulation, are only loosely linked to each other; hence dextrality and LH mediation of language often dissociate. Human language may be built upon pre-existing cognitive specializations in the LH for analytic–sequential processing (Bradshaw and Nettleton, 1981), possibly via primate vocalizations. We possess a specific-specific language processor in the LH, even though it may be built upon pre-existing, bilaterally represented mechanisms perhaps designed originally for mapping the occurrence of events in space. Hence early left hemispherectomy permits the development, later, of reasonable language competence by the RH; conversely, left hemispherectomy late in life, though severely disabling of language, is still compatible with a fully human conscious existence (see Chapter 6). Thus these specializations are probably relative or quantitative, rather than absolute or qualitative (see Chapter 5), and can perhaps be overridden in the event of injury. If 'modern' language first appeared around 50 000 years ago, it was probably not a sudden evolutionary innovation so much as the attainment of some kind of 'critical mass' in society.

IMPORTANT READINGS

Andrews, P. Fossil evidence of human origins and dispersal. *Cold Spring Harbor Symposia on Quantitative Biology*, 1986, **51**, 419–28.

Bradshaw, J. L. The evolution of human lateral asymmetries: New evidence and second thoughts. *Journal of Human Evolution*, 1988, **17**, 615–37.

Bradshaw, J. L. and Nettleton, N. C. The nature of hemispheric specialization in Man. *Behavioral and Brain Sciences*, 1981, **4**, 51–91.

Calvin, W. H. *The Throwing Madonna: From Nervous Cells to Hominid Brains*. New York: McGraw-Hill, 1983.

Cartmill, M., Pilbeam, D. and Isaac, G. One hundred years of paleoanthropology. *American Scientist*, 1986, **74**, 410–20.

Cherfas, J. Trees have made Man walk upright. *New Scientist*, 1983, January 20, 172–8.

Ebling, J. The mythological evolution of nudity. *Journal of Human Evolution*, 1985, **14**, 33–41.

Falk, D. Cerebral asymmetry in Old World monkeys. *Acta Anatomica*, 1978, **101**, 334–9.

Frost, G. T. Tool behavior and the origins of laterality. *Journal of Human Evolution*, 1980, **9**, 447–59.

Holloway, R. L. and de la Coste-Lareymondie, M. C. Brain endocast asymmetry in pongids and hominids: Some preliminary findings on the paleontology of cerebral dominance. *American Journal of Physical Anthropology*, 1982, **58**, 101–10.

Jaynes, J. *The Origin of Consciousness in the Breakdown of the Bicameral Mind.* Boston: Houghton-Mifflin, 1977.

Jerison, H. J. The evolution of biological intelligence. In R. Sternberg (ed.), *Handbook of Intelligence*. Cambridge: Cambridge University Press, 1982, pp. 723–91.

LeMay, M. Asymmetries of the brains and skulls of nonhuman primates. In S. D. Glick (ed.), *Cerebral Lateralization in Nonhuman Species*. New York: Academic Press, 1985, pp. 234–46.

Lieberman, P. *The Biology and Evolution of Language*. Cambridge, Mass.: Harvard University Press, 1984.

Lieberman, P. On the evolution of human syntactic ability: Its preadaptive bases—motor control and speech. *Journal of Human Evolution*, 1985, **14**, 657–68.

Lovejoy, C. V. The origin of Man. *Science*, 1981, **211**, 341–50.

McHenry, H. M. The pattern of human evolution: Studies on bipedalism, mastication and encephalization. *Annual Review of Anthropology*, 1982, **11**, 151–73.

Morgan, E. The aquatic hypothesis. *New Scientist*, 1984, April 12, 11–13.

Oakley, K. P. The emergence of higher thought 3.0 to 0.2 Ma B.P. *Philosophical Transactions of the Royal Society of London B*, 1981, **292**, 205–11.

Passingham, R. *The Human Primate*. San Francisco: Freeman, 1982.

Premack, D. *Gavagai or the Future History of the Animal Language Controversy.* Cambridge, Mass.: M.I.T. Press, 1986.

Richards, G. *Human Evolution: An Introduction for the Behavioral Sciences*. London: Routledge and Kegan Paul, 1987.

Ruhlen, M. Voices from the past. *Natural History*, 1987, **96**, 6–10.

Steklis, H. Primate communication, comparative neurology, and the origin of language re-examined. *Journal of Human Evolution*, 1985, **14**, 157–73.

Tobias, P. V. Ten climacteric years in hominid evolution. *South African Journal of Science*, 1985, **81**, 271–2.

Toth, N. Archaeological evidence for preferential right handedness in the lower and middle Pleistocene and its possible implications. *Journal of Human Evolution*, 1985, **14**, 607–14.

Wheeler, P. E. The evolution of bipedality and loss of functional body hair in hominids. *Journal of Human Evolution*, 1984, **13**, 91–8.

8

Handedness

Handedness is the most clearly evident, but perhaps one of the less fundamentally important aspects of human cerebral asymmetry, except for the possible pointer it may provide towards language organization. It would be almost as evident, though far less remarkable, if the *degree* of our hand asymmetries were no less strong, but instead as in certain other animal species the *direction* split 50/50 into dextrals and sinistrals. It is due to the fact that most of us are largely or entirely dextral, that left handers find a (largely right-handed) human world difficult at times, and indeed may even be subject to discrimination or ridicule. However, sinistrals have also long been suspected of a propensity towards neurological dysfunction, and, occasionally, of a propensity towards visuomotor excellence. We shall see that there may be some residual truth in such prejudices. Handedness (preference or performance—two indices which may not necessarily correlate) is of course only one manifestation of outward behavioral asymmetry, though footedness, eyedness and earedness are less immediately apparent. That of course does not mean that given adequate testing procedures we might not find one of the latter group, e.g. perhaps footedness, to be more predictively useful. This raises the question of whether a knowledge of parental handedness (or footedness) permits predictions to be made about their offspring's lateralization, either in terms of extent or direction. Conversely, we can ask whether environmental effects may operate, not just on sinistrals inhabiting a largely dextral world, but upon the fetus (e.g. via maternal and sibling hormones) and upon the newborn (e.g. birth stress or perinatal trauma). Again such questions are more socially useful if phrased in the context of associated neurological function (e.g. language or visuospatial abilities) than simply with respect to handedness; the latter is neurologically interesting only if it can in any way predict cognitive or psychomotor abilities. It is with such issues that this chapter is concerned.

In all cultures, sinistrals have long been regarded as a suspect minority. This is reflected in the words for left handedness, which invariably contain pejorative connotations, e.g. sinister, gauche, gawky (Old French—'bent'), cack-handed (faeces in colloquial English), lyft (Celtic—'weak'), laevus and scaevus (Latin and Greek—'ill omened'), link (Germanic—'clumsy'), zurdo (Spanish—'clumsy'), and mancino (Italian—'deceitful'). The left is of course the 'unhygienic' hand, while the political left and right date from the pre-revolutionary French assembly, with aristocrats on the right and peoples' leaders on the left—the left and right wings. The jails were often said to be full of left handers, and there are still claims of an excess among them of alcoholics, drug addicts, smokers and deviants . . . .

All too often to a neurologist sinistrality serves only to confound and dismay, to complicate neat models of neurological functioning, rather than to provide a rich natural source of individual differences in brain function, cognitive styles, abilities and deficits. Of course the real reason for studying handedness is the fact that it provides a relatively direct (if imperfect) approach to the far more interesting issue of language and cerebral organization, though there are stronger evolutionary and environmental pressures on handedness than on language lateralization, and the two are not all that closely tied, especially of course in sinistrals. For this reason we should be wary about claiming that both are driven by motor-sequencing mechanisms in the LH (see Chapter 7); indeed the correlation between handedness and the lateralization of visuospatial functions is even smaller. In fact we would need to study very large populations to obtain statistical information on brain lateralization from studies of handedness.

Prehistoric art, artifacts and tools indicate an approximately constant ratio of sinistrals to dextrals, right back even to *Homo habilis* (see Chapter 7) three million years ago. Sinistrality cannot therefore be totally deleterious, either for society (i.e. a balanced polymorphism may operate, if indeed group selection can occur) or for the individual. Thus reduced lateralization may protect against the effects of unilateral brain damage, though under primitive conditions any such serious injury would have probably resulted in death. There is also the sinistral advantage of surprise in combat—and today sinistrality does tend to occur more frequently than otherwise would be expected in those excelling at confrontation sports—though this might be at the cost of clumsiness in other aspects of a largely dextral world. Reduced cerebral lateralization may also provide for an increased ability in associating verbal and nonverbal modes of thought, with superior innovativeness and flexibility resulting; indeed sinistrals again occur in unexpectedly high numbers among students of mathematics, engineering, art and architecture, even though they may have an increased susceptibility to language disorders (see below) and maybe for that very reason perhaps choose nonverbal professions. Consequently sinistrality may be bimodally distributed at the two ends of the IQ distribution, i.e. at the ends corresponding to the least and the most able, with perhaps the uniformly lateralized dextrals in the middle. Again such effects are likely to be relatively small and statistical, and to require large numbers for their demonstration.

BEHAVIORAL INDICES OF SIDEDNESS

Overt sinistrality is rarer among Asiatics and members of conservative agrarian societies, compared to the far more laissez-faire hunters and gatherers, who presumably are less inclined to influence the handedness of sinistral offspring. Its incidence is also reduced among females and older people. While older cultures are of course typically more conservative and strict, it is also probable that hand preferences really do strengthen with increasing age, so that if we were to equate ambilaterality with sinistrality, sinistrality would appear to become gradually less common with advancing years. Asymmetries are strongest for handedness, and less so for footedness, eyedness and earedness in that order (Porac and Coren, 1981). There is often a poor correlation between them, or with language lateralization, especially for sinistrals.

Eye preference was measured as early as the sixteenth century; a staff would be placed before the subject's eyes, and when they were both open it would be aligned with a distant object. When the subject winked with alternate eyes, the dominant eye would be found as the one which seemed to keep the staff aligned with the distant object just as when both eyes were open. A minor variation of this procedure is of course still used. The above is strictly a performance measure of which eye is preferred for sighting. Other such performance indices include acuity and rivalry. The three intercorrelate poorly, and sighting dominance may perhaps best reflect any underlying lateralization. About 70% of dextrals are right eyed, while for sinistrals the figure is a chance 50%. 'Eyedness' is of course less subject to environmental pressures than handedness. However, it is doubtful whether crossed hand/eye dominance is deleterious (see Chapter 6); certainly sighting dominance correlates no higher with language lateralization than handedness.

Ear preference can be assessed by the ear chosen to listen to a watch tick, heart beat or a transistor radio play with the volume turned down. Ear performance indices include dichotic listening (see Chapter 4) and acuity thresholds. No relationship is apparent between ear preference and acuity; there is a weak relationship between dichotic performance and ear preference. Foot preference may be measured in terms of kicking, stepping on a chair, picking up objects with the toes, bearing the weight when relaxed, or putting on the first shoe, while the actual performance scores may perhaps best be obtained for tapping and manipulating. Of the four variables, hand, foot, eye, and ear, correlations are highest between the first two, and there are suggestions that foot preference may be a more sensitive index of cognitive and motor performance than hand preference. Nevertheless asymmetries are present at birth, e.g. the stepping reflex and the asymmetric tonic neck reflex (ATNR), see Chapter 10, both of which are thought to predict later handedness and language lateralization.

Despite earlier claims to the contrary, there seem to be few consistent asymmetries in foot length, though frontoparietal lesions in one hemisphere may result in reductions in the size of the contralateral limb (see below). In dextrals, the left leg is longer and heavier, an asymmetry which increases during development; this observation, together with the fact that the right arm is longer from an early age (Peters, 1988) suggests that stance and posture during active foot use, perhaps as a consequence of ongoing *manual* activity, may be important determinants. Indeed, in many activities, foot roles are determined by what the hands are doing, as in the stance adopted while throwing. In this respect foot roles are complementary and often subordinate to hand roles. If, however, we find that foot preferences relate to hand preferences in tasks where such complementarity is unlikely, then we may argue that the lateral specialization determining foot preferences cannot reside in the machinery guiding hand preferences, but must operate at a higher level. Foot preferences, moreover, are not dissociable from *leg* preferences, unlike the situation in the upper limb where writing places more emphasis upon hand and wrist movements than is the case e.g. in throwing and kicking. In both limbs there is the problem of role differentiation; in hands, the preferred hand realizes the goal of the movement, while the other hand lends support, a situation which may be particularly salient in natural bimanual activities. The same applies with respect to foot preferences; purposeful movements of one leg or foot cannot be performed in isolation from the other. Peters recommends that we define the preferred lower limb as the one used to manipulate or to lead as in jumping, the nonpreferred limb being the one used for support and postural stability. A good test for foot preference is ball work, though it should be noted that it combines two actions, fine manipulatory skill ('dribbling') and the ballistic application of force (kicking). Dextrals tend to prefer the right leg in these tasks (though just as with hand preferences in boxing, the left footed player may have the advantage of surprise). The right foot is also preferred for lifting objects, a task which when performed during standing forces a clear division of functional roles between limbs. The right foot is also the better *performer* in lifting, maneuvering and manipulating objects; it performs better in tapping tasks, and in coordinated tapping of a simple rhythm where one foot makes one tap for every two of the other, performance is better when the right foot takes the faster beat. The same is found with hands.

HANDEDNESS

Many of us, until tested, are unaware of our own sinistrality or ambilaterality. Indeed there may even be two different kinds of motor learning, pyramidal and axial (Geschwind and Galaburda, 1985). The former is concerned with programs dealing with the distal extremities, and is essentially contralateral. Axial control relates to the musculature of the head, trunk and eyes and to coordinated limb movements; outflow may be bilateral, even though, to avoid competition, control may ultimately need to be unihemispheric. These two aspects may dissociate with respect to hemispheric lateralization, e.g. neonates who when placed on their backs turn their heads to the right but later fail to become dextral (see Chapter 10), and those of us who can write large on the blackboard with one hand (employing largely axial musculature) and small on paper with the other hand (using pyramidal systems). Indeed mixed handers may even have pure axial dominance in one hemisphere, and pure pyramidal dominance in the other.

Hand preference

Note that people often seem, perversely, to prefer to use the less skillful hand. Questionnaires are often employed to assess hand preference, though in this case it is necessarily assumed that most of us are dextral, and that the writing hand is not the only manifestation of handedness or even the best; it is of course the simplest, and nicely demonstrates bimodality, with minimal overlap between left and right handers. It has to be remembered that people can be forced to change, and there is an implicit assumption of a difference between what people do naturally and what they do because of cultural and social pressures. It is also assumed that people actually do what they say they do. Nevertheless the question is still begged as to what is the best form of questionnaire, e.g. perhaps simply one which most clearly differentiates between self-professed sinistrals and dextrals. Also, should questionnaires provide for continuous or dichotomous gradations? They should be reasonably short, they should be reliable (some common items give poor test/retest correlations) and valid, except that people do *not* always do or know what they say they do; e.g. in threading a needle is the needle brought to the thread or vice versa? Typical questionnaires include such items as drawing, throwing, use of scissors and toothbrush, and maybe striking a match, use of a knife without fork, hand used to wield a tennis racquet or to open a lid on a box or jar. Scoring may be in terms of $(R - L)/(R + L)$; this gives a range from $+1$ (very dextral) to -1 (very sinistral). Apart from reliability and validity, other problems include memory accuracy, deliberate falsification (because of interest in or rejection of one's own sinistrality), deliberate practising of the nonpreferred hand, and change through pressure. Sinistrals typically show weaker scores than dextrals, strength

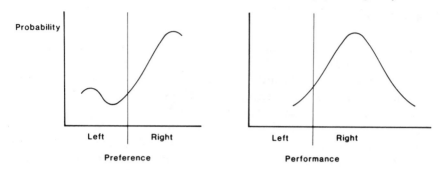

Fig. 1   Theoretical distributions of hand preference scores (mostly right, some left, few between) and hand performance scores (a normal unimodal distribution shifted to the right).

of handedness being continuously distributed, while its direction is dichotomous and bimodal; i.e. most people prefer right, fewer prefer left, while fewest of all fall between (see Figure 1, left side).

Hand performance

This was first studied by Sir Francis Galton in 1884, who assessed 7000 males at a health exhibition with hand dynamometers. Nowadays speed of moving pegs through a series of holes may be measured, or of fitting collars to pins, or other such speeded tasks are employed (see e.g. Tapley and Bryden, 1985). Such speed measures typically give a continuous distribution between left and right, i.e. one which is normal and unimodal with a rightwards shift (see Figure 1 right side). Thus most of us are moderately dextral. This distribution may in fact consist of two normally distributed sub-populations: the majority would have a population mean shifted to the right of the midpoint, while the minority (without such a rightwards shift, maybe 10 to 15% in all) would have a mean at zero. This approach, which we shall later discuss in the context of Annett's (1985) right shift model, has most sinistrals belonging to the leftwards half of the second group, though some will also fall in the far leftwards tail of the first group.

THE RELATIONSHIP BETWEEN HANDEDNESS AND CEREBRAL DOMINANCE

Clinical studies which have addressed this issue have employed unilateral ECT and amobarbital (see Chapter 2), together with examination of the effects of unilateral insult, see e.g. Bryden and MacDonald (in press), Fennell (1986)

Table 1 Handedness and lateralization of language

	Lateralization		
	Left (%)	Bilateral (%)	Right (%)
Right handers			
Carter *et al.* (1984)	99	0	1
Segalowitz and Bryden (1983)	95	0	5
Rasmussen and Milner (1977)	96	0	4
Left handers			
Carter *et al.* (1984)	23	66	11
Segalowitz and Bryden (1983)	61	20	19
Rasmussen and Milner (1977)	70	15	15

Table 2 Handedness and lateralization of visuospatial ability

	Lateralization		
	Left (%)	Bilateral (%)	Right (%)
Right handers	32	0	68
Left handers	30	32	38

(Data from Bryden and MacDonald, in press.)

and Segalowitz and Bryden (1983). (In this context, the problem with aphasia is that estimates of its incidence depend upon the number of nonaphasics included, and the latter may not present clinically after e.g. a mild stroke.) Overall, sinistrals are more likely than dextrals to suffer aphasia after *any* damage, left or right, while dextrals are the group more likely to suffer aphasia after LH damage, but are very unlikely to do so after injury to the RH; thus dextrals are the more polarized. Depending upon criteria and sources, some typical figures (percentages) for language dominance might be as shown in Table 1 (Bryden and MacDonald, in press).

For spatial abilities, lateralization is less extreme, demonstrating a lack of strict complementarity of function at the level of the individual subject, with verbal and spatial processes perhaps established semi-independently (Table 2).

Of course sex differences also enter into these figures; more males than females are sinistral or bilateral in motor terms, while the reverse is true for cognitive asymmetries. Indeed females are less likely to experience aphasia after LH injury (see Chapter 9), suggesting reduced asymmetries at the individual level.

MODELS OF HANDEDNESS

We cannot exclude the effects of environmental pressure upon change in handedness, though we must obviously seek some prior explanation for the fact that as a population we show a consistent lateral bias. Environmental pressures can involve imitation, as well as more direct action by caregivers, and tools and implements developed for a dextral world (vehicles, roads, water taps, can-openers, peelers and corkscrews) all may contribute to further polarization. Thus while sinistrality is unlikely to be imposed upon natural dextrals, the reverse is far from unlikely, especially in authoritarian settings. We have already discussed (above) age and sex effects in this context. However, the strongest argument for the position that the environmental component is far weaker than the genetic one comes from natural cross-fostering studies, where information is available about the handedness of both natural and adoptive parents.

The various genetic models are backed by a huge range of family studies, all bedevilled to various extents by such methodological problems as criteria for and validation of handedness. However, the general picture is that two sinistral parents are more likely than two dextrals to have sinistral offspring; though even then the probability barely exceeds 50%. With only one such parent, the probability is lower, though less so if the mother is the sinistral parent (suggesting the influence of extragenetic cytoplasmic factors) or if the child is female. Conversely many dextral parents have sinistral children, indicating the implausibility of any simple genetic model that e.g. argues for the determination of handedness by a single gene with two alleles, one from each parent. An example would be R (dominant) coding for dextrality, and l (recessive) coding for sinistrality; the RR dextral homozygote (perhaps also with LH language) and the ll sinistral homozygote (perhaps also with RH language) would contrast with the lR and Rl heterozygotes which should also be dextral due to dominance of the R gene. However, as we saw the homozygotes do not breed true, and if anything is under such genetic control it seems to be strength rather than direction of handedness. Indeed there is generally a poor concordance for handedness between siblings and twins; in fact both monozygotic (MZ) and dizygotic (DZ) twins show a lower concordance than fraternal siblings. The overall tendency to a higher rate of sinistrality in twins could be due to such pathological factors (associated with twinning) as intrauterine crowding and perinatal birth stress (see below). It is probably *not* due to 'mirror imaging' in twins, despite the argument that many singleton sinistrals may be the sole survivors of a twin pair, as *situs inversus* (true mirroring) is very rare, and in any case there is no higher incidence of sinistrality in MZ than in DZ twins. The raised incidence of sinistrality in all twins, and even in their parents and siblings, suggests a common hormonal explanation, e.g. fetal testosterone (see below), which indeed is more likely to be elevated with more than one fetus. Thus it is probably not the case that familial sinistrals (FS+, sinistrals with sinistral close relatives) are true genetic sinistrals, while nonfamilial sinistrals (FS−) are merely adventitiously sinistral, due to environmental factors such as early pathology. If this were the case, FS+ sinistrals should have the most anomalous brain organization, while both clinical and normal data tend to find (though there are exceptions) that *FS− individuals* are the more anomalous (due perhaps to that early pathology). Moreover if genetic factors were so important, then we might predict greater differences between FS+ and FS− *dextrals* (i.e. dextrals with or without familial sinistrality), since only FS− dextrals have absolutely *no* sinistrality, while both groups of sinistrals possess *some* sinistrality. Nevertheless there is no such strong evidence of behavioral or clinical differences between FS− and FS+ dextrals; in fact any evidence tends to point to interactions involving sex and the direction and strength of handedness (McKeever, 1986). Thus if we review major studies on the effects of handedness, familial sinistrality and sex on visual field asymmetries, there tends to be no main effect of familial sinistrality, only rather complex interactions with sex. Hormone levels may possibly act here as a moderator variable, with e.g. androgynous males (who have *intermediate* levels of testosterone) performing better than other males and females on spatial tasks. However, as most studies use less than 100 subjects, all usually drawn from an already highly selected population of students, findings may not be very secure.

Finally, given the above considerations, family size may no longer be a cause of concern in defining familial handedness. It used to be thought that a dextral with e.g. eight siblings, all dextral, was somehow more strongly or securely dextral than someone who only had one sibling anyway.

The two-gene model of Levy and Nagylaki (see Fennell, 1986) has been influential in the context of writing-hand posture. According to this account there are two relevant genes, each with a dominant and a recessive allele: one would code for language lateralization (the dominant L causing language to be lateralized to the LH, the recessive r bringing about the opposite asymmetry); the other would control whether the brain/hand relationship was contralateral (C, dominant) or ipsilateral (i, recessive). The following four combinations (CCLL, CiLL, CCLr, CiLr) would all lateralize language to the LH, with contralateral (i.e. right hand) control; the next two combinations (CCrr, Cirr) would all involve RH language with (again) contralateral (and now left hand) control; the next two (iiLL, iiLr) would all have LH language and ipsilateral (left hand) control, while the very rare double recessive iirr would involve RH language and ipsilateral (right hand) control. The authors claim that ipsilateral hand control is marked by a hooked or inverted writing posture, such that sinistral inverters employ ipsilateral pathways and are LH language dominant, while sinistral noninverters use contralateral pathways and are RH dominant, dextral noninverters use contralateral control and are LH dominant, and the (rare) dextral inverters use ipsilateral pathways and are RH language domi-

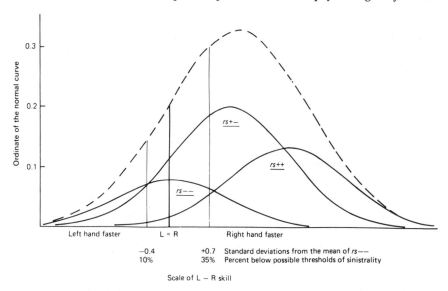

Fig. 2   Distribution of L–R skill assumed for the additive version of the right shift model proposed by M. Annett, *Left, Right, Hands and Brain: The Right Shift Theory*. London: Lawrence Erlbaum, 1985. (Figure reproduced with permission.)

nant. However, unfortunately, people again do not seem to breed true, and amobarbital (see Chapter 2) and behavioral tests fail to find the predicted patterns. Moreover there should be as many dextral inverters as sinistral inverters (there are not) unless the genes are linked, and finally the incidence of inversion in writing is heavily influenced by directionality of script, left-to-right for Western scripts and the reverse for many Eastern ones. Indeed sinistral inverters often change easily to a noninverting posture. Nevertheless it should be stressed that the genetic model could still stand, even if writing posture is not the true behavioral manifestation of hand control.

Perhaps currently the most widely accepted genetic model of handedness is that of Annett (1985), see Figure 2. She notes that the distribution of human handedness resembles the pawedness of other mammals and birds, except that it is shifted to the right, perhaps due to a byproduct of a factor inducing LH language lateralization. She invokes one gene with two alleles: $rs+$ (dominant, shift to the LH, right handed) and $rs-$ (recessive, absence of any such right shift). We thus obtain: $rs+-$ (with random mating, an expected 50% of the population; normal LH language and dextrality), $rs++$ (25%; a double dose of the 'right shift factor' which may lead to very poor performance with the nonpreferred hand, and to spatial deficits, i.e. a possibly disadvantageous situation), and finally $rs--$. This last genotype, representing 25% of the population, involves *absence* of consistent asymmetries rather than a reversal, the environment ultimately determining their direction. By chance half of these would therefore end up sinistral (i.e. 12 to 13%), a figure close to what actually occurs. Those homozygous for the *rs*− allele may be susceptible to reading disability, and those homozygous for *rs*+ may suffer from deficiencies in mathematical abilities and speeded motor skills. Thus the heterozygous *rs*+− configuration may be optimal, as well as the most common, at 50% under conditions of balanced polymorphism; this configuration may enhance the mediation of language by the LH since hand control is adjacent to speech, and both functions may receive mutual facilitation if efficiently organized within a single hemisphere. Of course such a balanced polymorphism cannot be directly linked to reading and mathematical ability, which have arisen too recently to have been operative in human evolution. Presumably other more fundamental aspects operated, perhaps in terms of advantages/disadvantages with respect to greater or lesser degrees of asymmetry. While it is possible that society benefits from the presence of the two minorities (the two homozygous groups) who might excel verbally and not spatially, and vice versa, nevertheless it is disputed whether evolution can operate at such a group level. Annett suggests that the genetic effects may operate via different rates of hemispheric maturation (and see below). The model accounts nicely for the 50% incidence of sinistrality in the offspring of two sinistral parents (though not everyone fully agrees with these figures), and for the lack of consistency (especially in sinistrals) between such indices as handedness, footedness, eyedness and earedness. However, why are not *all* the offspring of 'truly' dextral parents also dextral? Should not (according to her account) familial sinistrals (FS+) be more likely to have reversed (RH) language dominance than nonfamilial sinistrals (FS−)? As we shall see (below) we must also reserve a place for such environmental factors as birth trauma in the causation of both sinistrality and reversed dominance. Finally, the inherited presence or absence of the *rs* factor would make familial sinistrality a far more important predictor of cognitive lateralization than it currently appears. Indeed *rs*− sinistrals should have RH language lateralization 50% of the time; the figure is almost certainly smaller.

McManus (1984, 1985), like Annett, has developed a single-gene two-allele model, D (dextral) and C (chance), though now neither is dominant. Again we see a rightwards shift, together with chance influences, except that now the effects of the two alleles are additive in the heterozygote DC. Thus for the three combinations, CC, DD and DC we should find the following:

(1) CC—chance determines both handedness and language lateralization. Twenty-five percent (1/4) of individuals will be homozygous in this respect and will further break down as follows:
   (a) dextral and LH language: $1/4 \times 1/4 = 4/64$
   (b) dextral and RH language: $1/4 \times 1/4 = 4/64$
   (c) sinistral and LH language: $1/4 \times 1/4 = 4/64$

(d) sinistral and RH language: $1/4 \times 1/4 = 4/64$

(2) DD—dextral and LH language. Again 25% will be homozygous in this respect (16/64).

(3) DC—half (50%) will be heterozygous, with lateralization therefore being determined half by chance (C, i.e. 50% determination left or right) and half by D (100% dextral). If we assume a ratio of 75/25 for dextrality/sinistrality (75% is the mean of 50%−C and 100%−D), and a similar ratio for LH/RH language, and if we assume that handedness and language lateralization are statistically independent, then the heterozygote DC further breaks down as follows:

(a) dextral and
     LH language = $(3/4 \times 3/4) \times 1/2$ (as DC represents 50%) = 18/64
(b) dextral and
     RH language = $(3/4 \times 1/4) \times 1/2$ (as DC represents 50%) = 6/64
(c) sinistral and
     LH language = $(1/4 \times 3/4) \times 1/2$ (as DC represents 50%) = 6/64
(d) sinistral and
     RH language = $(1/4 \times 1/4) \times 1/2$ (as DC represents 50%) = 2/64

Combining across (1), (2) and (3) above, we obtain:

(a) dextral and
     LH language = 4/64 (CC) + 16/64 (DD) + 18/64 (DC) = 38/64
(b) dextral and
     RH language = 4/64 (CC) + 6/64 (DC) = 10/64
(c) sinistral and
     LH language = 4/64 (CC) + 6/64 (DC) = 10/64
(d) sinistral and
     RH language = 4/64 (CC) + 2/64 (DC) = 6/64

However, the full implications of this model remain to be worked out, though at first sight the incidence of dextrality with RH language seems rather high, and that of sinistrality with RH language rather low.

ENVIRONMENTAL PATHOLOGY AND LEFT HANDEDNESS

A disproportionate incidence of sinistrality has long been observed in clinical populations (see e.g. Nachshon and Denno, 1987), whether cognitively affected (e.g. retardates, stutterers, developmental dyslexics, spastics and epileptics) or suffering from affective disorders (e.g. autism, neurosis, schizophrenia, depression—maybe even criminality and excessive smoking!).

In the case of affective disorders it has been proposed (and see Chapter 2) that a damaged LH can no longer inhibit inappropriate emotional responses in the RH. Not only is the incidence of sinistrality generally higher, the worse the retardation of disability, but parents also are often sinistral, suggesting either an inherited tendency to e.g. birth stress, or the role of fetal hormones (e.g. testosterone, see below). Of course sinistrals could merely be more likely to experience birth stress (rather than the latter *causing* the former) if e.g. they are more likely to adopt an unfavorable aspect or position *in utero*.

According to Bakan (again, see Nachshon and Denno, 1987) *all* sinistrality stems from pre- or perinatal trauma. Thus its incidence should be higher in first or late born children, those born of very young or old mothers, where there have been many previously unsuccessful pregnancies, or prematurity, prolonged labor, Caesarean section, blue baby, breathing difficulties at birth, breech birth, Rhesus incompatibility, instrument birth or low birth weight, etc. (Note that not all of these risk factors originally appeared in Bakan's lists.) Sinistrality should also be increased in twins and males, who are more vulnerable at birth. However, there have been numerous nonconfirmations or at best weak or partial confirmations, especially in large well-controlled studies, and especially in the context of premature birth, prolonged labor, low birth weight and Caesarean section. There is also the problem of validation, hospital records obviously being superior to the mother's report or (worst of all) self report. The theory is 'too strong'; the evidence is not substantial and all too often sinistrals appear from normal births, and dextrals from births with many risk factors.

Satz (see e.g. Orsini and Satz, 1986, and Satz *et al.*, 1985) proffers a weaker version: some sinistrality stems from birth stress, while the rest is 'natural'. We have, therefore, two groups of left handers. The first is a small group of pathological left handers who would have been dextral except for early LH injury. They will perform very poorly with their nonpreferred (right) hand, much worse than dextrals with their left hand. Indeed Satz finds that children selected on the basis of poor performance with the nonpreferred hand are usually left handers, even though sinistrals *overall* tend to be *better* than dextrals with the nonpreferred hand. Satz's second (larger) group consists of 'natural' left handers, the result of genetic or (later) environmental factors; such individuals tend to be *better* than dextrals with the nonpreferred hand. Since in the absence of pathology more people are dextral, only a few sinistrals can become pathological dextrals (a group, incidentally, impossible for Bakan who denies the existence of 'natural' sinistrality), while many dextrals may become pathological simistrals. Moreover if pathological sinistrality is likely to lead to developmental dyslexia, then that condition should be common among sinistrals (and see Chapter 6). Indeed the LH is thought to be more susceptible to neonatal anoxia, especially in the fronto-parieto-temporal speech zones, because of morphological asymmetries in the distribution of blood supplies, and *in utero* the fetal LH is more vulnerable to pressure from the left sacral promontory of the mother. Satz suggests that clinical effects may be apparent even in those without overt evidence of pathology, and notes that cognitive and speech impairments are commoner in sinistrals with abnormally poor right hand performance. Thus a good index of *covert* brain impairment may be abnormally poor performance by the nonpreferred hand. Satz therefore nominates the following risk factors: a shift in manual dominance, motor impairment of nonpreferred hand, trophic changes in the extremities due to postcentral gyrus damage around birth (e.g. hypoplasia of right upper or lower extremities, including hand, foot, fingers and nails), transfer of language dominance to the RH, a resultant (due to 'crowding', see below) detriment, perhaps, of visuospatial functions, relatively preserved verbal functions, and a low probability of familial sinistrality. Thus we may find impaired left hand performance due to effects of a *functional* lesion (i.e. reorganization and 'crowding' of language functions into the RH), together with impaired right hand performance due to the effects of early structural damage to the LH. The relative sparing of speech and language functions in individuals with early LH injury suggests that such (partial) sparing may occur primarily via displacement and/or reorganization of language functions into the RH. (Satz claims that this 'crowding' effect occurs only with pathological sinistrality; others have invoked it even for 'normal' sinistrality. We shall see, below, that many sinistrals even demonstrate *superior* rather than inferior RH capacities.) Such considerations suggest that FS− sinistrals should be the anomalous performers in cognitive tasks, i.e. FS− sinistrals with early pathology, rather than FS+ sinistrals without such pathology, or sinistrals with pathology after about six years, or dextrals with early brain damage. There is some experimental evidence in support of such a view. However, as Bishop (1983) has pointed out, the kind of picture you get concerning ability, handedness and perinatal brain injury is very dependent upon your statistical approach, and far smaller sample sizes may suffice if the selection is based on e.g. comparing equal numbers of those with and without evidence of early insult, rather than comparing equal numbers of different handedness groups. Moreover Satz has not always been able to confirm his own predictions; thus sometimes verbal as well as performance scores have been decremented, though with unimpaired fluency, and right foot hypoplasia may be more evident than that of the hand. This last observation may perhaps apply because a larger cortical area is devoted to hands as compared to feet, and therefore only a small brain lesion may suffice for generating foot asymmetries. If so, it might be profitable to develop *performance* measures of foot asymmetry as possibly more sensitive indices of cognitive and motor performance than the current hand measures. Generally, studies show worse language deficits with later trauma, while early LH injury may lead to sinistrality and relatively unimpaired, though RH, language. Thus age at injury may be no less important than its severity; late lesions, when dextrality and language dominance in the LH are reasonably established, may lead to weak sinistrality, ambilaterality, language deficits but maintenance of language in the LH due to inadequate cerebral reorganization.

THE COGNITIVE CROWDING HYPOTHESIS

Independent of any pathological influences, is it possible that when language 'invades' the RH, it 'crowds out' that hemisphere's processing capacity for spatial functions, to their detriment (Levy, 1974)? The problem is that the data are very confused on whether sinistrals exhibit a language, spatial or overall deficit, or maybe are even superior in certain spatial or mathematical skills. The resolution may be to appeal to a bimodality of function with over-representation of sinistrals at each end of the spatial-ability continuum, to account for the disproportionate incidence of sinistrality among top mathematicians, architects and sports personalities, while 'average' sinistrals may tend to score rather lower on spatial skills. Note, however, that an excess of sinistrality at the two ends of the distribution of spatial ability, with a mean spatial score the same for both dextrals and sinistrals, would nevertheless still favor sinistrals, since competitive success depends primarily upon top scorers; the bottom-end tends not to count. Other factors probably relevant to the sinistrality/ability debate are strength of handedness, sex, age or rate of maturation (though see Chapter 10), and, possibly, familial aspects. It should be remembered that while females are less lateralized cognitively than males (see Chapter 9) like sinistrals, they are, unlike sinistrals, more lateralized in motor terms. Another problem for the cognitive crowding hypothesis is that while reduced lateralization (e.g. in sinistrals) could lead to a spatial deficit if language invades RH processing space, why then is not language ability correspondingly enhanced? The conventional picture is, of course, of a language decrement, as if *spatial* functions have invaded language space in the LH. Of course there are probably several types of sinistral, as we have already seen, and it would be foolish to seek a single explanation to cover all cases. An intriguing observation, though one which has been disputed (see Chapter 3) is that both females and sinistrals tend to have thicker tracts in certain regions of the corpus callosum. Whether these observations, if ultimately verified, relate in a causal way to cognitive abilities, and if so in what direction the causation may lie, is for the future to tell us.

DEVELOPMENTAL GRADIENT MODELS

According to Corballis and Morgan (1978) living systems may be subject to a left-to-right maturational gradient. The genes themselves are left–right agnosic and code the degree rather than the direction of any asymmetry, which may be expressed via nongenetic mechanisms. Dextrality and LH language would then stem from this maturational gradient, which will usually favor an earlier- or faster-developing left side; a switch will occur if this side (here equated with *hemisphere*) is damaged or restricted via environmental pressures or early pathology. Such factors may especially affect those who inherit weak expressions of asymmetry, e.g. Annett's *rs−* individuals. Since, according to this model, handedness develops later than language lateralization, sinistrals will continue to be more commonly language dominant in the LH rather than the RH. Maternal handedness may be more important than paternal, via nongenetic or cytoplasmic influences in the maternal oocyte. Unfortunately, evidence in favor of the hypothesis is at best controversial.

Geschwind and Galaburda (1985) have attempted to address possible mechanisms, and their equally controversial but thoroughly testable theory seeks, as in modern medical science, to avoid single-factor explanations. It tries to account for a number of intriguing observations, some of which we have of course already encountered: lateralization is often anomalous in developmental disorders of childhood; there is a raised incidence of such disorders (developmental dyslexia, stuttering, autism) among males; there is a raised incidence of sinistrality among males; males are better than females in spatial processing and worse in language skills; sinistrals (of either sex) and developmental dyslexics often exhibit superior spatial skills, there being more mathematicians and architects than expected; there is a raised incidence of immune disorders (migraine, allergies, thyroid and gastrointestinal disorders) among abnormally lateralized individuals, and those of high spatial ability. Hormones, especially fetal testosterone, are invoked as an intervening variable between genotype and phenotype; this permits operation of environmental factors, and avoids rigid, inflexible, genetic predispositions. The RH is said to develop earlier in the fetus, and to show reduced cell death, due to the action of fetal testosterone in slowing down the growth of parts of the LH. (In consequence, the RH, and the *rest* of the LH, will speed up, in competitive compensation, as may be observed with artificial lesions.) An alternative formulation is that slower maturation of the LH will result in it being vulnerable, for a longer period, to the deleterious effects of testosterone or any other environmental influence. While this idea is contrary to Corballis' proposal that the *LH* matures earlier, it may be noted that recent entirely independent evidence (see Thatcher, Walker and Giudice, 1987) does indicate differential rates of hemispheric maturation. It is also noteworthy that in a very recent reappraisal, Galaburda *et al.* (1987) conclude that changes away from a (usually leftward) asymmetry of the planum temporale involve an *increase* in the size of the *smaller* (i.e. usually right) side, rather than a *decrease* in the size of the *larger* (usually left) side. Thus brains which are symmetrical have two large plana, each equal in area to the larger planum of asymmetrical brains. The authors argue that testosterone, if it modifies brain asymmetry, must act not by slowing down one side (e.g. the left) and allowing the other (right) side to grow, but must instead directly promote growth of the smaller right side. Whether, however, testosterone retards growth of the left hemisphere, or enhances that of the right, Geschwind and Galaburda claim to find frequent evidence of anomalies in the LH language areas of developmental dyslexics. In some respects the model is a kind of mirror image of that proposed by Annett (above); she suggests an initial symmetry, with a genetically imposed shift to asymmetry. The present account proposes an initial asymmetry (i.e. LH dominance) with subsequent hormonal (not genetic) influences producing a shift towards increasing symmetry, via retardation of LH growth, or enhanced growth in the RH. Moreover only Geschwind, not Annett, can explain why sinistrality is more common in males; it is due to testosterone. Why is there an initial LH dominance? Geschwind and Galaburda, like Corballis, propose initial cytoplasmic asymmetries in the maternal oocyte, and note the closer relationship in lateralization between offspring and mother than between offspring and father; moreover the mother rather than the father seems to be at risk for producing offspring with defects of the neural tube. The most controversial aspect is the question of immune dysfunction. However, the patterns of disease which involve immune dysfunction do seem to be linked to sex and age. Many details remain to be verified, and the model cannot easily explain why males are cognitively and cerebrally more lateralized than females, and why the LH still usually ends up bigger. Nevertheless there is much independent evidence (see Chapter 1) from studies of rats and birds that testosterone affects the central nervous system. Moreover further strong support, which is circumstantial and independent, comes from Benbow's (1987, 1988) studies of mathematical genius in left handers. She has surveyed more than 100 000 twelve year old children taking the Scholarship Aptitude Test in the United States. She finds that the better the mathematical ability the more the boys outnumber the girls: 2 : 1 in the top 3% achievers; 4 : 1 in the top 0.5% and 13 : 1 in the top 0.2%. Similar findings have now been reported in Hamburg and Shanghai. She claims that social conditioning, enjoyment, encouragement or toy preferences cannot have acted to determine such specific effects. However, biology does seem to be relevant, as the top maths scorers also scored highly on allergies, sinistrality and (inexplicably, as yet) myopia. The first two observations of course nicely fit the testosterone theory. Further evidence has emerged that allergies and sinistrality are over-represented among those scoring extremely highly on *verbal* reasoning; however, as we saw (Chapter 6) verbal *reasoning* may closely involve the RH. It is possible that a brain organization which is heterogeneous, nonfocal and relatively symmetric may lead to a combination of superior spatial and verbal reasoning ability. However, one problem is why females, who traditionally exhibit reduced cognitive (though not motor) lateralization of this sort, are the *lower* maths scorers. Moreover such reduced cognitive lateralization in females is traditionally associated with superior verbal and inferior mathematical–spatial performance. Any relationship between degree of lateralization, sex, and either kind of cognitive performance would therefore appear to be complex and not solely in terms e.g. of testosterone levels (see Chapter 9). Indeed one possible, if trivial, reason for an apparent increase in sinistrality in mathematically and verbally precocious children is that teachers may not try to change handedness in such obviously able individuals, but may only be tempted to do so with their less fortunate peers (Searleman, in Commentary to Benbow, 1988). Nevertheless it does seem that these high scorers tended to have been conceived more frequently during months with the longest hours of daylight. Melatonin secretion is known to be affected by day length, and in turn affects reproductive hormones. Moreover these high scorers were more likely to be first born (a factor which we earlier considered in the context of potential perinatal birth stress), and as such would tend to be exposed to higher levels of progesterone. This hormone, *in utero*, has previously been linked with enhanced numerical ability.

SUMMARY AND CONCLUSIONS

Sinistrals have always been a suspect minority, with over-representation among both the least and the most able, with frequent pre-eminence in spatial and mathematical abilities, and their ratio to dextrals has varied little over the millenia. Asymmetries are strongest for handedness, which is studied because of its presumed correlation with language lateralization, and less so for footedness, eyedness and earedness. Hand preference, which is subject to environmental pressures including those of a right-handed world, though the biological contribution is stronger, may be assessed by questionnaire; the bimodal distribution results. Performance measures typically produce a continuous normal distribution which perhaps consists of two components, one of which (the larger) has a mean shifted to the right (and may involve heritable factors), while the other smaller distribution has a mean centred at zero (and may reflect chance environmental influences). With respect to language lateralization, both sinistrals and (*especially*) dextrals typically display LH dominance; dextrals are also more lateralized for visuospatial abilities, though these effects are weaker.

No simple genetic model can account for all the known facts, and neither dextrals nor sinistrals breed true. Nor does knowledge of familial dextrality/sinistrality have much predictive power with respect to cognitive asymmetries or abilities, though extreme dextrality may possibly be disadvantageous and nonfamilial sinistrals may exhibit the more anomalous performance. On the other hand neither is perinatal birth trauma a major determinant of left handedness, though certain aspects probably do bring about a condition of pathological left handedness. Such individuals may perform unusually poorly with their nonpreferred hand, and exhibit trophic changes to their (right) extremities, together with RH language, to the possible detriment of both verbal and spatial functions, due to 'crowding'. The raised incidence of sinistrality among twins, and their *families*, and an indication that a tendency towards what previously has been labelled 'birth stress' may be inherited, suggests a hormonal involvement. Fetal testosterone (which may possibly retard LH and promote RH growth) has been implicated in sinistrality, developmental learning disorders, and the raised incidence of sinistrality (and male sex) in such disorders. It has also been implicated in the raised incidence of immune dysfunction in sinistrals and developmental dyslexics, and in those who exhibit abnormally high spatial and mathematical skills, who also tend to be male and sinistral far more often than otherwise would be expected. This currently contested hypothesis has the virtue of offering many testable predictions.

IMPORTANT READINGS

Annett, M. *Left, Right, Hand and Brain: The Right Shift Theory*. Hillsdale, N.J.: Erlbaum, 1985.

Benbow, C. P. Possible biological correlates of precocious mathematical reasoning ability. *Trends in the Neurosciences*, 1987, **10**, 17–20.

Benbow, C. P. Sex differences in mathematical reasoning ability in intellectually talented preadolescents: Their nature, effects and possible causes. *Behavioral and Brain Sciences*, 1988, **11**, 169–232.

Bishop, D. V. M. How sinister is sinistrality? *Journal of the Royal College of Physicians of London*, 1983, **17**, 161–72.

Bryden, M. P. and MacDonald, V. The measurement of handedness and its relationship to neuropsychological issues. In R. S. Dean and C. R. Reynolds (eds.), *Assessment of Laterality: Issues, Techniques, Implications*. New York: Plenum Press, in press.

Corballis, M. C. and Morgan, M. J. On the biological basis of human laterality: 1. Evidence for a maturational left-right gradient. *Behavioral and Brain Sciences*, 1978, **1**, 261–9.

Fennell, E. B. Handedness in neuropsychological research. In H. J. Hannay (ed.), *Experimental Techniques in Human Research*. New York: Oxford University Press, 1986, pp. 15–44.

Galaburda, A. M., Corsiglia, J., Rosen, G. D. and Sherman, G. F. Planum temporale asymmetry, reappraisal since Geschwind and Levitsky. *Neuropsychologia*, 1987, **25**, 853–68.

Geschwind, N. and Galaburda, A. M. Cerebral lateralization: Biological mechanisms, associations and pathology I–III: A hypothesis and program for research. *Archives of Neurology*, 1985, **42**, 428–59, 521–52, 634–54.

Levy, J. Psychobiological implications of bilateral asymmetry. In S. J. Dimond and G. Beaumont (eds.), *Hemisphere Function in the Human Brain*. London: Elek Science, 1974, pp. 121–83.

McKeever, W. F. Influences of handedness, sex, familial sinistrality and androgyny on language laterality, verbal ability and spatial ability. *Cortex,* 1986, **22**, 521–37.

McManus, I. C. Genetics of handedness in relation to language disorder. In F. C. Rose (ed.), *Advances in Neurology, Vol. 42: Progress in Aphasiology.* New York: Raven Press, 1984, pp. 125–38.

McManus, I. C. Handedness, language dominance and aphasia: A genetic model. *Psychological Medicine Monograph Supplements,* 1985, whole No. 8, 1–40.

Nachshon, I. and Denno, D. Birth stress and lateral preferences. *Cortex,* 1987, **23**, 45–58.

Orsini, D. L. and Satz, P. A syndrome of pathological left handedness: Correlates of early left hemisphere injury. *Archives of Neurology,* 1986, **43**, 333–7.

Peters, M. Footedness: Asymmetries in foot preference and skill, and neuropsychological assessment of foot movement. *Psychological Bulletin,* 1988, **103**, 179–92.

Porac, C. and Coren, S. *Lateral Preferences and Human Behavior.* New York: Springer-Verlag, 1981.

Satz, P., Orsini, D. L., Saslow, E. and Henry, R. Early brain injury and pathological left handedness: Clues to a syndrome. In D. F. Benson and E. Zaidel (eds.), *The Dual Brain: Hemispheric Specialization in Humans.* New York: Guilford, 1985, pp. 117–25.

Segalowitz, S. J. and Bryden, M. P. Individual differences in hemispheric representation of language. In S. J. Segalowitz (ed.), *Language Functions and Brain Organization,* New York: Academic Press, 1983, pp. 341–72.

Tapley, C. M. and Bryden, M. P. A group test for the assessment of performance between hands. *Neuropsychologia,* 1985, **23**, 215–21.

Thatcher, R. W., Walker, R. A. and Giudice, S. Human cerebral hemispheres develop at different rates and ages. *Science,* 1987, **236**, 1110–13.

9

Sex differences

The external differences between the sexes are obvious. Women moreover tend to be somewhat shorter than men, and (at least in the first few decades of adult life) to possess a somewhat higher fat to lean-mass ratio. While they are generally not quite as strong as men, they may possess greater endurance, and they tend to live longer. Such a sexual dimorphism, occasioned genetically both directly and indirectly via hormonal mediation, may even extend to cognitive abilities and indeed biologically it would perhaps be strange if the different reproductive roles had not in some way influenced the evolution of brain function in men and women. As we saw in Chapter 1, this certainly seems to be the case with many species of bird, and the rat. Some of the apparent cognitive differences between men and women may relate to differences in hemispheric specialization. The latter may have a genetic origin, or may be under hormonal control (and thus in principle modifiable), or may be a more direct consequence of environmental forces, social pressures or adopted strategies. Indeed all three levels may differentially affect different aspects of hemispheric specialization; thus depending on task, experience and individual constitution, different patterns of cognitive ability and lateral asymmetry may be revealed. This chapter examines the nature of possible relationships between sex, cognitive ability, brain and behavioral lateralization.

Handedness and sex have been linked since antiquity. We can see this in the Pythagorean Table of Opposites, which actually predates the days of classical Greece. A mixture of numerology, number magic, mysticism and prehistoric mythology, it links 'left' with 'female', 'cold', 'dark', 'wet', 'crooked' and other pejoratives; while 'right' is linked to 'male' which in turn is characterized by an abundance of the superior element fire, which has the qualities hot and dry. The superiority of male over female is matched by the superiority of right over left, and if we assume that the right side of the body is hotter than the left, we arrive at a consistent theory of sex determination (Mittwoch, 1985), though the fine details may vary. Thus according to Parmenides, a child's sex is determined by its position, left or right, in the maternal womb, while Anaxagoras invoked the left or right testicle of the father, as the source of semen. Aristotle criticized both these theories on valid experimental grounds, though of course Anaxagoras was correct in that the father determines the child's sex. These beliefs persisted, with potential fathers tying off one or other testicle so as to 'determine' their child's sex, and pregnant mothers with an enlarged left breast were believed to be carrying a girl. Of course infants conceived at certain times of the female cycle do exhibit slightly different sex ratios, and while temperature does covary with cycle time, acidity changes in the cervix probably differentially affect the X or Y chromosomes carried by the sperm. Indeed, alligators and some other reptiles lack sex chromosomes; as incubation proceeds, the temperature in the nest determines the sex of the embryo. If the nest is cool, females result, while males predominate if the warmth of the nest exceeds a critical level.

HORMONAL EFFECTS

It has long been known that the sexes differ in physiology, aptitudes, abilities and temperament, but only recently have hormonal roles, throughout life, been studied. The hypothalamus releases luteinizing hormone releasing hormone (LHRH), which stimulates the pituitary to release gonadotrophins. These include follicle stimulating hormone (FSH) and luteinizing hormone (LH) which target gonads in either sex. Thus testosterone is produced in males, and estrogen in females, which feed back upon the hypothalamus and other brain targets. Three factors may therefore be involved in sex differences in cognition: the constitution of the sex chromosomes, the hormonal milieu during development (including fetal life and puberty), and finally existing hormones at time of testing, including even the stage of the female menstrual cycle.

The basic ground plan of the brain and body is female, unless male hormones make an early appearance. Hormones may have some or all of the following effects: they may differentially allocate total brain capacity (regardless of hemisphere) to the same abilities, e.g. spatial abilities may be given more processing space in males, and verbal abilities in females; they may establish differential hemispheric specialization between the sexes, with perhaps some functions more asymmetrically organized in males, and others in females; finally they may differentially activate cognitive strategies in the two sexes, even though the brain structures themselves are essentially similar. Indeed the brain may develop in either a generally male or female direction, depending upon the gonadal hormonal environment during critical stages of early maturation (Gordon and Lee, 1986; Hines and Gorski, 1985). If the fetus is treated with testosterone, both brain and genitalia can be masculinized. While hormonal differences are stronger at puberty, their actual effect, strangely, is weaker and more transient. Evidence from birds and rats indicates that hormonal effects on the brain may involve synapses, length and position of dendrites, and maybe even neuronal densities.

Generally, like handedness, sex differences are continuous rather than dichotomous, and may even partly depend upon uterine position. Thus a female fetus in a position to receive blood after it has contacted male siblings may be masculinized by the contained androgens; there is certainly evidence for this situation in nonhuman species. Moreover male fetal gonads produce very high testosterone levels in early stages, comparable to later adult levels, though they may drop before birth. The female fetus is also exposed to testosterone from the maternal ovaries and adrenals, and to estradiol. The latter, a breakdown product of maternal testosterone, has many effects (neural and behavioral, though not physiological) which are similar to testosterone. Finally the female fetus is also exposed to progesterone, which too can have a masculinizing effect.

COGNITIVE ABILITIES

Quite a number of cognitive effects may result from the influence of sex hormones, according to McKeever (1986, see also Gordon and Lee, 1986, and Kimura, 1987). High levels of female sex hormones may enhance verbal and sequential abilities, and the capacity to perform fine motor skills, relative to visuospatial capacities; the reverse may occur with low concentrations, again indicating the desirability of optimal (mid) levels, either for any one hormone, or for a balance between estrogen and androgen. Indeed excessively high androgenization in males may even lead to poor spatial scores, while a high level in females may lead to the good scores characteristic of normal males; low levels in females, conversely, may be associated with poor spatial scores. Women exposed prenatally to diethylstilbestrol (DES, an estrogen which, however, has a masculinizing effect on brain development) may give the large dichotic REAs which are characteristic of males, together with the male pattern of better spatial than verbal abilities. Follicle stimulating hormone (FSH) levels correlate negatively with visuospatial ability and positively with verbal ability, while luteinizing hormone (LH) levels correlate positively with verbal and sequential ability, and certain spatial capacities; testosterone levels correlate positively with other spatial abilities. Generally, mathematical and spatial abilities on the one hand, and verbal fluency on the other, vary reciprocally during the menstrual cycle, as a function of hormone levels. Moreover, postmenopausal women receiving estrogen therapy perform fine motor skills better on the days that they receive treatment. Estrogen and testosterone therefore, not only affect brain development before and after birth but may also affect brain function throughout life.

Waber (1985) originally hypothesized that delayed puberty correlates with poor verbal and good spatial abilities, with the reverse occurring when puberty is precocious. Thus she claimed that age at puberty is more important than gender, and that sex differences are absent if boys and girls are matched for levels of sexual maturation; otherwise, slow maturers will be better spatially than verbally, differing from early maturers only on spatial, not on verbal abilities. She suggested that slow maturation allows more time for language lateralization to develop (though, see Chapter 10, it probably does *not* develop); spatial skills would thus be enhanced if language develops first, itself a questionable assumption. Greater asymmetries would result from a longer opportunity for language to develop exclusively in the earlier-maturing LH (another questionable assumption), without encroaching upon RH functions, though at the cost of a longer period of potential vulnerability. Thus as observed by Vrbancic and Mosley (1988), there are in fact three facets to the Waber hypothesis.

(1) Spatial ability relates to rate of physical growth at adolescence, with late maturers possessing better spatial abilities than early maturers. There is some but not a great deal of independent experimental support for such an association between maturation rate and spatial ability, though it should be noted that many studies have used individuals with extremely early or late or otherwise aberrant puberty onset, due to endocrinological dysfunction.

(2) Late maturers possess greater hemispheric specialization (though it should be noted that usually only *verbal* lateralization has been assessed). Thus lateralization is seen as (probably erroneously) developing, and being halted by puberty, unless there is some characteristic of late maturation which is somehow otherwise associated with the possession of more pronounced hemispheric specialization. There *are* reports (see Chapter 10) of age-specific changes on some laterality tasks, e.g. face processing in a piecemeal or global manner, during early adolescence. Thus hemispheric specialization could be present during childhood but disrupted or altered at puberty during reorganization of cerebral and cognitive functions. Lateralization would therefore be associated with pubertal *status*, rather than pubertal *rate*, as indeed Vrbancic and Mosley (1988) found.

(3) There is a relationship between hemispheric specialization and spatial ability, with individuals who possess greater hemispheric specialization having the better spatial abilities. This argument stems from a greater LH specialization for *language* functions resulting thereby in less encroachment of such functions upon RH spatial processing capacities. Alter-

natively, it could of course be argued that *reduced* RH specialization for *spatial* abilities (i.e. more bilateralization) would permit more processing capacity, and better spatial abilities, if the LH can also participate. In any case, LH specialization for language functions and RH specialization for spatial functions may not necessarily be linked or 'complementary' (see Chapter 5)—and as observed above, usually only *verbal* asymmetries have been dichotically assessed. Indeed hemispheric specialization for LH and RH functions may differ with respect to spatial and verbal abilities, to maturation rate and to maturational status.

Waber's hypothesis, at least in its original form linking cognitive ability and maturation rate, maturation rate and hemispheric specialization, and hemispheric specialization and cognitive ability, does not therefore receive much current empirical support, unless perhaps extra-biological factors are appealed to. Thus early and late maturers may have been exposed to different modes of socialization; moreover small pre-existing biological differences (see Figure 1) could be magnified by experience, social reinforcement or self-selection of activities, leading to strategy differences in the way tasks are approached by the two sexes. We shall return to this below.

We should perhaps consider chromosomal abnormalities in this context (see e.g. Netley and Rovet, 1983). Some baby boys, suffering from Klinefelter's syndrome, have an XXY sex chromosomal pattern instead of the usual XY, i.e. an extra X chromosome. Though phenotypically male at birth, at puberty they develop breasts. Likewise in Turner's syndrome (XO) some baby girls are missing an X, suggesting that the presence/absence of the Y chromosome determines gender, the actual number of X chromosomes being irrelevant at least in this context. It has been reported in Turner's syndrome that there are reduced or reversed dichotic asymmetries, a normal verbal performance, and poor spatial performance. With Klinefelter's syndrome (XXY) the opposite situation generally obtains, poor verbal and normal spatial performance, with smaller asymmetries on LH tasks and larger ones on RH tasks than normal controls. This might suggest a failure of the LH to gain dominance over the RH in language processing, and a greater involvement of the RH than normal in both verbal and nonverbal processing. Thus the RH might inefficiently assume the LH's normal language functions and exaggeratedly participate in nonverbal processing, perhaps due to slower fetal growth rates as a consequence of an extra X chromosome. (The absence in these syndromes of a correlation between hormone levels and enhanced RH processing seems once again to indicate a role for growth-related events, though now perhaps more at a prenatal level, in determining patterns of lateralization, and cf. Geschwind's developmental gradient hypothesis, discussed in Chapter 8). The abnormal presence or absence of an X chromosome may therefore affect the development of either verbal or nonverbal abilities, though it should be noted that

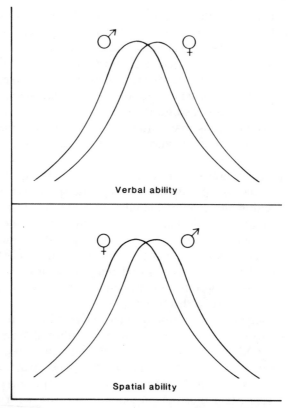

Fig. 1   Though the differences are usually very small and 'statistical', i.e. only apparent when very large samples are compared, females tend to outperform males in certain verbal abilities, while the reverse may be true for certain spatial abilities.

other supernumerary chromosomal conditions (XYY and XXX) also seem to be associated with lower overall functioning, especially verbal. In any case it does not seem possible to identify a completely consistent relationship between the presence and number of X and Y chromosomes, hormonal levels, and verbal and spatial abilities, though growth rates may act as an intervening variable. Indeed the general hypothesis of an X linked recessive gene for high spatial ability, of the kind traditionally held to favor males, and often believed to be transmissible in e.g. certain families of gifted mathematicians, is itself refutable if father–son transmission is discovered. This is the case because sons only receive their Y chromosome from their fathers, and their X chromosome comes instead from the mother.

Sexually dimorphic behaviors, therefore, are not simply reproductive; they also include social play, differences in activity levels and maze performance, active and passive avoidance learning, taste preferences, aggression, lateralization patterns, and of course verbal and spatial abilities (Browne, 1983; Halpern, 1986; Linn and Petersen, 1985; McGlone, 1986; Segalowitz and Bryden, 1983; Signorella and Jamison, 1986). Nevertheless differences between normal males and females tend to be small and often merely statistical. The fact that such sex differences in cognitive abilities appear in infancy suggests that they are unlikely to be purely experiential, though the fact that they may further change around puberty suggests the possibility of further hormonal or experiential factors. Girls typically learn to speak earlier, and have bigger vocabularies and greater fluency of expression; their incidence of stuttering, autism, developmental dyslexia and delayed speech is a quarter that of boys, and they also show greater manual dexterity and perceptual speed. Boys on the other hand explore more, and talk, socialize and tell stories less. They perform somewhat better on mazes, picture assembly, block design and mechanical skills, and at disembedding figures, and aligning rods to the gravitational vertical. In mathematics and chess (there are *only* grand 'masters') the differences in favor of boys can be very much greater. While huge sex differences in medical, engineering and legal studies have been largely eliminated within one generation of social change, social factors do not seem to account for sex differences in mathematics and chess. However, few can agree on how to clarify these nonverbal sex differences (Browne, 1983). One way is in terms of four kinds of test: visualization, orientation, directional sense and Piagetian conservation. Visualization tests assess the ability to perform mental manipulation and rotation of images, and the ability to appreciate the relative changes which result, e.g. topology, geometry, constructing and rotating three-dimensional images from two-dimensional representations. Orientation tests, however, now place the observer into the scene as a part thereof, as a reference point for objects in space. Thus in the rod and frame test a luminous rod is to be adjusted to the true vertical in a frame which is possibly tilted. With respect to directional sense, the subject decides whether a represented body part (hand or foot perhaps) is left or right; in the road-map test of directional sense, the subject memorizes a schematic map and describes a standard route from memory. Mazes may also be used. Finally, in Piagetian conservation tests, subjects draw the correct liquid surface on pictures of tilted containers, or undertake tests of conservation of mass, volume, length, number or area. Males generally outperform females in all of these tests, though there is considerable disagreement on details, and of the effects of age, strategies and experience.

LATERALITY DIFFERENCES

Do these sex differences in cognitive abilities (males: spatial, females: verbal) reflect asymmetries (RH: spatial, LH: verbal)? Do both relate to sex dif-

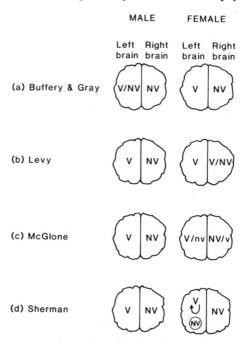

Fig. 2   Possible models of the distribution of verbal (V) and nonverbal (NV) abilities in
the two sides of the male and female brain (see text; figure redrawn, with permission,
from J. Inglis and J. S. Lawson, Sex, intelligence and the brain. *Queens Quarterly*, 1984,
91, 37–54.)

ferences in strength of lateralization, e.g. are males more lateralized in
cognitive terms, and less so with respect to motor aspects (see e.g. McGlone,
1986)? Note first, however, that these effects are small and often are of
marginal significance, though no studies show e.g. *bigger* REAs in females. It is
also difficult to seek lines of causation among three-way correlations, sex
versus lateralization, sex versus cognitive abilities, and cognitive abilities
versus lateralization. There is the question whether strength or direction of
cognitive lateralization is the more important variable, just as is the case with
handedness (see Chapter 8). In some respects, indeed, females and sinistrals go
together (just as in the Pythagorean Table of Opposites): both have tendencies
to cognitive *bilaterality*, though they certainly do not resemble each other in
cognitive *ability*. Finally, note that the possible effects of strategies should not
be underrated. Thus females using inappropriate verbal strategies in spatial
tasks may in consequence show both poor spatial performance and apparent
reductions in asymmetry, even though the use of strategies could itself stem
from pre-existing biological differences between the sexes.

A number of models have been proposed to describe and account for sex differences in lateralization (Figure 2, and see McGlone, 1986). According to that of Buffery and Grey, females are *more* lateralized for nonverbal functions than males (who possess an additional nonverbal component in their left, verbal hemispheres), because of an earlier establishment in them of language dominance in the LH. (However, as we shall see in Chapter 10, dominance probably does not develop.) Females, furthermore, are said by Buffery and Gray for this reason to possess more verbal and less nonverbal capacity. However, adult females are generally thought to be less rather than more lateralized, though see below. Indeed Levy adopts just this position: language is less lateralized in females, who are therefore spatially disadvantaged, as verbal functions encroach (i.e. 'crowd', see Chapter 8) on the spatial processing capacities of the RH. Of course sinistrals also should therefore be spatially disadvantaged; some of course may be, but as we saw, many are spatially *superior*. McGlone instead proposes that females possess some extra, minor nonverbal mechanisms in the LH, and likewise some additional verbal mechanisms in the RH; this 'double dose' of language apparently helps them, though it is not clear why the same is not true of spatial functions, or indeed, why the invasion of some spatial functions into the verbal LH does not cancel the verbal advantage of extra language representation in the RH. Sherman's pattern for males (a neat dichotomization of LH verbal, RH spatial) agrees with that of McGlone and of Levy for males. However, for females, strategies are now invoked as an intervening variable. Female verbal precocity leads to a preference for verbal strategies which involve the LH, even for inefficiently solving nonverbal 'RH' problems; hence a nonverbal deficiency occurs in females, who nevertheless are helped verbally by their reliance upon verbal processing strategies.

Lesion data seem generally to support the idea of greater hemispheric specialization among males, while for females LH lesions typically lead to both verbal and nonverbal deficits; this would eliminate Levy's model and support that of Sherman, especially since RH damage in females may have little or no verbal effect, just as happens with males. Kimura (1987), however, disputes such considerations. She notes that the relative decrement in Performance IQ after RH (compared to LH) damage is *not* greater in males than in females, and that females, just like males, have a very low incidence of aphasia after RH damage. While females do indeed suffer less aphasia than males after LH damage, she argues that this does not necessarily imply that female brains are less asymmetric, since in females aphasia is far commoner after anterior (motor) lesions of the LH than after posterior damage; in males the situation is said to slightly reverse. (Fresh data compatible with such a view are reported by Vignolo *et al.*, 1986.) Consequently, in what is almost a reversal to the Buffery and Gray position, she argues that speech and manual praxis are more focally represented in females, and that anterior regions of the LH are especially important for that sex; in males, speech representation is rather more diffuse,

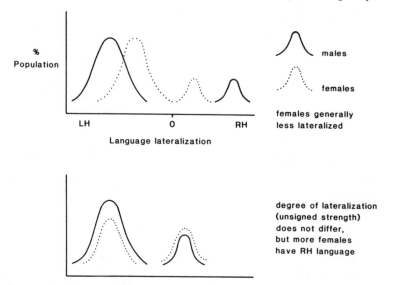

Fig. 3 Are females generally less lateralized than males, irrespective of the direction of asymmetries at the level of individual subjects, or do more females (than males) show a reverse pattern of lateralization, without differing from males in the degree of lateralization? (Figure suggested by M. P. Bryden)

perhaps with a slight posterior emphasis, a conclusion for whose support she cites electrophysiological evidence. She therefore puts down the lower incidence of aphasia in females after LH damage to this greater concentration of language in the anterior regions of the LH. Since vascular accidents causing restricted damage tend to affect posterior regions more than anterior, thus avoiding the critical anterior regions in females, women *appear* to be less affected in speech and praxis by LH damage. However, the absence of an increased incidence of aphasia (and apraxia) after RH damage in females, indicates that they are not in fact less lateralized than males. Of course the (rarer) aphasia in females should be severer, as it will have involved a more vital focal area. As yet there is no evidence for this. While Kimura could explain differences in dichotic and tachistoscopic asymmetries between the sexes in terms of strategies, she notes that such studies, being perceptual, will address largely *posterior* regions; consequently asymmetries in males may appear larger if (in males) the posterior regions are more important. Otherwise evidence (see Chapter 8) that in *motor* aspects, like handedness, females are more lateralized, fits in with her thesis that language and praxis are more focally represented anteriorly in females. Of course while Kimura's hypothesis may be attractive, it should be noted that as yet it is by no means secure, and a more focal representation of language in the female LH might be expected to lead to *reduced* language competence in that sex, compared to males.

In the context of normal subjects' cognitive asymmetries, we must ask whether the apparently reduced degree of female asymmetry is present at the level of individual subjects (i.e. irrespective of the *direction* of any asymmetry), or, alternatively, whether it is an artifactual consequence of averaging across subjects (Figure 3). In the latter case, individual females may be no less lateralized than males, but instead more females may simply *reverse*. The latter alternative, for which there is some experimental support, argues against the idea that in most females some RH processing space is given over to verbal processes, and is more compatible with Kimura's position (above). Of course we can then no longer seek directly to explain a verbal superiority (or spatial inferiority) in females compared to males in terms of differences in cognitive asymmetries.

We cannot study sex differences without reference to handedness in this context; many of the mutually contradictory findings in both sets of literature stem from examining one factor without controlling the other. Recently, evidence has emerged of complicated interactions between sex and handedness (see Chapter 8). Moreover according to the Geschwind hypothesis (Chapter 8, and see Benbow, 1988) males (and sinistrals) are more likely to excel on spatial tasks. Indeed other moderator variables should also probably be included, e.g. strength of handedness, possibly even familial sinistrality, as well as type of task, strategy, ability and developmental age.

Finally, there have been reports that females exhibit a thicker trunk of the corpus callosum, though these findings are now disputed (see Chapter 3). Could this be a cause, or an effect, of reduced lateralization? (The evidence reviewed above may in any case now go against the idea that lateralization is reduced in females; they may merely include more 'reversers', in which case callosal differences would not necessarily be expected.) Nevertheless an increase in the size of this structure could facilitate interhemispheric communication, though even then this would only be relevant if hemispheric specializations are absolute and depend upon transfer of information, rather than reflecting relative differences in efficiency (see Chapter 5). Some schizophrenics and sinistrals have also been said to possess thicker corpora callosa, together with reduced lateralization at an *individual* level, where, unlike perhaps the case with females, this is not simply an artifactual consequence of averaging across subjects. Of course many other factors also operate in the case of schizophrenia.

SUMMARY AND CONCLUSIONS

'Female' has been linked with 'sinistral' and other pejoratives from time immemorial. The sex hormones are known to target the brain, as well as the body, and may account for sex differences in (verbal and spatial) cognitive abilities, and for cognitive asymmetries. An intermediate hormonal level may be optimal. Like handedness differences, sex differences tend to be continuous rather than dichotomous, though they are usually small in magnitude. Girls, however, score far better than boys on measures of verbal fluency, and are much less likely to suffer from stuttering, autism, developmental dyslexia and delayed speech; however, their spatial abilities may be slightly inferior. Males generally tend to appear more lateralized in cognitive tasks (though less so for simple motor functions). However, there are disagreements about how to interpret such findings, and differences in strategies may be important. From clinical evidence it is even possible that speech and manual praxis are more focally represented in the brains of females, especially in the anterior LH. Indeed some recent data from normal subjects tend to indicate that individual females are no less lateralized than males, but perhaps more females may reverse. However, much of the confusion and contradiction in the experimental data stems from failures adequately to control for handedness; both factors almost certainly interact in a complex fashion.

IMPORTANT READINGS

Benbow, C. P. Sex differences in mathematical reasoning ability in intellectually talented pre-adolescents: Their nature, effects and possible causes. *Behavioral and Brain Sciences*, 1988, **11**, 169–232.

Browne, R. J. Sex differences in neuropsychological functioning. In C. J. Golden and P. J. Vincente (eds.), *Foundations of Clinical Neuropsychology*. New York, Plenum Press, 1983, pp. 429–58.

Gordon, H. W. and Lee, P. A. A relationship between gonadotrophins and visuospatial function. *Neuropsychologia*, 1986, **24**, 563–76.

Halpern, D. F. *Sex Differences in Cognitive Abilities*. Hillsdale, N.J.: Erlbaum, 1986.

Hines, M. and Gorski, R. A. Hormonal influences on the development of neural asymmetries. In D. F. Benson and E. Zaidel (eds.), *The Dual Brain: Hemispheric Specialization in Humans*. New York: Guilford, 1985, pp. 75–96.

Kimura, D. Are men's and women's brains really different? *Canadian Psychologist*, 1987, **28**, 133–47.

Linn, M. C. and Petersen, A. L. Emergence and characterization of sex differences in spatial ability: A meta analysis. *Child Development*, 1985, **56**, 1479–98.

McGlone, J. The neuropsychology of sex differences in human brain organization. In G. Goldstein and R. E. Tarter (eds.), *Advances in Clinical Neuropsychology*, Vol. 3. New York: Plenum Press, 1986, pp. 1–30.

McKeever, W. F. Influences of handedness, sex, familial sinistrality and androgyny on language laterality, verbal ability and spatial ability. *Cortex*, 1986, **22**, 521–37.

Mittwoch, U. Erroneous theories of sex determination. *Journal of Medical Genetics*, 1985, **22**, 164–70.

Netley, C. and Rovet, J. Relationships among brain organization, maturation rate, and the development of verbal and nonverbal ability. In S. J. Segalowitz (ed.), *Language Functions and Brain Organization*. New York: Academic Press, 1983, pp. 245–66.

Segalowitz, S. J. and Bryden, M. P. Individual differences in hemispheric representation of language. In S. J. Segalowitz (ed.), *Language Functions and Brain Organization*. New York: Academic Press, 1983, pp. 341–72.

Sherman, J. A. *Sex-related Cognitive Differences*. Springfield, Illinois: Charles C. Thomas, 1978.

Signorella, M. L. and Jamison, W. Masculinity, femininity, androgyny and cognitive performance: A meta analysis. *Psychological Review*, 1986, **100**, 207–28.

Vignolo, L. A., Frediani, F., Boccardi, E. and Caverni, L. Unexpected CT-scan findings in global aphasia. *Cortex*, 1986, **22**, 55–69.

Vrbancic, M. I. and Mosley, J. L. Sex-related differences in hemispheric lateralization: A function of physical maturation. *Developmental Neuropsychology*, 1988, **4**, 151–67.

Waber, D. P. The search for biological correlates of behavioral sex differences in humans. In J. Ghesquiere, R. D. Martin and F. Newcombe (eds.), *Human Sexual Dimorphism*. London: Taylor & Francis, 1985, pp. 257–81.

10

Developmental aspects

The form and function of a living organism is subject to both genetic and environmental influences, which may interact in a complex fashion. As the creature develops, form and function unfold, and may continue to do so as long as it lives. The realization of genetic potential may depend upon environmental adequacy; conversely, environmental influences may mask the expression of genetic predispositions. Cerebral lateralization is no different in these respects. Early in fetal life asymmetries may be apparent, and given appropriate environmental circumstances may sequentially unfold at different stages, even though the expression at each stage may only be probabilistic, and may depend upon exposure to the 'right' sort of influences. Thus viewed at a population level, a sequence may be perceived linking asymmetries in brain morphology, head and limb posture, auditory and electrophysiological asymmetries, and lateralization in the use of one or both hands, followed by the 'traditional' visual-field and dichotic asymmetries. At an individual level, however, breaks and inconsistencies may appear anywhere in the chain, occasioned perhaps by early injury, isolation, deafness or blindness, and the age at which such misadventures may occur is critically important. Thus a debate has arisen concerning the 'development' of lateralization, early hemispheric equipotentiality, and the possibility of plastic reorganization. Much of the disagreement stems from differences in age at injury, and at testing. As we depend so extensively upon language, most theoretical and experimental work has been directed to developmental disorders in such predominantly LH functions. Recently, however, nonverbal processes (e.g. face recognition) have also been studied in the context of development, lateralization, and (to a lesser extent) dysfunction; such studies, as we shall see in this chapter, have highlighted the important role of strategic control and strategy differences.

In considering the question of developmental aspects of cerebral asymmetry, perhaps the key point to be made is that cerebral asymmetry almost certainly does not develop; asymmetries, morphological and behavioral, are present *ab initio*, and the most that can be said is that they may unfold.

STUDIES WITH NEONATES AND CHILDREN UP TO THREE YEARS

Neonates usually lie, if placed on the stomach, with the head turned to one side, with arm and leg extended to that side (usually the right side) and the opposite limbs flexed, as if in a fencer's posture (Harris and Fitzgerald, 1983; Lewkowicz and Turkewitz, 1983; Trehub, Corter and Shosenberg, 1983); this is known as the asymmetric tonic neck reflex (ATNR). Indeed babies of dextral parents are more likely to exhibit such a rightwards ATNR, and they in turn are more likely later, as infants or adults, to show right hand preferences. Nevertheless all three links in the chain are far from strong, and infantile asymmetries are very unstable. Indeed nurses in maternity wards traditionally tend to turn babies on to their right. There is, however, a suggestion that intrauterine arm and head position may itself determine the ATNR. The reflex seems to be truly motor, and is not the result of asymmetric visualization of e.g. the right hand, since the congenitally blind show a normal ATNR and incidence of dextrality, whatever the case may be with respect to language lateralization (see Chapter 6). Nevertheless neonates are more sensitive to all stimuli on the right, perhaps because a rightwards ATNR exposes the right side, even though the reverse is not true—the reflex is not due to differential sensitivities of the exposed and occluded sides. Finally, neonates' stepping reflex also shows a right leg bias.

By one to four months, the right hand is typically preferred for visually directed reaching and touching, and unimanual grasping, while the left may be used more for nondirected activity (see e.g. Young *et al.*, 1983). By six months this right hand preference extends to unimanual manipulation of objects, and may correlate with the onset of 'duplicated babbling'. By thirteen months the right hand preference extends to bimanual manipulation of objects, which correlates well with later hand preferences, though the bias is still less extreme than in adults (see e.g. Michel, 1983; Ramsay and Weber, 1986); maybe dextrality and lateralization of language to the LH mutually facilitate each other. By three years, an adult pattern has emerged of dextrality (i.e. with the same ratio of sinistrals to dextrals as in adults) for unimanual skills and unimanual tapping; thus there is a greater decrease in tapping rate for the right than for the left hand during concurrent recitation (see Chapter 4). Likewise by three years there is the adult trend of a left hand superiority in copying patterns of finger movements and hand gestures, as long as they are meaningless, and of greater use of the right hand for gesturing, during speech. In general terms, voluntary responses (e.g. reaching and manipulation) seem to be better indices than early involuntary reflexes, perhaps just as in adults hand preferences are less asymmetrical than hand performance measures (see Chapter 8), though obviously the latter are unavailable in the very young. It should be noted also that much of this research is bedevilled by poor methodology and weak criteria. Thus when assessing reaching behavior, do we determine which hand is first used, or the hand used most often, or the one holding on to something longest, or even the first hand to drop an object in favor of something new? It is often claimed that the onset of hand preferences correlates with the onset of speech; however, it is unclear whether unimanual or bimanual behavior is under consideration, and one- or two-syllable babbling, or use of words or even of syntax. Nor is it clear whether a causal connection is implied, and if so in which direction. Finally it should be noted that unfolding does not necessarily imply development of lateralization.

OTHER BEHAVIORAL INDICES: DOES LATERALIZATION DEVELOP?

Auditory asymmetries are present even in neonates and infants (Molfese and Molfese, 1983, and see also Lewkowicz and Turkewitz, 1983). Neonates may demonstrate activation of the right-ear/LH system during exposure to speech sounds, with opposite asymmetries occurring during presentation of musical notes, as demonstrated by EEG or ERP indices or even where amount of recovery of the cardiac orientating response is assessed. Adult procedures with conventional dichotic testing are possible by three years; there is no evidence of a developmental increase in lateralization, though consistencies certainly improve, together with the ability to attend to the nonpreferred side, giving the spurious appearance of a developmental trend in lateralization (Beaumont, 1982; Bryden and Saxby, 1986; Curtiss, 1985; Hahn, 1987). Of course such problems as memory, report order, directional attention etc., which we encountered with adult studies (see Chapter 4) may be more intractable with children (Bryden and Saxby, 1986). Similar observations apply to dichhaptic techniques, though a left hand superiority for the recognition by feel of nonsense shapes and real objects seems to be secure by two years. Early asymmetries are also evident with tachistoscopic measures, though again problems to do with stimulus quality (i.e. duration, luminance and familiarity—see Chapter 4) can lead to the spurious appearance of RH mediation. Indeed while lateralization may not develop, our ability to process degraded stimuli may do so, and to extract information therefrom, again leading to the spurious appearance of developing asymmetries. Moreover one must be able to read to be able to show RVF superiorities to letters or words; even adults learning new scripts may show LVF advantages (see Chapter 6). Again it is the reading ability which is developing, not the lateralization. However, six year old children show the adult patterns of LVF or RVF superiorities respectively to physical (AA, bb) or nominal (Aa, Bb) matching (see Chapter 4), and no age-related trends in asymmetries are apparent in the dual-task interference of left or right hand tapping during recitation.

Of course all these indices are inferential, with relatively poor reliability and maybe (as we saw) even doubtful validity as pure indices of hemispheric lateralization. While the latter most emphatically does not develop, the associated skills or abilities do unfold, and this may happen at different rates in different socioeconomic groups; this fact, together with our earlier observations on the importance of familiarity with language or script to generate the 'normal' asymmetries, may account for the apparent emergence of asymmetries at different ages in different groups. Moreover disruption of the normal stages of language acquisition, e.g. through extreme social isolation (see Curtiss, 1985), deafness, autism, even developmental dyslexia (see Chapter 6), may lead to abnormally lateralized behavior. Indeed lateralization surely 'proceeds' (not 'develops') normally in the blind and deaf, as long as some form of language is available, e.g. signing. Thus for the normal establishment and manifestation of LH mediation of its pre-existing specializations, speech *per se* may even perhaps be less important than e.g. grammar or the 'computational' aspects of language.

According to the position of Lenneberg, the two hemispheres are equipotential at birth; damage to either has equally insignificant long-term effects. He argued that language lateralization is impossible before the development of language, and that the former commences along with the onset, at two years, of both language and handedness. Thereafter the lateralization of language to the LH increases (and the contribution of the RH decreases) until puberty. Finally, recovery (after injury) of language functions depends on the degree of lateralization, and brain lateralization is tied to language. Thus there is no recognition by Lenneberg that a system may be prelateralized before an ability unfolds (with the development of lateralization seeming to occur due to such unfolding), and no recognition of anatomical brain asymmetries in the fetus or of behavioral asymmetries in neonates. Lenneberg's views stem largely from the childhood aphasia studies of the early 1960s, which suggested that transient aphasia would occur whichever hemisphere was injured, with aphasia after RH injury commoner in children than in adults. These studies also indicated that LH injury in infancy has less serious consequences than in adulthood, and that the RH can take over the functions of the damaged LH. However, these findings have recently been disputed with better controlled studies. The earlier findings failed to distinguish between two kinds of information: lateralization at the *time of injury*, which can be ascertained by e.g. any aphasia apparent immediately after insult, and, secondly, the extent of any neural or functional plasticity, which is given by the relative ease of recovery *subsequent* to the injury (see e.g. Bullock, Liederman and Todorovič, 1987; Witelson, 1985, 1987). Thus recovery from childhood aphasia tells you that the system is 'plastic', not that language was not established in the damaged (usually left) hemisphere.

TESTING IMMEDIATELY AFTER INJURY

Testing should therefore take place immediately after injury, to provide us with information about the actual status, *then*, of hemispheric asymmetry. This of course poses problems if the child is too young to speak. With children old enough to talk, aphasia is commoner after LH injury than after RH damage, just as in adults, though in childhood, despite an LH specialization for language which is manifest by two years, the RH may possibly play a more important language role than later in life. Maybe we *need* our RHs to *learn* to speak and read, though it is quite possible that an apparently greater language involvement by the infantile RH stems from the fact that in such small brains bilateral damage cannot easily be excluded. Indeed in such cases we have no premorbid data on language; nor do we know what hand preferences there otherwise would have been, and in any case language in such young patients probably was not very secure. Curiously, no such apparent developmental shift occurs in sinistrals; thus sinistral children show approximately the same incidence of aphasia after RH damage as sinistral adults. Perhaps being strongly dextral causes a language shift from the RH (in children) to the LH when older, while the intrinsically less likely reverse phenomenon does not happen in sinistrals.

TESTING MANY YEARS AFTER THE TIME OF ORIGINAL INFANTILE INJURY

Information from this source can tell us a lot about the system's capacity for plastic recovery, but not much about its asymmetric status at time of injury. We cannot therefore conclude from such data whether the hemispheres are initially equipotential, or whether lateralization develops. Nevertheless such later testing reveals considerable residual syntactic deficits (though see Chapter 6), even though recovery is still better than is the case with adult injury. However, such deficits may be no less for injuries incurred before the onset of speech than when they occurred with fully functional speech. Hemispherectomy or hemidecortication is of course potentially the cleanest source of evidence for functional or neural plasticity, and in theory can circumvent many of the problems associated with lesion data. However, even when subjected to the operation in infancy, such individuals tested as adults with only a RH remaining show worse syntactic and grammatical deficits than right hemidecorticates, who show visuospatial deficits. Of course there are not many such patients to test, some of the findings have recently been subjected to criticisms of methodology, statistics and interpretation (see Chapter 6), and we do not know the extent to which strategies adopted to cope with deficits may obscure real effects. Nevertheless from such studies we can be sure that surviving functions can only be mediated by the remaining hemisphere, and that the RH, even in adults, may be able eventually to take over some of the LH's functions, though such plasticity is far less complete than is the case with children. Moreover in the absence, now, of e.g. the LH, we can be sure that the RH is free from any inhibitory influences from that source. Thus in the congenital absence of the corpus callosum the RH may immediately start to develop unwanted language functions.

There are probably limits, less perhaps in the case of early injury, to the possible extent of functional plasticity. Recovery of function may be fullest for specific aspects normally mediated by the damaged area, and less complete for the general, nonspecific cognitive aspects accompanying brain damage; indeed these aspects, which encompass e.g. problem solving and capacities for reasoning, may be the more significant, especially with lesions incurred early in life. Such aspects of cognition are indeed often thought to be typical of the RH (see Chapter 6), so we need careful tests to separate out the effects of specific and general deficits. In this way we can perhaps resolve the apparent paradox that certain deficits may be worse with early rather than late lesions— if the deficits involve *general* rather than specific, clearly circumscribed abilities. Thus neural plasticity may be better able to rectify specific cognitive deficits (e.g. speech), decreasingly so perhaps with maturation, while the capacities for general problem solving may be far less amenable to plastic recovery. However, at the *other* end of the age spectrum, 'fluid' performance intelligence (i.e. general problem-solving capacities, of the sort often ascribed to the RH, see Chapter 6) may decline faster than 'crystallized' verbal intelligence, mediated by specially dedicated processing mechanisms in the LH.

After early injury, does language take precedence over visuospatial functions? Thus is the RH able to take over language functions to some extent if required, without the LH being correspondingly able to mediate visuospatial aspects? While some have claimed just such an asymmetry in the direction of plastic takeover, these aspects could instead be merely a manifestation of the general cognitive aspects of problem solving, which we saw (above) related more to the RH; thus the LH's specializations may not permit it to handle the sort of general cognitive processing which includes both 'fluid' problem solving and (related) visuospatial aspects. Yet another explanation invokes differences in the rates of hemispheric maturation (Thatcher, Walker and Giudice, 1987). Thus both neuro-anatomical and psychological data (e.g. that of Corballis, see Chapter 8) have been invoked to suggest earlier LH maturation, with Geschwind claiming the opposite. In any case the study of Thatcher *et al.* now provides us with good independent evidence of complex asynchronous cycles of hemispheric maturation; none of this implies that lateralization develops, as, if a cognitive task cannot yet be performed, we cannot say that the appropriate lateralization has not yet developed, merely that the task ability has not yet unfolded. As we have seen, there is little evidence that asymmetries maturationally increase for tasks that *can* be done, or that greater skill leads to greater lateralization. Nevertheless there may be functional reorganization of language substrates during development even *within* a hemisphere; they may gradually become more focalized, so that early damage *anywhere* in the LH may lead to difficulties in speech production, while later only *anterior* damage may have this effect, as if development leads to a *specialization* of language subtypes. (We have already met something similar in the context of possible sex differences in the nature of language specialization, see Chapter 9.) Of course it is far easier in the very young to test for speech production than comprehension, and such biases may lead to faulty conclusions about changes in the nature of language specialization and subtypes during development. Conversely, a child may 'grow into' a deficit which only manifests subsequently, when the damaged area has now become critical for that function as it unfolds. Nevertheless the existence of hemispheric specialization before the onset of speech itself suggests that something more fundamental than specialization for language underlies LH lateralization, e.g. perhaps control of fine, sequential, analytic, temporal processing (see Chapter 7).

DEVELOPMENTAL CHANGES IN FACE RECOGNITION

It is not only LH functions such as language which may unfold maturationally. The ability to recognize faces, not surprisingly, also improves with age (Young, 1986). We can see this in terms of a change in the nature of errors in response to the presence of distracting paraphernalia like moustaches, hats and spectacles. Before ten years, face recognition may depend more upon the recognition of isolated, piecemeal features, suggesting a LH mediation. Thereafter, configurational information, relational aspects, distances between but otherwise independent of features ('meta features') may become important, suggesting an increase in RH involvement (Levine, 1985). After ten years, inversion (which seems to affect the encoding of configurational information far more than that of piecemeal, feature aspects, see Figure 1) may have a far more detrimental effect upon the recognition of faces than of the other mono-orientated, symmetrical and familiar stimuli like house fronts; before ten years, inversion of either type of stimulus may be equally detrimental. However, not everyone finds a shift at age ten from piecemeal (LH?) to configurational (RH?) encoding of upright faces. Maybe after ten, unfamiliar faces can be

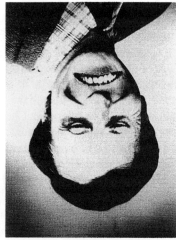

Fig. 1   An inverted face in which the eyes and mouth remain the normal way round still appears inverted, but otherwise unexceptional. However, when the page is rotated through 180° so that both faces are now normally oriented, it can be seen that an appreciation of a face's overall configuration and expression can only be gained when it is upright. (Reproduced with permission from material kindly supplied by D. M. Thomson.)

more efficiently processed in a configurational fashion, while by six years *familiar* faces can be recognized in an adult fashion, ignoring irrelevant aspects, paraphernalia etc. There are in fact according to Levine three possibilities concerning a possible change in RH involvement in the development of face recognition. According to the first, there may in fact be no such change, especially if the RH is differentially involved in the recognition of unfamiliar (and familiar) faces at *all* ages. Secondly, the RH may not be differentially involved in face recognition in young children, but does become so, after ten years, for both familiar and unfamiliar; there would therefore be a developmental change in favor of the RH, but one which is unrelated to any general developmental change in the ability to recognize *unfamiliar* faces. Finally, the RH may be differentially involved in recognizing *familiar* faces before *unfamiliar*, with familiar ones being recognized in the adult mode at an earlier age. Such a model of RH involvement in face recognition relates to developmental changes in how *unfamiliar* faces are recognized, as the RH can perhaps recognize familiar faces as early as six years via the adult mode, but may only be able to cope with unfamiliar ones by ten. Levine in fact finds that the LVF/RH superiority in recognizing *unfamiliar* faces emerges between eight and ten years, and is coincident with developmental changes in how these faces are recognized, and may even temporarily disappear around puberty (fourteen

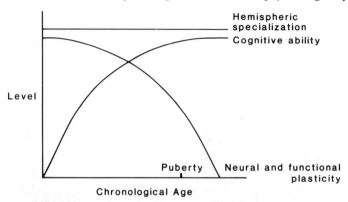

Fig. 2   Theoretical relationships between age and hemispheric specialization (constant), cognitive ability (increasing) and plasticity (decreasing to puberty). (Figure redrawn and modified from other versions in S. F. Witelson, Neurobiological aspects of language in children. *Child Development*, 1987, **58**, 653–685.)

years). Interestingly, a similar dip around puberty has been noted for recognition scores in voice recognition and tonal memory also. Finally we should remember (see Chapter 4) that there is some evidence of a *left* hemisphere involvement in the recognition of familiar faces by adults.

It can be safely concluded that hemispheric specialization does not develop, but is present, in both hemispheres, *ab initio*. Nevertheless with maturation more cortical areas become functional, and as they unfold more skills may become 'available for lateralization'. The genetic phenotype of course requires an appropriate environment for such 'unfolding' to occur, e.g. a language, *any* language, continuously heard during infancy. The resultant 'unfolding' must be allowed to take place at pre-ordained critical periods (infancy and puberty being significant milestones for the acquisition of first and subsequent languages, respectively); after this the resultant product becomes more or less permanent. There may also be changes in strategy with maturation, and greater familiarity with certain aspects of a task, and these aspects may themselves become differentially lateralized, e.g. phonology versus semantics (see Chapter 6). Floor and ceiling effects may themselves also suggest developmental changes in lateralization, and different indices or measurements may lead to different conclusions. Nor is there anything incompatible in the coexistence of early hemispheric asymmetry and early plasticity (see Figure 2); the latter does not imply any reduction in the former, even though the limits of plasticity may be partly determined by existing functional specialization. Thus plasticity may be greatest in the least-committed, slowest-maturing association areas, even though specific functions may perhaps recover in these regions at the expense of their original capacities for general problem solving. Plasticity is presumably only 'released' in the event of injury, when neural reorganization must occur; were it to operate in a healthy developing organism it would necessarily detract from specialization of function and hemispheric asymmetry. Indeed even in adult primates, the primary cortical projection areas for fingers can be reallocated should a finger be lost. We do not need to invoke the idea of a developmental increase in lateralization superimposed upon a preexisting asymmetry, or increasing interhemispheric inhibition of the subsidiary functions of a minor hemisphere.

SUMMARY AND CONCLUSIONS

Neonates exhibit an asymmetric tonic neck reflex, which may possibly predict future handedness, and may even stem from asymmetries in intrauterine position. In the first few months, unimanual asymmetries appear for grasping, followed by manipulation (unimanual, then bimanual), though much of the research is open to dispute. By three years many adult patterns of cognitive and motor asymmetry appear fixed. Even neonates may demonstrate 'verbal' REAs if appropriate techniques are employed. Contrary to much accepted opinion, asymmetries cannot be said to develop, though they may unfold along with the developing abilities which are their substrate, and there may be a reduction in performance variability, and difficulty in directing attention. Indeed task unfamiliarity, which even in adults is associated with RH involvement, may also explain why cognitive asymmetries can appear to increase during development. Moreover disruption of the normal stages of language acquisition, through extreme socialization, deafness, autism or developmental dyslexia may lead to abnormally lateralized behavior. We cannot therefore conclude that the hemispheres are equipotential at birth, or that lateralization develops, though plasticity certainly does diminish during the early years. Early damage to the LH may be less disabling than that incurred later, but detectable sequelae (e.g. difficulties with complex syntax) can probably still be measured in later years. Plastic recovery may be fullest for specific aspects normally mediated by the damaged area, and less complete for nonspecific cognitive aspects associated with general ability—often those normally ascribed to the RH. Deficits of the latter sort may, therefore, apparently paradoxically be worse with early lesions, and may lead to conclusions that language takes precedence over visuospatial functions. Developmental changes have been reported both in face recognition and in the associated tachistoscopic asymmetries, involving perhaps a shift from piecemeal to global processing. There is also debate about how children perceive unfamiliar and inverted faces, and other mono-orientational stimuli.

IMPORTANT READINGS

Beaumont, J. G. Developmental aspects. In J. G. Beaumont (ed.), *Divided Visual Field Studies of Cerebral Organization*. New York: Academic Press, 1982, pp. 113–28.

Bryden, M. P. and Saxby, L. Developmental aspects of cerebral lateralization. In J. E. Obrzut and G. W. Hynd (eds.), *Child Neuropsychology*, Vol. 1. New York: Academic Press, 1986, pp. 73–94.

Bullock, D., Liederman, J. and Todorovič, D. Reconciling stable asymmetry with recovery of function: An adaptive systems perspective on functional plasticity. *Child Development*, 1987, **58**, 689–97.

Curtiss, S. The development of human cerebral lateralization. In D. F. Benson and E. Zaidel (eds.), *The Dual Brain: Hemispheric Specialization in Humans*. New York: Guilford Press, 1985, pp. 97–115.

Hahn, W. K. Cerebral lateralization of function—from infancy through childhood. *Psychological Bulletin*, 1987, **101**, 376–92.

Harris, L. J. and Fitzgerald, H. E. Postural orientation in human infants: Changes from birth to three months. In G. Young, S. J. Segalowitz, C. M. Corter and S. Trehub (eds.), *Manual Specialization and the Developing Brain*. New York: Academic Press, 1983, pp. 285–306.

Levine, S. C. Developmental changes in right hemisphere involvement in face recognition. In C. T. Best (ed.), *Hemispheric Function and Collaboration in the Child*. New York: Academic Press, 1985, pp. 157–91.

Lewkowicz, D. J. and Turkewitz, G. Relationships between processing and motor asymmetries in early development. In G. Young, S. J. Segalowitz, C. M. Corter and S. Trehub (eds.), *Manual Specialization and the Developing Brain*. New York: Academic Press, 1983, pp. 375–94.

Michel, G. F. Development of hand-use preference during infancy. In G. Young, S. J. Segalowitz, C. M. Corter and S. Trehub (eds.), *Manual Specialization and the Developing Brain*. New York: Academic Press, 1983, pp. 33–70.

Molfese, D. L. and Molfese, V. J. Hemispheric specialization in infancy. In G. Young, S. J. Segalowitz, C. M. Corter and S. Trehub (eds.), *Manual Specialization and the Developing Brain*. New York: Academic Press, 1983, pp. 93–110.

Ramsay, D. S. and Weber, S. L. Infants' hand preference in a task involving complementary roles for the two hands. *Child Development*, 1986, **57**, 300–7.

Thatcher, R. W., Walker, R. A. and Giudice, S. Human cerebral hemispheres develop at different rates and ages. *Science*, 1987, **236**, 1110–13.

Trehub, S. E., Corter, C. M. and Shosenberg, N. Neonatal reflexes: A search for lateral asymmetries. In G. Young, S. J. Segalowitz, C. M. Corter and S. Trehub (eds.), *Manual Specialization and the Developing Brain*. New York: Academic Press, 1983, pp. 257–74.

Witelson, S. F. On hemisphere specialization and cerebral plasticity from birth: Mark II. In C. T. Best (ed.), *Hemispheric Function and Collaboration in the Child*. New York: Academic Press, 1985, pp. 33–85.

Witelson, S. F. Neurobiological aspects of language in children. *Child Development*, 1987, **58**, 653–88.

Young, A. W. Subject characteristics in lateral differences for face processing by normals: Age. In R. Bruyer (ed.), *The Neuropsychology of Face Perception and Facial Expression*. Hillsdale, N.J.: Erlbaum, 1986, pp. 167–200.

Young, G., Segalowitz, S. J., Misek, P., Alp, E. and Boulet, R. Is early reaching left-handed? Review of manual specialization research. In G. Young, S. J. Segalowitz, C. M. Corter and S. Trehub (eds.), *Manual Specialization and the Developing Brain*. New York: Academic Press, 1983, pp. 13–32.

11

Hemisphericity and cognitive style

AN OVERVIEW

In previous chapters, we have examined the evidence for asymmetries of form and function in living creatures other than ourselves. Indeed we saw that systematic 'population-level' asymmetries occur in the biochemistry of protein and amino acids, and may even stem from an asymmetric action of subatomic forces. While left–right asymmetries are grossly absent in the natural world, and our two sides are at least superficially left–right mirror images of each other, our predominant dextrality and LH mediation of language seems at first sight to set us apart from our fellow creatures. However, analogies and even homologies abound; the LH of passerines mediates song, and in other bird species may be dominant for the acquisition of visually guided behaviors, imprinting, visual discrimination learning, auditory habituation and attention switching. In both birds and rodents, the RH may subserve spatial relationships and emotional responsivity, and in several species of mammal there are intriguing suggestions that the LH is involved, as perhaps in birds, in communication. Certainly in primates asymmetries in brain morphology appear, in regions which subserve language in ourselves. Evidence for such a LH mediation of language functions comes from the various new imaging techniques, and from studying the effects (aphasia, alexia) of localized brain trauma. Similar though weaker asymmetries, often in the opposite direction, are found clinically for such nonverbal functions as face recognition and the perception and expression of emotion. Similarly, hemineglect, predominantly of events to the left, seems to be largely a RH dysfunction. Appropriate (if sophisticated and somewhat artificial) testing of patients whose forebrain commissures have been surgically disconnected largely confirms such clinical observations, while raising additional questions. These include whether the operation inevitably results in perceptual disunity, noncortical transfer of information, differences in processing strategies between the hemispheres, the status of the RH as a fully conscious ratiocinating entity which possesses its own independent will, whether the two hemispheres maintain independent processing capacities and modularity of function throughout the brain.

Normative studies provide the third major source of evidence for human cerebral asymmetry, though such asymmetries may represent the algebraic sum of a multiplicity of independent modular functions, themselves subject to a bewildering range of task and subject factors. This partly accounts for the contradictions and inconsistencies in the literature. While 'RH' functions therefore tend to be less consistently lateralized than simple articulatory responses (e.g. right-field superiorities with vocal naming latencies), faces provide strong tachistoscopic asymmetries; this leads to questions about the possibility of a specialized RH processor for faces complementary to a LH language processor. However, recent findings indicate the important role of directional attention, and coding in terms of the perceived origin of stimulation with respect to various coordinate systems. Indeed the nature of inter-hemispheric interaction via the commissures, excitatory and inhibitory, is still far from clear. While clinical studies may suggest absolute or qualitative specialization, and other studies indicate that this state of affairs may result from inhibitory processes, with asymmetries which instead are relative, yet other suggestions have been made in terms of complementary hemispheric specialization. Such complementarity may not necessarily apply for individual subjects at a gross level (e.g. LH verbal therefore RH visuospatial), but attractive models have been developed at a micro modular level, e.g. 'mirror-image negativity' of subprocessors. Thus it is no longer counterintuitive to talk about a RH contribution to language, perhaps more in terms of connotative meaning, context, prosody or emotional aspects than phonology. Such a RH contribution, extending maybe even on occasion to phonology, may be stronger in certain groups. e.g. sinistrals, maybe females, or those who have experienced early trauma, or who are illiterate, socially isolated or congenitally deaf, or with material which is novel, unfamiliar, degraded or excessively 'concrete'. It may even apply, perhaps only briefly, to those learning a second language. Two pathologies, stuttering and developmental dyslexia, have also been associated with RH language, though again this may be a matter of adopted strategies, or the differential activation of certain groups of sub-processors. Alternatively, the RH may normally only make a contribution in the event of LH dysfunction.

As human beings we are unique in simultaneously employing language, tool use and an upright bipedal posture. How was the latter selected for? Did gesture precede true language, or might language have preceded gesture and tool use? Is language somehow 'special', or is it continuous with earlier primate call systems? Should we invoke a multifactorial and interactive scenario involving cortical expansion, bipedal locomotion, foraging, a material culture and a unique mode of reproduction? Did LH language mediation and hand lateralization evolve semi-independently from ancestral syntactic, rule-governed processes in the LH? Dextrality certainly goes back to our earliest *Homo* ancestor, *H. habilis*, who *may*, just possibly, have managed *some* form of verbal communication. Moreover sinistrals, long a suspect minority in a largely dextral world, seem to have persisted in about the same incidence ratio to dextrals for millennia, suggesting a possible evolutionary advantage for such a balanced dimorphism. Certainly, extreme dextrality may be no less disadvantageous than extreme sinistrality, though the patterns of disadvantage may differ. However, no simple genetic model can account for all the various performance and preference aspects. While perinatal birth trauma no longer seems likely to be a major determinant of left handedness (though pathological sinistrality certainly may continue to play a role), evidence is growing for a hormonal involvement, perhaps involving fetal testosterone. This hypothesis links the male sex hormone with sinistrality (and a raised incidence of sinistrality among males), developmental learning disorders, abnormally high mathematical and spatial skills, and immune dysfunction. To what extent may the various sex hormones (otherwise known to target the brain) generally account for sex differences in verbal and spatial cognitive abilities, and in cognitive asymmetries? Hormone levels, as opposed to the dichotomous phenotype male/female, are continuously distributable, and an intermediate level may perhaps be optimal. However, girls generally fare better than boys in verbal functions both within and outside of normal limits, while the reverse may be true of spatial performance. Males tend to be more lateralized than females at a cognitive level, though strategies may play a part, while the reverse may be true (perhaps in many species) motorically. Clinical data even suggest that language and manual praxis may be more focally represented in the female brain, especially in the anterior LH, an observation which can in fact even be interpreted so as to explain sex differences in lateralized cognitive performance. However, much of the confusion may stem from failure to control adequately for handedness differences.

If differences in adopted strategies may account for some of the above sex differences, can such asymmetries be said to develop, as a consequence either of environmental pressures or of an ontogenetic unfolding? A weakly predictive chain may be discerned commencing with asymmetric reflexes in the neonate (themselves possibly influenced by intrauterine posture), through grasping and on to unimanual and later bimanual manipulation. On the other hand brain and even ear asymmetries, not too different from those of the adult, are also reported in neonates. We certainly cannot conclude that the hemispheres are equipotential at birth, or that lateralization develops, though lateralized abilities certainly unfold, a grossly abnormal environment may lead to abnormal lateralization, and the potential for plastic reorganization diminishes during the early years. Again, differences in adopted strategy or experience may play a role in empirical performance asymmetries. So can we therefore characterize individuals in terms of different personality characteristics and cognitive styles, and thereby predict their patterns of lateralization—or even use observations about the latter to generalize about the former? This issue is the subject of this final chapter.

HEMISPHERICITY AND COGNITIVE STYLE

The umbrella-discipline 'Psychology' ranges from the borderlands of anthropology and sociology, to physiology, genetics, pharmacology, biochemistry and ethology, with a central core of experimental interest clustering around sensory and perceptual processes, cognition, motor skills, learning theory and ergonomics. Neuropsychology is even more of a popular and hybrid newcomer, with diverse roots in physiological, clinical and educational psychology, neurology, cognitive science, psycholinguistics, pattern recognition, perception and motor skill. The study of human cerebral asymmetry, because of its tacit acceptance of localizationist principles concerning language and spatial processes, two of our highest cognitive functions, has recently come to preoccupy both clinical and experimental neuropsychologists. Moreover, because of the often dramatic nature of findings with commissurotomized patients, the popular press has tended to emphasize left–right differences, often ignoring other equally important distinctions, e.g. anterior–posterior, and cortical–subcortical. It has also tended to concentrate upon the *dichotomous* nature of such distinctions (specialization of course does not necessarily presuppose a dichotomy), and upon dominance and minor–major relationships. Realization since the end of World War II, that the so-called minor hemisphere may have an equally important if different role to play to that of the left hemsiphere, has led to an almost political interest in its functions, in a manner akin to current social debates concerning racism and sexism: to be right (as opposed to left) is not necessarily to be inferior. A superficial reading of such debates has led to claims that the educational system has become biased in its dealings with the young. However, as Harris (1985) observes, educators have tried to apply neuropsychological findings right from the days of Broca, in the early 1860s. Wigan (1844) mused a century and a half ago as a general practitioner upon the duplex nature of the brain. This led to an 'ambidextrality' cult, and to attempts to double our brain capacity by training in the equal use of our two hands. It was even believed that we might thereby be able to create a doubling of our language centers. The pendulum swung the other way with Orton's (1937) attempts (see Chapter 6) to enhance *asymmetry* and *left* hemisphere processing to overcome left–right confusions, directionality problems (as in reading scans) and, ultimately, developmental dyslexia in children. Orton, as we saw, assumed that while the dominant hemisphere (usually the left) records letters and words in the correct orientation, the other hemisphere does so in a reversed orientation; moreover mixed motor dominance (inconsistent hand preference, or a disjunction of hand from foot or eye preference) reflects, he thought, incomplete or mixed cerebral dominance. He thus incorrectly assumed that lateral asymmetries develop (see Chapter 10). He suggested remediation to *enhance* dominance, though his cautious approach has not been followed by modern enthusiasts like those of the Doman–Delacato group (see e.g. Delacato, 1966). Of course we now know (see earlier chapters) that sinistrals do not usually have visual language control in the RH, that dominance is not progressive or liable to be somehow slowed or halted, that the minor hemisphere does not record percepts (whatever may happen to memory traces) in mirror reversed form, and that mixed or incomplete motor dominance is not simply or directly related to either cerebral dominance or to reading disability. Nor, as is sometimes claimed, is there any evidence that unilateral dominance for language functions can be enhanced by direct training of the contralateral limb.

However, the latest modern fad, 'neuromythology' or 'neurophrenology' as Harris (1985) observes, is a return to the RH, to campaign for its role as a kind of 'endangered species', in music, art, mathematics, visualization, creativity, imagination, empathy and intuition, and to propose educational exercises for its development. There is of course little evidence that creativity is related to exclusive or even greater use of the RH, even though highly creative individuals may somehow differ in their modes of cognitive processing, their 'cognitive style', which may possibly be shown someday to relate to strategic or even individual differences in hemispheric arousal or use (see below). So far, however, regional cerebral blood flow (rCBF) studies have not been promising in this context. There is certainly no evidence that only one hemisphere is involved in any one task. Both hemispheres may be differentially specialized for analytic–holistic processing functions (see e.g. Chapters 5 and 7); however, they inevitably interact and cooperate, and even commissurotomy patients employ strategies for engaging both hemispheres, except under the most artificial of experimental lateralizing procedures.

The modern concept of hemisphericity claims that individuals have a preferred left or right cognitive mode, according to the extent that they exhibit characteristics associated with the left (verbal, analytic) or right (spatial, holistic) hemisphere. Cognitive styles, implying predominant activity by one or other hemisphere, are thus viewed as reflecting not only individual differences in perceptual processes, but also intellectual, social–interpersonal and personality variables, including reasoning, thought and abnormal states. As Beaumont, Young and McManus (1984) observe, cognitive development and educational aspects are emphasized, together with creativity, problem solving, an interest in poetry and mysticism, the origins of human consciousness, psychiatric states, and social issues in art, architecture, religion, life style and above all education. We have already observed the absence of support from rCBF studies; the same can be said of electrophysiological approaches. Thus while there is no *conclusive* evidence that EEG measures are laterally asymmetrical to verbal and nonverbal tasks, given for example the possibility of artifacts from underlying morphological asymmetries (see Chapters 1 and 4), the evidence is even weaker that individuals differ in left/right ratios with respect to different cognitive tasks. A second line of evidence, conjugate lateral eye movements (cLEMs), is equally suspect. Thus it is claimed that the gaze deviates laterally, in opposite directions, during verbal and spatial processing. However, we have already seen (Chapter 4) that the cLEMs literature is unreliable, and so we should treat with caution the proposal (similar to that of Kinsbourne) of Levy, Heller, Banich and Burton (1983). They note the great individual differences in magnitude and direction of dextrals' laterality effects, and propose that rather than reflecting differences in hemispheric specialization *per se*, they index individual differences in task-dependent asymmetries of hemispheric arousal. As evidence they invoke turning biases in animals, mediated by asymmetries in the dopaminergic motor system (which undoubtedly occur, see Chapter 1, but may relate little to human cognitive asymmetries), EEG α symmetries, rCBF effects, cLEMs and Kinsbourne's attentional model (for which empirical support is, at best, ambivalent; see Chapter 5). Electrophysiological and blood-flow measures do, of course, index *local* regions of processing activation; and it cannot be denied that lateral biases in attention underlie the clinical phenomenon of unilateral neglect (Chapter 2), or our behavior when confronted with chimeric or composite faces under conditions of free viewing (Chapter 1). The distinction, moreover, between hemispheric specialization (absolute, relative or in terms of combinations of subprocessors or availability of resources), variations in hemispheric arousal, and variations in hemispheric reliance or utilization (e.g. strategic) is certainly conceptually useful; however, at best the evidence is weak that individuals with a strong leftwards bias on nonverbal tasks and a reduced rightwards asymmetry on verbal tasks show relatively enhanced nonverbal and reduced verbal performance, compared to individuals with opposite lateral biases. Similarly, attempts have been made to correlate responses to questionnaires with performance upon cognitive tests ('verbal' and 'spatial', often with little attempt at *independent* validation of tests selected or developed *ad hoc* for the task) and with scores on dichotic and tachistoscopic tasks. The latter, as we have seen, only indirectly index cerebral lateralization, via a number of intervening variables. Thus the hemisphericity literature, though apparently supported by some prominent neuropsychologists, may suffer from some serious underlying flaws. A major problem relates to the important distinction between individual differences (personality, ability, cognitive style) and strategy. Do people *invariably* and *involuntarily* approach problems in one or other way, as the hemisphericity literature implies, or do they *choose* one or other strategy or processing mode, perhaps in a biased fashion, for particular problems? Tests of cognitive mode may be quite adequate to characterize the individual's current general approach to problem solving, and his or her relative skill on spatial–holistic tasks compared to verbal–analytic ones, but it is misleading to use cognitive mode to characterize people as being dominated by one hemisphere or the other. Hemispheric differences, strategic or otherwise, are as we have seen often small and quantitative, rather than substantial or absolute. Thus while it is undoubtedly true that by virtue of cerebral specialization some cognitive processes are primarily controlled by one hemisphere, the other hemisphere is not thereby *incapable* of such activities. Especially in the immature individual the other hemisphere may well take over many of the functions of the damaged specialist hemisphere. When a hemisphere is removed, patients do not suddenly adopt a different cognitive style. The disconnected hemisphere in the commissurotomized patient does not indulge in a newly liberated cognitive style: rather, it adopts the same mental set that the person had before, merely less efficiently if the processing mode of the moment is one for which the other hemisphere is the more specialized. Thus we must distinguish between specialization for cognitive processes and the selection of a cognitive style. There is no systematic evidence that one hemisphere would choose to cope with a task in one style and the other in another. The individual as a whole surely has an idiosyncratic personality or cognitive style that is probably little affected by lateralized hemispheric damage. He or she is merely now less efficient at those functions that were mediated by the now-damaged hemisphere. It is far too simplistic to claim that an individual is either characterized by a left hemisphere analytic or right hemisphere holistic cognitive style, or that the individual selects one or the other mental set to solve problems that can be solved in either mode. Neurologically normal individuals never have one hemisphere so 'dominant' that the other is rarely activated, even in such 'lateralized' activities as speaking (compare the role of subprocessors, discussed earlier); likewise they rarely use or under use one hemisphere, whatever may be the strategic or idiosyncratic differences in thinking styles between verbally or artistically creative individuals. Nor do the hemispheres work in isolation from each other; as we saw, even commissurotomy patients employ strategies to engage both hemispheres in cognition.

In conclusion, while individuals undoubtedly differ in 'cognitive style', there are no grounds for explaining these differences in terms of 'hemisphericity'. While the left hemisphere demonstrates a powerful control of articulatory output, in all other respects cognitive differences are small, quantitative and subtle. Any observable brain-related differences in cognition are likely to be pre-existing, rather than amenable to variation by educational mode, and to be gross, e.g. relating to verbal or performance IQ, rather than subtle and relating to cognitive style. Thus Yeo *et al.* (1987) reported that morphological asymmetries of hemispheric volume $[(L-R)/(L+R) \times 100]$, obtained by CT scan, correlated ($r = 0.57$, $p < 0.001$) with the verbal minus performance IQ difference. It is perhaps along directions such as these that substantive progress may be made, rather than by characterizing an individual's permanent (or momentary) cognitive style as left- or right-hemispheric, on the basis of questionnaire, laterality or even metabolic/activational procedures. Without question, as Harris (1985) observes, the new 'right brain education movement' is trendy, faddist and superficial, celebrating or at least excusing anti-intellectualism, irrationality and illiteracy. Music, and the visual and the plastic arts, have a natural place in education and intuition; imagination and visualization deserve encouragement, on their own merits, and not under the guise of pseudopsychological jargon which promotes simple-minded dichotomies and superficial learning styles.

SUMMARY AND CONCLUSIONS

Psychology is an umbrella discipline, and neuropsychology is a hybrid of several disciplines. The study of human cerebral asymmetry has latterly become a major clinical and experimental preoccupation, with popular over-dramatization of many of the findings. Nevertheless only comparatively recently has the RH come into its own, in fact it may be receiving an unhealthy popular emphasis, nowadays, despite the fact that the duplex nature of our brains has been under scrutiny for at least one-and-a-half centuries, and over 100 years ago attempts were made to 'double' our processing capacities. Fifty years ago, on the other hand, attempts were made to increase rather than reduce asymmetries, for the treatment of developmental dyslexia, and certain modern propagandists continue in this tradition. However, there is little evidence that creativity and a host of recent preoccupations are the exclusive prerogative of the RH, and the modern concept of hemisphericity or cognitive style, according to which individuals have a preferred left or right cognitive mode, is a dangerous oversimplification. Similar objections can be made to the study of conjugate lateral eye movements; there is no evidence that they usefully index either an individual's current or dominant mode of information processing.

IMPORTANT READINGS

Beaumont, J. G., Young, A. W. and McManus, I. C. Hemisphericity: A critical review. *Cognitive Neuropsychology*, 1984, **1**, 191–212.

Delacato, C. H. *Neurological Organization and Reading*. Springfield, Ill.: C. C. Thomas, 1966.

Harris, L. J. Teaching the right brain: Historical perspective or a contemporary educational fad? In C. T. Best (ed.), *Hemispheric Function and Collaboration in the Child*. New York: Academic Press, 1985, pp. 231–74.

Levy, J., Heller, W., Banich, M. T. and Burton, L. A. Are variations among right handed individuals in perceptual asymmetries caused by characteristic arousal differences between hemispheres? *Journal of Experimental Psychology: Human Perception and Performance*, 1983, **9**, 329–59.

Orton, S. T. *Reading, Writing and Speech Problems in Children*. New York: Norton, 1937.

Wigan, A. L. *A New View of Insanity: The Duality of the Mind Proved by the Structure, Functions and Disease of the Brain, and by the Phenomena of Mental Derangement, and Shown to be Essential to Moral Responsibility*. London: Longman, Brown, Green and Longmans, 1844, and republished by Joseph Simon, 1985.

Yeo, R. A., Turkheimer, E., Raz, N. and Bigler, E. D. Volumetric asymmetries of the human brain: Intellectual correlates. *Brain and Cognition*, 1987, **6**, 15–23.

Author index

Allen, M., 112, 119
Alp, E., 193, 202
Andrew, R.J., 11, 21
Andrews, P., 148, 157
Annett, M., 139, 164, 168, 169, 174, 175, 177
Anzola, G., 118, 119
Aoki, C., 135, 145
Armin, D., 47, 52

Babcock, L.E., Frontispiece
Bakan, P., 171
Banich, M.T., 206, 211
Beale, I.L., 5, 21
Beaumont, J.G., 194, 202, 207, 210
Becker, J.B., 14, 22
Beecher, M.D., 19, 22
Bellugi, U., 136, 146
Benbow, C.P., 175–177, 189. 190
Benson, D.F., 29, 51
Besner, D., 127, 146
Bigler, E., 24, 53, 209, 211
Bihrle, A.M., 131, 144
Bishop, D.V.M., 124, 139, 145, 172, 177
Black, S., 24, 52, 56, 73
Boccardi, E., 187, 191
Boder, E., 142
Bogen, J.E., 60, 72
Borod, J.C., 49, 51, 53
Boulet, R., 193, 202
Bradshaw, J.L., 1, 8, 10, 12, 16, 17–19, 21, 43, 51, 76, 81–86, 92, 96–98, 101–103, 106, 108, 151, 157
Bromage, T.G., 152

Browne, R.J., 185, 190
Brownell, H.H., 131, 144
Bryden, M.P., 48, 51, 92, 94, 108, 111, 119, 134, 139, 145, 146, 164, 165, 177, 178, 185, 188, 191, 194, 202
Buffery, A.W.H., 186
Bullock, D., 196, 202
Burden, V., 92, 96, 108
Burton, L.A., 206, 211

Calvin, W.H., 153, 157
Camp, D.M., 14, 22
Caramazza, A., 33, 51
Carey, S., 90, 108
Carroll, W.M., 58, 72
Cartmill, M., 154, 158
Castro, S.L., 136, 145
Caverni, L., 187, 191
Cherfas, J., 158
Chiarello, C., 83, 108, 134, 145
Chomsky, N., 156
Chui, H.C., 24, 52
Code, C., 145
Collins, R.L., 10, 12, 13, 21
Coltheart, M., 34, 35, 52, 124, 126, 130, 133, 145
Cook, N.D., 115, 116, 119, 126–129
Corballis, M.C., 5, 21, 111, 119, 140, 173–175, 177, 197
Coren, S., 161, 178
Corter, C.M., 193, 202
Cosiglia, J., 174, 177
Coslett, H.B., 47, 52
Cronin-Golomb, A., 64, 65, 72, 73

Crosson, B., 33, 52
Curtiss, S., 194, 195, 202

Damasio, A.R., 36–39, 52
Damasio, H., 37, 38, 52
Davidson, R.J., 25, 52
De Haan, E.H.F., 38, 52
Delacato, C.H., 207, 210
de la Coste-Lareymondie, M.C., 152, 158
Deneberg, V.H., 14, 21
Denno, D., 170, 171, 178
Deutsch, D., 97
Deutsch, G., 92, 122, 146
Diamond, M.C., 14, 21
Diamond, R., 90, 108
Dingwall, W.O., 155
Doty, R.W., 58, 72
Dougher, M.J., 47, 53

Ebling, J., 158
Eccles, J.C., 72
Eisenberg, H.M., 122, 146
Ellis, A.W., 139, 143, 145
Ellis, H.D., 85, 108
Engel, M., 41

Falk, D., 152, 158
Farah, M.J., 91, 108
Fennell, E.B., 164, 167, 177
Fitzgerald, H.E., 193, 202
Foundas, A.L., 24, 52
Fox, P.T., 25, 27, 53
Frediani, F., 187, 191
Friedrich, F.A., 43, 53
Frost, G.T., 153, 158

Gainotti, G., 47, 52
Galaburda, A.M., 16, 18, 22, 163, 174, 175, 177
Gallese, V., 45, 53
Galton, F., 164
Gardner, H., 131, 144
Gazzaniga, M.S., 60, 66, 67, 70, 72, 133, 145
Geschwind, N., 10, 18, 22, 29, 34, 51, 141, 145, 163, 174, 175, 177, 189. 197
Giudice, S., 174, 178, 197, 198, 202
Glick, S.D., 14, 22
Goodale, M.A., 6
Goodman, R.A., 124, 145

Gordon, H.W., 139, 141, 145, 180, 181, 190
Gorski, R.A., 180, 190
Grafman, J., 47, 52
Gray, J.A., 186

Hahn, W.K., 194, 202
Halliday, A.M., 58, 72
Halligan, P.W., 47, 53
Halpern, D.F., 185, 190
Hardy, A., 153
Harris, L.J., 139, 145, 193, 202, 206, 207, 210, 211
Heilman, K.M., 42, 46, 52
Heller, W., 206, 211
Hellige, J.B., 75, 76, 79, 108, 109
Henderson, V.W., 24, 52
Henry, R., 123, 146, 171, 172, 178
Henson, R.A., 50, 52
Hines, M., 180, 190
Hiscock, M., 105, 106, 108
Holloway, R.L., 152, 158
Howell, J., 24, 52, 56, 73
Hughes, L.F., 92, 108
Humphreys, G.W., 36, 52
Hung, D.L., 135, 138, 146
Hynd, G.W., 142, 146

Isaac, G., 154, 158

Jamison, W., 185, 191
Janowski, J., 41
Jarman, P.J., 15
Jay, B.S., 58, 72
Jaynes, J.R., 4, 69, 156, 158
Jerison, H.J., 154, 158
Johnson, L.E., 64, 72
Jones, E.A., 135, 145
Jones, E.G., 55, 65, 73

Kertesz, A., 24, 29, 52, 56, 73
Kimura, D., 92–94, 102, 187–190
Kinsbourne, M., 93, 104, 115, 117, 119
Klima, E., 136, 146
Koff, E.I., 24, 49, 51, 52
Kolb, B., 2, 10, 22
Kosslyn, S.M., 91, 108

La Barba, R.C., 137, 146
Ladavas, E., 43, 53
Lambert, A.J., 122, 125, 145
Lecours, A.R., 136, 145

Lee, P.A., 180, 181, 190
LeMay, M., 17, 22, 152, 158
Lenneberg, E.H., 195
Levin, H.S., 122, 146
Levine, H.L., 24, 52
Levine, S.C., 38, 53, 198, 202
Levy, J., 167, 174, 177, 186, 187, 206, 211
Lewine, J.D., 58, 72
Lewkowicz, D.J., 193, 194, 202
Ley, R.G., 48, 51
Lichtheim, L., 29, 30
Lieberman, P., 155, 158
Liederman, J., 196, 202
Lindblom, B., 20, 22
Lindeboom, J., 64, 73
Linn, M.C., 185, 190
Lovegrove, W.L., 142, 145
Lovejoy, C.V., 148, 154, 158
Luppino, G., 118, 119

McCarthy, R.A., 36, 53
McCloskey, M., 33, 51
MacDonald, V., 164, 165, 177
McDonald, W., 58, 72
McGlone, J., 185–187, 190
McHenry, H.M., 154, 158
McKeever, W.F., 76, 83, 85, 108, 167, 178, 181, 190
McManus, I.C., 169, 178, 207, 210
McMullen, P.A., 134, 146
MacNeilage, P.F., 20, 22, 137, 146
Marcotte, A.C., 137, 146
Marshall, J.C., 32, 34, 47, 53
Martin, F., 142, 145
Mehler, J., 136, 145
Mesulam, M.-M., 42, 46, 53
Michel, G.F., 193, 202
Michelow, D., 131, 145
Milner, B., 2, 10, 22
Mintun, M., 27
Misek, P., 193, 202
Mittwoch, U., 179, 190
Molfese, D.L., 194, 202
Molfese, V.J., 194, 202
Moody, D.B., 19, 22
Moore, B.D., 122, 146
Morais, J., 136, 145
Morgan, E., 153, 158
Morgan, M.J., 173–175, 177
Moscovitch, M., 75, 81, 88, 108, 112, 115, 117, 119

Mosley, J.L., 182, 191
Myers, J.J., 63–65, 73

Nachshon, I., 170, 171, 178
Naeser, M.A., 24, 52, 53
Nagylaki, T., 167
Nass, R., 41
Netley, C., 183, 190
Nettleton, N.C., 17, 19, 43, 51, 92, 96, 98, 101–103, 108, 157
Newcombe, F., 38, 52
Nonneman, A.J., 10, 22
Nuding, S., 34, 145

Oakley, K.P., 149, 150, 158
Obler, L.K., 135, 146
Ojemann, G.A., 28, 53
Orsini, D.L., 123, 146, 171, 172, 178
Orton, S.T., 139, 143, 206, 211
Otto, M.W., 47, 53

Pappanicolaou, A.C., 122, 146
Parente, M.A., 136, 145
Passingham, R., 151, 158
Patterson, K., 127, 146
Peters, M., 162, 178
Petersen, A.L., 185, 190
Petersen, M.R., 19, 22
Petersen, S.E., 25, 27, 53
Pieniadz, J.M., 24, 52
Pierson-Savage, J.M., 43, 51
Pilbeam, D., 154, 158
Pirozzolo, F.J., 142, 146
Poizner, H., 136, 146
Polk, M., 24, 52, 56, 73
Porac, C., 161, 178
Porro, C., 118, 119
Porter, R.J., 92, 108
Posner, M.I., 25, 27, 43, 53
Premack, D., 151, 158
Puccetti, R., 70, 73

Rafal, R.D., 43, 53
Raichle, M.E., 25, 27, 53
Ramachandran, V.S., 64, 73
Ramsay, D.S., 193, 202
Rayner, K., 142, 146
Raz, N., 24, 53, 209, 211
Richards, G., 158
Riddoch, M.J., 36, 52
Ringo, J.L., 58, 72
Risberg, J., 24, 53

Rizzolatti, G., 45, 53, 118, 119
Robinson, T.E., 14, 22
Robison, R.A., Frontispiece
Roeltgen, D.P., 130, 146
Rogers, L.J., 11, 22
Rosen, G.D., 174, 177
Ross, E.D., 48, 53, 130, 146
Rovet, J., 183, 190
Ruhlen, M., 156, 158

Sackeim, H.A., 49, 53
Saffran, E., 47, 52
Saslow, E., 123, 146, 171, 172, 178
Satz, P., 123, 146, 171, 172, 178
Saxby, L., 139, 145, 194, 202
Schweiger, A., 130, 147
Searleman, A., 121, 125, 146
Segalowitz, S.J., 165, 178, 185, 191, 193, 202
Senehi, J., 134, 145
Sergent, J., 65, 66, 73, 75, 76, 79, 80, 108, 109
Shallice, T., 36, 53
Shankweiler, D., 95
Shapiro, R.M., 14, 22
Sherman, G.F., 174, 177
Sherman, J.A., 186, 187, 191
Shosenberg, N., 193, 202
Sidtis, J.J., 60, 63, 64, 66, 73, 96, 109, 146
Signorella, M.L., 185, 191
Silberman, E.K., 47, 53
Slaghuis, W.A., 142, 145
Smylie, C.S., 133, 145
Solazar, A.M., 47, 52
Sperry, R.W., 56, 60, 63, 69, 70, 73
Springer, S.P., 92, 109
Stebbins, W.C., 19, 22
Steklis, H., 152, 154, 158
Stiles-Davis, J., 41
Studdert-Kennedy, M.G., 20, 22, 95
Sussman, H.M., 96, 109, 137, 146
Sutherland, R.J., 10, 22
Swinkels, J.A., 64, 73

Tapley, C.M., 164, 178
Taylor, L., 2, 10, 22
Temple, C.M., 126, 146

Thatcher, R.W., 174, 178, 197, 198, 202
Thomson, D.M., 199
Tobias, P.V., 148, 158
Todorovič, D., 196, 202
Toth, N., 149, 150, 158
Tranel, D., 37, 52
Trehub, S.E., 193, 202
Turkewitz, G., 193, 194, 202
Turkheimer, E., 24, 53, 209, 211
Tzeng, O.J.L., 135, 138, 146

Umiltà, C., 118, 119

Vadeboncoeur, A., 136, 145
Valenstein, E., 42, 46, 52
Vance, S.C., 47, 52
Van Lancker, D., 144, 146
Vignolo, L.A., 187, 191
Vrbancič, M.I., 182, 191

Waber, D.P., 182, 191
Walker, J.A., 43, 53
Walker, R.A., 174, 178, 197, 198, 202
Wapner, W., 131, 145
Warrington, E.K., 36, 42, 53
Watson, R.T., 42, 46, 52
Weber, S.L., 49, 53, 193, 202
Weiner, J.M., 24, 52
Weingartner, H., 47, 52, 53
Weiskrantz, L., 38, 53
Westbury, J.R., 96, 109
Wheeler, P.E., 158
Whishaw, I.Q., 10, 22
Whitaker, H.A., 124, 145
Wigan, A.L., 55, 206, 211
Witelson, S.F., 95, 109, 196, 200, 202
Wolf, M.E., 6

Yeo, R.A., 24, 47, 53, 209, 211
Young, A.W., 38, 52, 85, 86, 108, 109, 146, 198, 202, 207, 210
Young, G.W., 193, 202
Yutzey, D.A., 14, 21

Zaidel, E., 60, 62, 63, 73, 112, 120, 130, 132, 133, 147·
Zoloth, M.D., 19, 22

Subject index

Abstract–concrete effects, 134
Agnosia, 36–42
Alexia, *see* Dyslexia
Allergies, *see* Geschwind's hormonal hypothesis
Amobarbital (amylobarbitone) test, *see* Wada test
Amusia, *see* Music
Analytic–holistic processing, 28, 39, 61, 87–91, 198–200
Androgen, *see* Hormonal effects
Annett's right shift model, 164, 168–169, 174
Aphasia, 29, 60, 122–125, 187–188, 196–198
Aprosodia, *see* Prosody
Aquatic phase in hominid evolution, 153
Asymmetric tonic neck reflex, 162, 193
Attentional biases, 92–94, 98, 101–102, 104
Auditory asymmetries, 92–102
Australopithecus, 149, 152
Axial dominance, 163

Beta decay, 8
Bilateral visual presentations in humans, 77–79, 87
Bilingualism, second languages, 85, 135–136
Bipedalism, *see* Evolutionary aspects
Birds, 10
Birth stress, 170–173
Blindsight, 38, 47, 58
Blood flow, *see* Imaging techniques

Brightness asymmetries, 85, 117

Calcichordates, 10
Canaries, 11
Carbon molecule, 9
CAT scans, *see* Imaging techniques
Category-specific deficits, 36
Cats, 16
Chaffinches, 11
Chicks, 10, 12
Chimeric composites, 61–62
Chirality, 8–9
Chomsky's nativist account, 156
Chromosomal abnormalities, 183
cLEMs, *see* Conjugate lateral eyemovements
Coelenterates, 8
Cognitive crowding hypothesis, 122, 172–173
Cognitive style, 206–211
Color asymmetries, 85, 117
Commissures, *see* Corpus callosum
Commissurotomy operation and effects, 54–73, 132–134
Complementarity and dominance, 111
Concurrent cognitive loads, tasks, 85, 105–106, 117–119
Conjugate lateral eyemovements, 48, 106
Consciousness, 'unconscious awareness', 66–71
Corpus callosum, 55–73, 189
Cross cueing strategies, 65–66

Deaf hand signs, 85, 136
Delayed auditory feedback (DAF), 99
Developmental aspects, 90, 122–125, 131, 133, 173, 192–202
Dichhaptic studies, *see* Tactual asymmetries
Dichotic studies, *see* Auditory asymmetries
Diethylstilbestrol, 181
Direct lexical access, 34, 62
Directional scanning, 84, 140–141
Dogs, 16
Dopamine, 14–16
Double tasks, *see* Concurrent cognitive loads, tasks
Dowel balancing, 105
Drawing deficits, and unilateral lesions, 39–41
Dyslexia
   deep, 34, 125–130, 133–134, 143
   developmental, 125, 138–143, 170, 185

Ear preference (*see also* Auditory asymmetries), 161
Electroconvulsive therapy (ECT), unilateral, 29, 47
Electroencephalographic measures, 25–27, 134, 208
Electrostimulation, 28, 136
Emotion, emotionality, 3–4, 14, 47–50, 101
Enantiomers, 8
Estrogen, *see* Hormonal effects
Evoked potentials, *see* Electroencephalographic measures
Evolutionary aspects, 148–157
Exposure duration (visual presentations), 76
Eye preference, 161
Eyetracking devices, 62, 75, 82

Faces, face asymmetries, face composites, 2, 4, 49, 61–2, 75, 85–92, 198–200, 208
Familial sinistrality, 167
Familiarity, 87–88, 90, 198–200
Foot preference, 161–162

Geschwind's testosterone hypothesis, 141–142, 174–176, 183
Gesture, 153

Gorillas, 20

Hand preference, 160–177, 189
Haptic asymmetries, *see* Tactual
Hemi-inattention, *see* Hemineglect
Hemineglect, 42–47, 70, 132, 208
Hemiretinal division, 76
Hemispace asymmetries, 102–104
Hemispherectomy, 124–125, 196–197
Hermaphroditism, 1
Homo erectus, 17, 149, 152
Homo habilis, 149, 152–153, 160
Hormones, 10–12, 166–167, 171, 174–176, 180–189
Humor, 131–132

Illiteracy, 136
Imagery, 82, 91
Imaging techniques, 24–27, 134, 207–208
Immune dysfunction, *see* Geschwind's hormonal hypothesis
Impala, 15–16
Interhemispheric communication in absence of commissures, 63
Inversion of visual stimuli, 90, 199

Japanese scripts, *see Kana* and *Kanji*
Java Man, *see Homo erectus*

Kana and *Kanji*, 134–135, 138
Kartagener's syndrome, 9
Kimura's structural model, 92–94
Kinsbourne's activational account, 93, 104–105, 115, 117
Klinefelter's syndrome, 183

Lateral limits technique, 63, 65, 82
Lesion effect vs. dominance effect, 125
Letter processing, 81–82
Lexical decisions, 83–84

Mathematical ability, 173–175, 181, 184
Maturation, *see* Developmental aspects
Mice, 12–13, 16
Mirror-image-negativity relationships between the hemispheres, 115–119, 127–9
Mirrors, 1–2
Models of interhemispheric interaction, 110–120
Monaural asymmetries, 98–102
Monkeys, 17–20

Motor pathways and limbs, 58
Mouth asymmetries, 4, 6
Music, 50, 101, 200

Neanderthal Man, 151, 156
NMRI, *see* Imaging techniques
Noncomplementarity hypothesis, 95
Novel scripts, 85, 134, 138

Parietal operculum, 17, 151
Parrots, 11
Pathological sinistrality, *see* Birth stress
Peking Man, *see* Homo erectus
PET scans, *see* Imaging techniques
Phonological processing, 34–35, 62–63, 121, 124–126, 130, 132, 135, 138
Physical/nominal identity matching (letter pairs), 81–82
Piagetian tests, 185
Pigeons, 7
Planum temporale, see Temporal planum
Plasticity (neural) in the immature, 122–125, 197–198, 200
Primates (nonhuman), 16–20
Priming, 83
Process limiting variables, 81–92
Progesterone, *see* Hormonal effects
Prosimians, 20
Prosody, 48, 130–132, 135
Prosopagnosia, 37–39
Pyramidal dominance, *see* Axial dominance
Pythagorean table of opposites, 179, 186

Radiolaria, 8
Rats, 12, 14–16
rCBF, *see* Imaging techniques
Reaction time analyses, optimal procedures, 76–77
Report order, 84, 92, 102–103
Resources, within and between hemispheres, *see* Concurrent cognitive loads, tasks
Right hemisphere language, 62–66, 121–147

Scanning, *see* Directional scanning
Second languages, *see* Bilingualism
Secondary tasks, *see* Concurrent cognitive loads, tasks
Semantic paralexia, *see* Dyslexia, deep

Semantic priming, *see* Priming
Semantic processing, 65, 82–83
Sex differences, 174–176, 179–191
Shapes and patterns, asymmetries, 85–91
Singing, *see* Music
Situs inversus, 9, 166
Sivapithecus, 149
Social isolation, 155, 195
Société de Linguistique de Paris, 148
Spatial ability, 174–176, 181–185
Spatial frequencies and hemispheric specialization, 78, 142
State limiting variables, 78–81
Stereopsis and depth asymmetries, 85
Strategies, 81, 181–189, 206–209
Stroop effects, 84
Stuttering, 137, 170, 185
Subprocessors, 83, 116
Sylvian fissure, 16–18, 151–152

Tachistoscopic presentations of lateralized material, 60, 65–66, 76–92
Tactual asymmetries, 102
Tapping, 105–106
Temporal planum, asymmetries, 17–18, 174
Testicular asymmetry, 1
Testosterone, *see* Hormones *and* Geschwind's testosterone hypothesis
Tonal asymmetries, 99
Tool manufacture and use, *see* Evolutionary aspects
Trilobites, 10
Turner's syndrome, 183
Turning biases, 14, 16
Twins, 166

Unilateral neglect, *see* Hemineglect

Vibrotactile reaction times, 103–104
Visual pathways, 57, 61
Voice pathways, 57, 61
Voice recognition, 200

Waber's hypothesis, 182–185
Wada test, 29, 95, 122, 137

Zaidel ('Z') scleral contact lens, 62, 82, 132–133